"WHOLE-BRAIN THINKING does what the best books in any category do—it makes you think. But it also promises to give you more brainpower to do it with."

Forbes

"The concepts and findings of split-brain research are conveyed in stimulating and readily understandable fashion."

Los Angeles Herald Examiner

"Creativity has been a key part of the forty years of success that our company has seen. We have worked hard to encourage and to accentuate this skill among our people. Creativity requires the right and left brain skills'—the discipline and inspiration so skillfully dealt with by Jacquelyn Wonder and Priscilla Donovan in this book."

A. Bruce Boehm, President
Dow Corning U.S.A.

WHOLE-BRAIN THINKING

WORKING FROM BOTH SIDES OF THE BRAIN TO ACHIEVE PEAK JOB PERFORMANCE

JACQUELYN WONDER & PRISCILLA DONOVAN

BALLANTINE BOOKS • NEW YORK

Library of Congress Catalog Card Number: 83-19381

ISBN 0-345-32204-5

This edition published by arrangement with William Morrow and Co., Inc.

Manufactured in the United States of America

First Ballantine Books Edition: June 1985
Ninth Printing: January 1990

ACKNOWLEDGMENTS

We wish to thank the many individuals who have helped us in writing this book:

Jerry Conover for his gift of creative criticism, tireless navigation, and constant encouragement

Family members Don, George, Maryann, Nora, Michael, Jeff, and Jennifer Donovan, who submitted to various tests and endless conversations about the research

Dugan, Donovan, Daniel, and Mary Mahoney for interviews, ideas, and enthusiasm

Pam, Beth, and Margo Conover for their support

Loving parents who provided self-confidence and guidance: Mattie Lee Blanton Thompson and Earl George Thompson, and Elizabeth Wasson Wonder and Edward Frank Wonder

Colleagues Pat McClearn, Shari Robertson, Leroy Thomas, Larry Kessenick, and Ted Conover for their encouragement and manuscript suggestions

Sandy Dunlap and Kay Lowder for their expert typing and eagle-eyed proofing

A right-brained agent who understands the bottom line, Peter W. Livingston

A left-brained editor who respects nuance and egos, Alison Brown Cerier

And seminar students and study participants, whose cooperation enabled us to define concepts and gather data.

CONTENTS

WHOLE-BRAIN
THINKING

Sometimes I am provided with too much information at one time and simply can't absorb it. I have no chance to ask questions or put the information to use, so my mind wanders. How can I listen effectively in these marathon sessions?

I believe I was hired as superintendent by the School Board for my business expertise. Now, I find that the teachers, counselors and staff in the district resent my bottom-line, production-oriented attitude. Everyone is polite but distant. What do I do next?

I'm a loan analyst for a large mortgage company and often visit the site of an organization applying for a loan. I need to remember pertinent information told to me as I walk through the building. I've found that if I take notes, it is distracting and unnerving to my clients.

I am a manager at Cobe Labs. We have been growing rapidly. I'm expected to do extraordinary things in my division, yet my staff and workers are simply ordinary people. How do I get ordinary people to do extraordinary things?

Problems of communication, listening, memory, management, organization, stress—these are the dilemmas facing American business. Increasingly, business is recognizing that they cannot be solved by logic, discipline and attention to detail alone. They require not only these traditionally valued skills, but also intuition, free-spirited invention and comprehension of the overall picture. In other words, we must learn how to draw on both the left side of the brain, home of logic and efficiency, and on the right side of the brain, home of intuition and inspiration.

In 1981, neurosurgeon Roger Sperry won the Nobel Prize for his proof of the split-brain theory, which says that our problem-solving skills, physical and mental abilities, and even personality traits are strongly influenced by our habit of using one side of the brain more than the other. Brain bias explains why one person is a math whiz while "creative types" often flounder when trying to balance their checking accounts.

Not only individuals, but also organizations have brain bias. Consider the following profiles of left-brained and right-brained companies, from the points of view of employees with the opposite brain-style, to their dismay:

Four years ago I joined a large organization with an attractive reputation for low employee turnover, excellent benefits, a fatherly concern for employees and a prestigious position in the community. Now I am disillusioned and depressed by the company's rigid, bureaucratic ways. There is no flexibility, no altering working hours and no comp time. Procedures are cumbersome—everything must be in triplicate! Advancement is tied to a strict schedule with no allowances for exceptional work. I'm fed up and don't know what to do next.

I work for a spice and herb company which started as a cottage industry in the sixties and has grown into a phenomenally successful, national corporation. While it's exciting to be part of such a dynamic organization, I'm going bananas. There's no structure, no routine, no follow-through or even goals. The letters are handwritten, there's a constant milling about of people and the noise is unbelievable. The informal attitude and all the rest offend my sense of how a business should operate, and yet I feel guilty because everyone's so darn nice.

Both individuals and organizations need to learn how to shift consciously from one brain-style to another to meet each demand.

The secret to peak job performance and satisfaction is learning how to use both sides of your brain. You also need to learn to recognize the thinking styles of others, and to alter or adapt to them. Finally, you need to discover your organization's style and how you can modify your job within it.

Successful managers and entrepreneurs have learned naturally how and when to use both sides of their brains, combining detail and logic with a sense of overview and invention. One reason that Japanese management techniques are so successful is that they make far greater use of right-brained holistic talents than do most managers in the West.

Whole-Brain Thinking tells how everyone can combine "the Oriental perspective" with good old American pragmatism. For the first time, the practical applications of the split-brain theory can be put to work on the job.

The authors of *Whole-Brain Thinking* have been testing these practical uses for five years. Jacquelyn Wonder, a mangement consultant, has led dramatically successful seminars on whole-brain thinking for such innovative companies as IBM, ARCO, Kodak, Sperry Rand and Dow

Corning. Priscilla Donovan, an adult-education coordinator, has conducted brain lateralization research at the Biofeedback Institute of Denver under the direction of Dr. Thomas Budzynski.

Their whole-brain thinking system has three phases. First, you will learn about the split-brain theory and will take an intriguing self-test to discover your brain-style's place on a continuum from total left to total right.

Next, exercises called mind movers will teach you how to shift between the brain's hemispheres:

INTERNAL BRAINSTORMING—freeing, then evaluating, ideas
CINEMATICS—envisioning scenes
INSIDE OUTS—turning the facts upside down to find fresh solutions
SUSPENDERS—overstimulating the left to free the creative right
HEARINGS—moving into either brain-style at will
UPRIGHTS—shifting left when the situation demands

In the third phase, case studies show how the mind movers have been used to solve actual dilemmas like those at the beginning of this introduction.

Whole-Brain Thinking will teach you how to work effectively with ease, creatively with pleasure.

BRAIN AND
PERFORMANCE

1

THE SPLIT-BRAIN THEORY

The chief function of your body is to carry your brain around.
—Thomas Alva Edison

BECAUSE OF OUR SPECIFIC GENETIC INHERITANCE, OUR family life, and our early training, most of us prefer to use one side of the brain more than the other. This bias can be helpful to us in honing special talents or skills, but it can also be harmful to our health, happiness and success.

Researchers have delved into the mechanics of the brain's operation and found that we have two distinct thinking processes: one that's analytical and verbal housed in the left half of the brain, and another that's intuitive and visual and seated in the brain's right hemisphere. There is a connector, the corpus callosum, through which these two halves communicate. Typically, we use our left hemisphere when speaking or balancing the checkbook and the right when painting the porch or listening to our favorite record album. We shift back and forth between these hemispheres as we change activities. (See THE BRAIN CONNECTOR.)

Some of us make these shifts quite easily; others move hesitantly between them, or into the wrong hemisphere. To understand how this shifting process affects both your private life and job performance, you need to know something about the two halves of your brain.

For an ever-ready model, clench both hands into fists, placing fist and second knuckles together with your thumbs

---

THE BRAIN CONNECTOR

Throughout history, artists, writers, and philosophers have referred to the dual nature of the human being, but it was not until the 1960s that a physiological basis was identified.

Neurosurgeons began performing commissurotomies on epileptic patients with advanced, life-threatening convulsions.* Their seizures ceased and their behavioral patterns seemed unchanged. However, in follow-up studies of nine cases by Roger Sperry and Michael Gazzaniga (1967), subtle changes were discovered that indicated that the corpus callosum serves the vital purpose of letting the right hand know what the left hand is doing.

Each hemisphere was tested separately by masking one eye and then the other, and it was found that each hemisphere absorbed information in a different way and was unaware of the other's learning.

The left could identify, verbally, what fell in its line of vision; the right could point to or touch items in its line of vision.

The few verbal expressions that came as a result of right-brained viewing were emotional and disjointed. Sperry and Gazzaniga observed that the right hemisphere has very poorly developed grammar, is incapable of forming the plural of a given word, and lacks a "feel" for syntax.[1]

*The operation severs the corpus callosum, thus disconnecting the two halves of the brain.

---

toward your body. Your fists in this position are the approximate size of your brain, unless you have the hands of a wide receiver. There is a correlation between the appearance of your hands and the brain's abilities. The bumps created by the knuckles, veins, and scars of work-worn hands roughly approximate the neocortex, the outer layer of your brain. The more folds and creases the neocortex has, the more information it stores. A baby's brain is nearly as smooth as its bottom because it has not yet experienced learning. (See WRINKLED BRAIN.)

WRINKLED BRAIN

The wrinkledness of the neocortex (the outer layer of the brain) is a visible indication of intelligence. The more convoluted the surface of the brain of a species, the greater its relative intelligence; also, the larger the size of the brain in proportion to total body weight, the more intelligent the animal.

Human babies are born with a brain relatively larger than that of other species. By the time humans are six years old, their brains have reached 90 percent of their total size. Further brain growth results from increasing the number of connectors between neurons through learning experiences. Since brain mass increases but skull size is static, folds develop in the brain's surface and the entire surface of the brain becomes more enfolded.[2]

Now imagine that you have a gray glove on your left hand and a white one on the right. There are, in fact, slight differences in color between the two hemispheres caused by different rates of development. (See GRAY AND WHITE MATTER.) The mismatched-glove concept will help you remember that the left side of the brain has gray matter, the stuff that makes you smart by society's standards: facts, figures, dates, and more.

As you look at your "handy" model, imagine you see a wart on the back of your left hand. Name that wart Broca

GRAY AND WHITE MATTER

The left brain has more gray matter relative to white matter than the right.[2a] The white color occurs because of myelination, in which cells are coated with an insulating substance called myelin. Myelination reduces interference noise, allowing nerve cells to process signals more clearly and transmit them more quickly. Myelination in humans occurs with need; the areas of the brain that are most concerned with survival myelinate first. Thus, the right brain is more myelinated than the left, since it houses the essential intuitive, feeling, reactive skills. The left brain does not need this sheathing as sorely as does the right, since its cognitive functioning requires organization of separate facts rather than a picture of the entire scene. Therefore, when the expression "he's got lots of gray matter" implies intelligence, it is correct in this sense: The gray matter on the left side *is* an indication of how many organized facts you have mastered. The right brain's "white matter" can process a wide variety of visual, emotional, and sensory information, culminating in a hunch or gut feeling. This talent is especially valuable in emergency situations.

in honor of a nineteenth-century French investigator, Paul Broca, who discovered that the left half of the human brain has an extra lump that houses language. The ability to speak

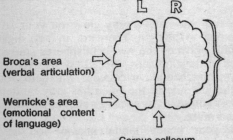

Broca's area (verbal articulation)

Wernicke's area (emotional content of language)

Right-side speech skills include whole-body response to commands (dancing). Detects others' spelling errors but cannot spell well itself

Corpus callosum

and form thoughts into words rests primarily in the left hemisphere of most persons. (For interesting exceptions, see RIGHT-BRAIN LANGUAGE.)

Your left brain has other talents, too: It puts things in sequential, logical order. For example, when you're planning the day's schedule, your left brain will tell you to leave ten minutes early so that you can drop off your dry cleaning on the way to work. It will have settled on a cleaners that opens early enough to visit during your usual drive, and it will have chosen one on the right side of the street so no turns or traffic problems will impede you. The left brain is determined to keep your life sensible, organized, and on schedule. Since it speaks for you, reads for you, and computes for you, it is a vital part of you.

If you were an A student in grade school, excelling in math, reading, and debate, you were probably functioning with a well-developed left brain. But chances are you flunked playground because it is the domain of the right brain,

---

RIGHT-BRAIN LANGUAGE

Studies of brainwave activity show that language is experienced at higher levels in the right hemisphere in the following situations:

- The Japanese have two writing systems, one phonetic, the other (*kanji*) ideographic. The latter is pictorial and is processed in the right side of the brain.
- Bilinguals who learn their second language during the teen years or later use right-brain strategies such as detecting the melodic or graphic features of words.
- Lower socioeconomic classes usually use language with more right-hemisphere characteristics. These languages are more rhythmic and pictorial.
- Hopi children show more brain activity on the right when learning their native language. Anthropological linguist Benjamin Lee Whorf believes this is because Hopis view reality and themselves as part of the total environment. This global philosophy is a right-brained perception.[3]

---

which controls your ability to move easily, take flights of fancy, and *scream*. The right brain is host to motor skills, intuition, and emotion, and is a ready receptor of music and cadence. As a problem-solver, it looks at the whole situation, and often the solution materializes as if by magic.

Cases of individuals who have experienced some type of brain injury show clearly the brain's hemispheric differences.

For example, a nun who was beaten severely by a robber was not allowed to testify at her assailant's trial because the damage to her brain's left hemisphere had resulted in loss of judgment and memory for details. Although she could still speak, her language was inexact and subject to the emotions of the moment. According to the prosecuting attorney, if she had testified, she would probably have hugged the accused when asked to identify him. Her ability to discriminate the details required in positively identifying the robber was destroyed by the injuries to the left side of her brain. Her right brain took over speech and produced childlike language—emotional, loving and uncritical.

In contrast is the young woman employed by a dining club company. Her job was to sort membership cards and match them to restaurant invoices (this was before small companies could afford computers). She underwent brain surgery to remove a large tumor from her brain's right hemisphere and lost some brain tissue. Afterward she could not remember or develop a pattern for classifying the cards and invoices. Furthermore, it was difficult for her to coordinate the physical movements required.

She reported great difficulty in performing other spatial tasks as well. She could not remember how to put on pantyhose or get in and out of automobiles. She analyzed these activities step by step, planning a proper sequence of movements and then rehearsing them until she could carry them out. Although she was able to use this left-brained approach, she did not feel comfortable with it. When she was distracted in the middle of these seemingly simple tasks, she had to review the steps and start over. Because she remained

---

RIGHT STROKES

Research at the University of Texas suggests that the emotional quality of speech is derived from right-brain involvement. Victims of right-hemisphere strokes could not communicate emotion via their voices even though vocabulary, grammar and articulation stayed normal.

One of the subjects was a thirty-nine-year-old schoolteacher who found her voice was weak, monotonous, unmodulated, and lacked changes in pitch. Classroom discipline was impossible without an ability to express emotion. At home, when she "meant business" with her own children, she prefaced angry and determined remarks with: "Goddammit, I mean it."[4]

---

highly articulate (there was no injury to the left brain), she was shifted to answering telephone inquiries, a task for which she was still well suited because she retained her verbal, left-brained abilities. It is likely that much of her right speech area remained intact; otherwise, the tone and quality of her voice would have been affected. (See RIGHT STROKES.) While articulation and grammar are seated in Broca's area on the left side, the emotional tone of phrasing and voice derive from the right side of the brain.

It is easier in an industrial society to adapt to right-hemisphere brain damage than to a loss in the left, because the skills of the left center around communication, math and logic, all required by technology. In primitive societies, the inability to dance, create visual images, and understand intuitively would have been just as debilitating. For a technological society, an ideal brain model includes these characteristics:

- highly developed skills in the hemisphere suited for a particular activity (speech on the left and image making on the right).
- backup skills in the less appropriate hemisphere—that is, some right-brain speech capabilities producing a pattern

of speaking that is impassioned as well as logical. They also offer an auxiliary speech system in case of injury to the left.

But which combination of development produces the ideal person? The chemist (left-brained occupation) who also enjoys dancing and also gets along well with fellow workers is one example. Another would be the artist (right-brained) who keeps accurate accounts of sales and campaigns for more efficient city government. In short, the ideal person has strong skills in each hemisphere and can move into the appropriate one when that skill is needed.

When a chemist is titrating or computing, he can be careful, logical and accurate. When he is dancing, he shifts to his right brain and feels the steps. The artist is operating at optimal levels when he uses his right brain to visualize new design and moves left to make an accounting of his sales. Although the chemist is probably more comfortable performing left-brained tasks, he balances his life-style with some right-brained activities. The artist balances his preference for the right with left-brained tasks.

The matter of brain preference is important to you in your job because it predisposes you to certain likes and dislikes, skills and failings. In Chapter 2, you will discover which side you use predominantly and prefer. These preferences are developed early in life and become more extreme because of the natural tendency to follow the broken trail. If you are a good piano player and poor reader, you will spend more time playing the piano than reading. The more you play the piano, the better you become and the more you neglect reading ... and the more one-sided your abilities and personality become.

Although humans seem to be born with these tendencies and are heavily influenced by family and society, it is possible to develop that less preferred side.

A case in point is Theodore Roosevelt, the twenty-sixth President of the United States. As a child, he was quite studious, shy, and reclusive, probably because he was sickly.

As he grew older, he resolved to overcome his physical problems. He involved himself in exercise and the outdoor life. This athletic, more flamboyant view of him is the one emphasized in history texts—for example, the Rough Rider of San Juan Hill. However, as he changed, he retained his scholarly, left-brained skills, as evidenced by extensive writing in the fields of politics, history, and wildlife. His political policies are also a study in contrasting brain-styles. His domestic programs were serious and reasoned, while his foreign relations tended to be intuitive and adventuresome. Perhaps this well-known description of his foreign policy best exemplifies his balanced approach: "Speak softly . . . but carry a big stick."

A less laudatory but equally dramatic example of "balancing" one's brain is Paul Gauguin, the French post-impressionist artist. He was a successful banker who at age thirty-five suddenly left his family and job to become an itinerant painter in the South Pacific islands.

Gauguin's abrupt change also demonstrates a characteristic of brain organization typical of males—a high degree of lateralization. Men tend to shift farther left or right than do women. This accounts for some of the differences in the way men and women typically perform tasks. (Box on MALE/FEMALE THINKING STYLES.)

Persons who are highly lateralized move almost totally to the right or left depending upon the task. Those who have a more generalized thinking style perceive the whole scene, not just the task at hand.

Most modern cultures encourage this pattern of lateralization in men and generalization in women. The difference probably dates back to prehistoric days, when survival of the species depended upon such division of labor.

Since early woman was the childbearer and nurturer, she cared for the children until they could survive on their own. She stayed at the home site, where she was aware of simultaneous crises and responded immediately to the most important one. When the meat fell in the fire, wild animals were threatening from the sidelines and the children were

WHOLE-BRAIN THINKING

MALE/FEMALE THINKING STYLES

At birth there are basic differences between male and female brains. The female cortex is more fully developed. The sound of the human voice elicits more left-brain activity in infant girls than in infant boys, accounting in part for the earlier development in females of language. Baby girls have larger connectors between the brain's hemispheres and thus integrate information more skillfully. This flexibility bestows greater verbal and intuitive skills. Male infants lack this ready communication between the brain's lobes; therefore, messages are routed and rerouted to the right brain, producing larger right hemispheres. This size advantage accounts for males having greater spatial and physical abilities and explains why they may become more highly lateralized and skilled in specific areas.

Some researchers claim that these differences can be attributed to socialization, and without doubt, cultural expectations do play a major role. Physical differences also play a major role, and it is not clear which came first. Perhaps this agreement between neurosurgeon Karl Pribram and researcher Diane McGuinness forms an acceptable premise: "Women and men are different from the very beginning; what needs to be made equal is the value placed upon these differences."[5]

toddling off toward danger, she needed to be able to observe everything and react immediately. Her first priority was to to rescue the baby.

The hunter-provider husband, on the other hand, found that single-mindedness was better for pursuing game. Basically, he used the trial-and-error method with its deductive logic, trying one thing at a time until he found a sequence of successful strategies. A few million years later, his descendant might have been the Henry Ford who found that refining car production into limited steps and sequencing them in a logical order yielded an extremely efficient, cost-effective method for mass-producing automobiles.

It is difficult to see the significance of broad changes

while in the middle of them, but the recent increase of women in the workworld and in stereotypical male jobs suggests several possibilities. Individual women might become more highly lateralized as they adapt to the demands of business and industrial work. Men might become less lateralized if the more generalized approach produces effective results.

Also, in the future, the ability of machinery to perform so much of the left-brain work could shift the emphasis of human work to right-brain skills. (Computers are not expected to replicate right-brain functions in the foreseeable future.)

Whichever of these scenarios evolves (most likely all three will blend into one), you will be better prepared for them by strengthening the less preferred half of your brain and improving your ability to move into the hemisphere appropriate to the demands of the situation.

DRIVING ON BOTH SIDES

You already know how to shift from one side of your brain to the other. You do it every day. Here is an example:

You're driving down the highway, your mind a thousand miles away, thinking about the vacation you're going to take soon. You see a sandy beach, you feel the sunlight warming you, you smell the salt air and the suntan lotion, you hear the waves lapping at the shoreline. You're humming to yourself when suddenly someone cuts in front of you without so much as a horn beep. You instantly come back to reality, braking just enough to avoid a collision, but not so hard that the car will flip or sideswipe the truck to your right.

You have just moved from your right brain to your left in a highly appropriate shift. The left brain makes the computerlike adjustments to the facts and logically organizes things in proper sequence, while the right converts immediately from the sandy beach to a sense of traffic conditions and a feel for the proper physical responses. In a split second you shift constantly between hemispheres in a way that is vastly superior to that of the most sophisticated computer.

WORLDS OF DIFFERENCE

Researchers refer to the left brain as the dominant hemisphere and the right as the nondominant one, because the skills of the left brain are dominant in our society. Money, technology, efficiency and power are thought to be the rewards of left-brain planning. Conversely, right-brain factors are nondominant. For example, cultures that prefer mystical, intuitive, intangible, and artistic values are not politically or socially powerful in our country. American Indian, black, and Hispanic groups generally have right-brain values. These minorities may soon be dominant in numbers, but the chances are great that they will not be dominant in power until they develop left-brain skills (not, one hopes, at the expense of their unique right-brain qualities). This development is already evident in the blacks, Indians, and Hispanics who have acquired middle-class and higher status. For the most part, these "successful" minority members have acquired the left-brain skills and priorities necessary to make this trip across the social and financial barriers. Society at large (including the minorities left behind) considers this trip to be progress, a step from the nondominant world into the dominant. One aim of this book is to show why right-brained thinking and performance should be more accepted in the workplace.

Another reason it's a left-brained world might be the Broca wart. Since communication is so important to the human condition, the left-brain cultures would most likely continue to be dominant even if technology and money were not important. However, the human potential movement toward communication of feelings, not just facts, is a step in the "right" direction.

FRANK AND ERNEST by Bob Thaves   Reprinted by permission. © 1982 NEA, Inc.

DOUBLE-CROSSING WAYS

Contralaterality is another important discovery of split-brain research. The term means that your left hemisphere controls the actions, hearing, seeing and sensations of the right side of your body, and vice versa. Since this society is a left-brained one, 85 percent of the population is right-handed—or is it that since most Americans are born right-handed, the culture is left-brained? This is one of those chicken-or-the-egg questions that left-brainers love to discuss. (You can read about some research conducted on this question in LEFT-HAND HISTORY.)

If you are left-brained, you'll probably do that now, since you typically enjoy research and study. Readers of both persuasions should check with a light pencil mark the information boxes you've read thus far in this book. You'll be using this later as part of the self-test in Chapter 2.

TALKING OUT OF BOTH SIDES

It would be easier to understand brain theory if one could assume (because of the contralaterality phenomenon) that left-handers are dominant rights, have few language skills, and prefer doing things in a right-brained manner. However, if you think of some of the left-handers you know, you'll realize that many of them are very articulate as well as fully equipped with artistic and intuitive skills. These

LEFT-HAND HISTORY

The world's population is approximately 15 percent left-handed. This poses an interesting question: Why are there so few or, conversely, why any at all? Animals show no preference for handedness. Cave drawings of prehistoric men indicate they created with the right, and the meager tools and implements they left behind indicate right-hand use.

Some researchers feel that the human preference developed during the Bronze Age, when tools became more refined and required precise skills so one hemisphere became dominant in these matters. This still does not explain why the right hand was selected. Perhaps Carlyle's rationale a century ago is still the most logical: Man's need to shield his heart in battle while wielding his weapon developed because the heart is on the left side and could most easily be covered by the left hand.

The sociobiologist would not stop here but would ask: Why did the heart settle down in the left side instead of the middle, where it could be protected by either hand? A possible answer could lie in the efficacy of the lateralization. If there were no specialization of hemispheres, then talents would not be as refined as a technological society requires, and competition between the hemispheres would be constant and damaging.[6]

Because left-handers have to assert themselves in a right-hand world, they are likely to be extreme natural right-brainers. On the other hand, righthanders could be right-brained persons who found adaptation easier than fighting the left-brained system. In 1932 2 percent of the U.S. population was left-handed; today the estimate is 15 percent. This growth is attributed to the discovery that thwarted left-handedness often causes stuttering and emotional problems. This indicates how powerful are social taboos and pressures.[7]

anomalies occur because left-handers, in adapting to the right-handers' society, often develop compensating talents, becoming mixed dominants out of necessity rather than because it comes most easily. They frequently have linguistic capabilities in the right brain as well as in the left. When the two work in concert, their speech is poetic, rich in expression and metaphor.

A mixed dominant has refined talents in both hemispheres and the ability to shift appropriately between them. There are mixed dominants who *don't* develop clear brain lateralization, thus creating a competitive tension between the two language centers. The outcome may be stuttering or dyslexia—the person seems to be ambivalent and indecisive because two internal speakers are forever engaged in debate.

Another anomaly that may have occurred to you is that since speech is a left-brained task, why are women so good at it as well as at the right-brained skills of intuition and emotional sensitivity? Part of the explanation for this apparent inconsistency lies in the difference in maturation rate of males and females. Females develop speech earlier. They are encouraged in it, which accelerates the rate of verbal learning and leaves less time for spatial development. By the time boys develop language skills, the optimal time to receive reinforcement for verbal learning has passed. These are generalizations, of course, and early parental support and stimulation of speech improve levels for both males and females. On the other hand, the males tend to acquire superior spatial skills because they are not as involved in communicating verbally.

SUMMARY

As you continue to read this book, keep in mind these major points:

1. The human brain's two halves have different but overlapping skills or ways of thinking:

WHOLE-BRAIN THINKING

"It's finally happening, Helen. The hemispheres of my brain are drifting apart."

Drawing by Lorenz;
© 1980 The New Yorker Magazine, Inc.

Left		Right
	Intuitive	
Positive		
Analytical	Spontaneous	Holistic
Linear	Emotional	Playful
Explicit	Nonverbal	Diffuse
Sequential	Visual	Symbolic
Verbal	Artistic	Physical
Concrete		
Rational		
Active		
Goal-oriented		

2. Individuals have a tendency to *prefer* one side or the other, which affects their approach to life and work. Although individuals do not change dominance or preference, it is possible to develop the skills of the less-

preferred hemisphere. One may experience a thrust to an opposite brain-style because of changing responsibilities and opportunities and because of the body's innate need for balance (homeostasis).

3. Whichever your dominance or preference, you still use both sides of your brain and shift them, depending upon the skills needed and your particular brain organization.

4. Lateralization is the degree to which brain functions are performed in the task-appropriate hemisphere (balancing the checkbook in the left and recalling a loved one's face in the right). Highly lateralized individuals move more completely into the task-appropriate hemisphere (the usual case with males), while less lateralized persons (the usual case with females) will perform a task in both hemispheres.

In the next chapter, you'll discover which, if either, brain-style you prefer and how this preference affects your behavior.

2

KNOWING YOURSELF
—RIGHT OR LEFT

What lies behind us and what lies before us are small matters compared to what lies within us.

—Ralph Waldo Emerson

THE IDEAS BEHIND SPLIT-BRAIN RESEARCH WILL BE OF much greater value when you can translate them into personal terms. Without further ado, you are invited to take the following test to determine your hemispheric dominance.

Please do not analyze the questions. Answer them quickly, checking the answer that first feels right to you. When there are multiple choices, select the one that most closely represents your attitude or behavior.

BRAIN PREFERENCE INDICATOR TEST

1. In a problem-solving situation, do you:
   - ___ a. take a walk and mull solutions over, then discuss them?
   - _✓_ b. think about, write down all alternatives, arrange them according to priorities, and then pick the best?
   - ___ c. recall past experiences that were successful and implement them?
   - ___ d. wait to see if the situation will right itself?

2. Daydreaming is:
   - ___ a. a waste of time
   - _✓_ b. amusing and relaxing
   - ___ c. a real help in problem-solving and creative thinking
   - ___ d. a viable tool for planning my future

3. Glance quickly at this picture.

Was the face smiling?
___ a. yes   _✓_ b. no

4. Concerning hunches:
   _____ a. I frequently have strong ones and follow them
   _____ b. I have strong hunches but don't consciously follow them
   _____ c. I occasionally have hunches but don't place much faith in them
   _____ d. I would not rely on hunches to help me make important decisions

5. In thinking about the activities of your day, which is most typical of your "style"?
   _____ a. I make a list of all the things I need to do, people to see
   _____ b. I picture the places I will go, people I'll see, things I'll do
   _____ c. I just let it happen
   _____ d. I plan the day's schedule, blocking out appropriate times for each item or activity

6. Do you usually have a place for everything, a system for doing things, and an ability to organize information and materials?
   _____ a. yes   _____ b. no

7. Do you like to move your furniture, change the decor of your home or office frequently?
   _____ a. yes   _____ b. no

8. Please check which of these activities you enjoy:
   _____ swimming   _____ travel
   _____ tennis   _____ bicycling
   _____ golf   _____ collecting
   _____ camping/hiking   _____ writing
   _____ skiing   _____ chess
   _____ fishing   _____ bridge
   _____ singing   _____ roulette
   _____ gardening   _____ charades
   _____ playing instrument _____ dancing

WHOLE-BRAIN THINKING

___ home improvements	_✓_ walking
___ sewing	___ running
_✓_ reading	___ hugging
_✓_ arts/crafts	_✓_ kissing
___ cooking	___ touching
___ photography	___ chatting
___ doing nothing	___ debating

9. Do you learn athletics and dancing better by:

both ___ a. imitating, getting the feel of the music or game?

___ b. learning the sequence and repeating the steps mentally?

10. In sports or performing in public do you often perform better than your training and natural abilities warrant?

___ a. yes   _✓_ b. no

11. Do you express yourself well verbally?

_✓_ a. yes   ___ b. no

12. Are you goal-oriented?

_✓_ a. yes   ___ b. no

13. When you want to remember directions, a name, or a news item, do you:

___ a. visualize the information?

___ b. write notes?

_✓_ c. verbalize it (repeat it to yourself or out loud)?

___ d. associate it with previous information?

14. Do you remember faces easily?

_✓_ a. yes   ___ b. no

15. In the use of language, do you:

___ a. make up words?

___ b. devise rhymes and incorporate metaphors?

_✓_ c. choose exact, precise terms?

16. In a communication situation, are you more comfortable being the:
    ____ a. listener?   ____ b. talker?

17. When you are asked to speak extemporaneously at a meeting, do you:
    ____ a. make a quick outline?
    ____ b. just start talking?
    ____ c. shift the focus to someone else or say as little as possible?
    ____ d. speak slowly and carefully?

18. In an argument, do you tend to:
    ____ a. talk until your point is made?
    ____ b. find an authority to support your point?
    ____ c. just become withdrawn?
    ____ d. push chair or table, pound table, talk louder—yell?

19. Can you tell fairly accurately how much time has passed without looking at your watch?
    ____ a. yes   ____ b. no

20. Do you prefer social situations that are:
    ____ a. planned in advance?
    ____ b. spontaneous?

21. In preparing yourself for a new or difficult task, do you:
    ____ a. visualize yourself accomplishing it effectively?
    ____ b. recall past successes in similar situations?
    ____ c. prepare extensive data regarding the task?

22. Do you prefer working alone or in a group?
    ____ a. alone   ____ b. group

23. When it comes to "bending the rules" or altering company policy, do you feel:
____ a. rules and policy are to be followed?
__✓__ b. progress comes through challenging the structure?
____ c. rules are made to be broken?

24. In school, did you prefer:
____ a. algebra?   ____ b. geometry?

25. Which of these handwriting positions most closely resembles yours?
__✓__ a. regular right-hand position
____ b. hooked right-hand position (fingers pointing toward your chest)
____ c. regular left-hand position
____ d. hooked left-hand position (fingers pointing toward your chest)

26. In notetaking, do you print:
__✓__ a. never?   ____ b. frequently?

27. Do you use gestures to
____ a. emphasize a point?
__✓__ b. express your feelings?

28. Do you instinctively feel an issue is right or correct, or do you decide on the basis of information?
__✓__ a. feel   ____ b. decide

29. I enjoy taking risks.
____ a. yes   __✓__ b. no

30. After attending a musical:
__✓__ a. I can hum many parts of the score
____ b. I can recall many of the lyrics

31. Please hold a pencil perpendicularly to the ground at

arm's length, centered in your line of vision and lined up with a frame, board, or door. Holding that position, close your left eye. Did your pencil appear to move?
____ a. yes

Close your right eye. Did your pencil appear to move?
____ b. yes

32. Sit in a relaxed position and clasp your hands comfortably in your lap.

Which thumb is on top?
____ a. left   ____ b. right   ____ c. parallel

33. Check as many of these items as you feel are true about you:
____ I can extract meaning from contracts, instruction manuals, and legal documents
____ I can understand schematics and diagrams
____ I strongly visualize the characters, setting, and plot of reading material
____ I prefer that friends phone in advance of their visits
____ I dislike chatting on the phone
____ I find it satisfying to plan and arrange the details of a trip
____ I postpone making telephone calls
____ I can easily find words in a dictionary, names in a phone book
____ I love puns
____ I take lots of notes at meetings and lectures
____ I freeze when I need to operate mechanical things under stress
____ Ideas frequently come to me out of nowhere

34. I have:
____ a. frequent mood changes
____ b. almost no mood changes

35. I am:
  _____ a. not very conscious of body language. I prefer to listen to what people say
  _____ b. good at interpreting body language
  _____ c. good at understanding what people say and also the body language they use

36. How many research boxes did you read in Chapter 1?

_____

Here's the scoring key to the self-test. List the numbers of each answer you checked.

1.	a. 7		5.	a. 1
	b. 1			b. 7
	c. 3			c. 9
	d. 9			d. 3
2.	a. 1		6.	a. 1
	b. 5			b. 9
	c. 7			
	d. 9		7.	a. 9
				b. 1
3.	a. 3			
	b. 7			
4.	a. 9			
	b. 7			
	c. 3			
	d. 1			

8.			
swimming	9	travel	5
tennis	4	bicycling	8
golf	4	collecting	1
camping/hiking	7	writing	2
skiing	7	chess	2
fishing	8	bridge	2
singing	3	roulette	7
gardening	5	charades	5

playing instrument	4	dancing	7
home improvements	3	walking	8
sewing	3	running	8
reading	3	hugging	9
arts/crafts	5	kissing	9
cooking	5	touching	9
photography	3	chatting	4
doing nothing	9	debating	2

9. a. 9
   b. 1

10. a. 9
    b. 1

11. a. 1
    b. 7

12. a. 1
    b. 9

13. a. 9
    b. 1
    c. 3
    d. 5

14. a. 7
    b. 1

15. a. 9
    b. 5
    c. 1

16. a. 6
    b. 3

17. a. 1
    b. 6
    c. 9
    d. 4

18. a. 3
    b. 1
    c. 7
    d. 9

19. a. 1
    b. 9

20. a. 1
    b. 9

21. a. 9
    b. 5
    c. 1

22. a. 3
    b. 7

23. a. 1
    b. 5
    c. 9

24. a. algebra 1
    b. geometry 9

25. a. 1
    b. 7
    c. 9
    d. 3

26. a. 1
    b. 9

27. a. 2
    b. 8

28. a. 9
    b. 1

29. a. 7
    b. 3

30. a. 9
    b. 1

31. a. 8
    b. 2

32. a. 1
    b. 9
    c. 5

33.

contracts	1		postpone	7
schematics	7		find words	1
visualize	9		puns	3
advance	2		notes	1
chatting	3		freeze	3
plan trip	1		nowhere	9

34. a. 9
    b. 1

35. a. 1
    b. 7
    c. 5

36. Score as follows:
    9 a. if you read 0 to 1 boxes all the way through
    5 b. if you read 2 to 5 boxes all the way through
    1 c. if you read 6 to 8 boxes all the way through

Now add the number of points you scored and divide the total by the number of answers you checked. (This latter number will vary among testers, since questions 8 and 33 have a large number of parts.) For example: if your points totaled 300 in 40 answers, your Brain Preference Indicator (BPI) would be 7.5.

Left _____ Right
  1   3   5   7   9

    The questions in this self-test cover the most salient differences between dominant rights and lefts. The ques-

tions have been posed to individuals who underwent an
EEG dominance test at the Biofeedback Institute of Denver. (See **BRAIN DOMINANCE**.) In its final form, the self-test
has been given to more than five hundred people in the
Wonder seminars. The results of the self-test and the lab
test correlated.

Your Brain Preference Indicator (BPI) indicates a general thought style that results in a consistent pattern of

---

BRAIN DOMINANCE

The hypothesis of a study at the Biofeedback Institute of
Denver was that researchers could predict a subject's brain
dominance by choice of occupation. For example, it was
assumed that lawyers, mathematicians and accountants
would be left dominants because these occupations require
logical, sequential skills. Musicians, athletes and artists were
expected to be right dominants, since these occupations
require visuospatial, artistic talents. Therefore, subjects were
limited to those occupations.

The EEG or electroencephalogram test involved attaching
electrodes to the left and right sides of the head, on three
locations for each side. These measured the electrical
emissions from the brain's two sides, while mental tasks
were assigned by the tester. When output varies between
hemispheres it can be determined which hemisphere is in
dominance and the degree of that dominance. Half the tasks
were right-handed (listening to music, visualizing) and half
were left-brained (counting out loud backward, defending a
point of view). More than four hundred persons were tested
in this manner.

Individuals in occupations involving highly structured
procedures (accountants, chemists) were clearly left
dominants, while those in work with less structure (athletes,
painters) were right dominants. Furthermore, within specific
occupations distinctions were noted; lawyers who practiced
corporate and contract law were more left-brained than those
who were in domestic and criminal law. Classical musicians
were left dominants (most likely because of the discipline of
their studies), while rock musicians were right dominants.[8]

---

behavior in all areas of your life. Recognizing and understanding the components of this pattern allow you to develop alternative approaches where needed. To help you interpret your BPI, an analysis of each question or related questions follows.

Questions 1 and 5

The left-dominant person is more apt to solve a problem by following an organized approach: defining the problem, researching and recording possible solutions, eliminating impossible solutions, assigning priorities to the most viable, and then implementing the plan. The extreme dominant right will wait to see what happens. The other two answers describe moderate degrees. Moderate rights will get a feel for what will work and need frequent support from others. The moderate left will check the record and repeat strategies that were previously successful.

Questions 2 and 4

These are attitudinal questions. Extreme and moderate rights typically place their trust in daydreaming and hunches, while lefts find such things as intuition entertaining at most.

Question 3

Dominant lefts are usually "right-eyed" and first look at the left side of the paper. Therefore they see the down-turned side of the mouth in the test picture.

Question 6

Good organizational skills and habits are typical of the left-dominant person. New York therapist Selwyn Mills has found that artists are right dominants and sloppy, whereas craftsmen are left dominants and neat. When counseling families about the phenomena of two neat parents rearing a sloppy child, he suggests that the problem usually stems from differences in brain dominance between the parents and the child rather than in parenting style or the child's stubbornness. Mills has found that right- and left-brain dominants are attracted to each other; he conducts "Odd

Couple Seminars" to help them benefit from their differences.[9]

Questions 7, 23, and 28
Right-brained dominants like change because they are visually and physically oriented. They like the unusual, the discordant, the different. Because lefts like order and stability, they are willing to adhere to rules and adapt themselves to structure. Rights "feel" the approach that is proper for them, whereas left dominants analyze and compare society's standards.

Question 8
By their nature, some sports invite more comparisons and evaluations than others and are preferred by left dominants. Lefts like to "play" competitively, whether it's in their garden or on the golf course. Their flowers are entered in shows and their scores posted on the club notice board. Rights thrive on freedom and dread comparison; when they play tennis they simply enjoy hitting the ball, and their hikes have no destination in mind. When lefts play tennis they prefer to start scoring faster. And a hike less than ten miles is to them a failure. These same tendencies toward competitiveness and goal-setting versus recreation for relaxation and having fun are also evident in work. The thrill of doing is enough for the right-brain person, but the left wants a product to result from crafts or gardening.

Questions 11 and 12
Left dominants have good verbal skills and usually have definite objectives in mind when speaking. They are more apt to be structured and disciplined in seeking those goals. Right dominants have vague feelings about wanting to express something—but often are not quite clear what! Occasionally they have a full-blown picture of the outcome they desire but grope for words to describe it.

Questions 13 and 14
Right-brain types easily recognize faces and associate vis-

ual information with them (what the person wore, whom he danced with, whether she drank white or red wine). The left-brained person, however, remembers best by recording the information or talking about it. This is a disadvantage when meeting strangers at cocktail parties: Lefts repeat the name, even spell it, but usually forget it quickly if the person mumbles the name or moves on quickly. Also, lefts need specific directions—"Three blocks north, one south"— every step of the way. Rights do better with visual and emotional cues: "It's out by that swinging singles place with the green and yellow neon sign."

Question 15
Left dominants are more precise in their use of language, while rights favor colorful, emotional, sweeping terms. Rhyming and using metaphors require both.

Questions 16 and 17
Because lefts' verbal skills are more highly developed, they feel more at home talking than do rights. In public speaking, right dominants are prone to wander, often failing to reach a conclusion. They relate information to personal experiences—a practice that is useful for remembering and understanding but bad for logic and clarity. Mixed dominants tend to speak slowly because they are often simultaneously listening to an internal debate between left and right thoughts. Rights are more reluctant to speak in public— quite the opposite of left dominants, who know what they think and are glad to tell you! Their confidence in their well-defined logical opinions often makes them persuasive speakers.

Questions 19 and 22
Lefts are very conscious of time, schedules, etc., whereas rights frequently lose contact with the here and now. It is not so much that they lack a sense of responsibility (although it is often interpreted that way) as that they find themselves in another reality, where time seems to go either slowly or quickly. Along the same line, lefts become impatient with

time-consuming aspects of group work (meetings, committees), while rights are oblivious to the passage of time and enjoy the personal interaction.

Question 20
Right dominants are impulsive and like impromptu occasions. Lefts tend to believe that if an occasion is not planned and structured, it is not very worthwhile. This combination also makes rights risk-takers—physically, financially, and emotionally. They like change and don't like to plan, so they are more easily involved in new ideas and projects. Lefts, though, will seldom take risks until they have scrutinized most of the speculative factors out of the situation (for example, analyzed an investment until they *know* they can't lose money). Since they are not as likely to observe the body language of others or credit their own intuition, lefts often fail in spite of their reasoned analyses, which in turn reinforces their suspicions of risk-taking and makes them more reluctant to take chances again.

Questions 21 and 32
Left dominants prepare for a project by organizing and structuring facts. If rights plan at all, they usually do so by visualizing the desired outcome and getting a sense of the current situation. For example, in assembling a child's swing set or a radio kit, a left would lay out all the parts, count them to be sure the set is complete, gather the necessary tools and then follow the directions. A dominant right would typically glance at the diagram or schematic and then begin with whatever tools were there, sensing how the parts fit together. It can be maddening to the left type that this nonsystem often works better than the reasoned approach, which frequently breaks down when the manufacturer's instructions are incorrect.

Question 24
Since algebra is the mathematics of logic and deduction, using analysis and comparison, it is usually easier for left dominants to understand than geometry. Geometry is more

spatial and graphic. While it too is logical, it is visually comprehensible and therefore more likely to be preferred by right-brain dominants.

Question 25

In studies of the four handwriting positions (normal right, normal left, hooked right and hooked left), it was found that left-handers who hold the pencil in a normal handwriting position and right-handers who use a hooked handwriting position both have primary speech functions in their right hemispheres. This is a disadvantage for language skills, since the left is most appropriate for logical, articulate speech.

The same research showed that persons who have the normal right-hand style have primary language in the left hemisphere, as do left-handers who write with a hooked-hand position, an advantage to language skills.[10]

Question 26

Printing is more pictographical than script and is therefore preferred by many rights, especially if they disliked the structure and precision of handwriting classes.

Question 31

This exercise determined your "eyedness," the tendency to use one eye more than the other. The eye that was open when your pencil stayed still is your dominant eye. Eyedness is also contralateral—that is, if you are right-eyed, you are apt to be a left-brained dominant. Similarly, individuals are handed and footed, and these preferences also correlate with brain dominance. However, handedness is not a reliable means of testing dominance because of society's strictures against left-handedness—natural lefts often take the "right" way out. Footedness can be determined by noting which foot you kick with, jump on, or put forward first when engaging in a sport or other physical activity.

Question 32

This test is one used by hypnotists to determine how easily a person can be hypnotized. Persons who are most com-

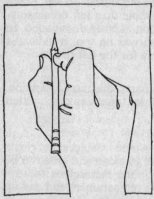

Normal right-hand writing style: primary language in left brain.

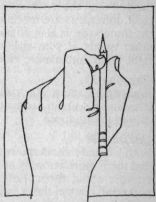

Normal left-hand writing style: primary language in right brain.

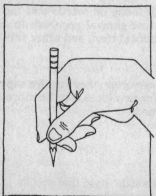

Hooked right-hand writing style: primary language in right brain.

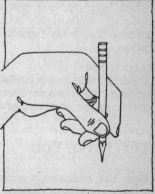

Hooked left-hand writing style (60 percent of left-handers write this way): primary language in left brain.

fortable with the right thumb on top are more easily hyp-notized than those who prefer the left thumb on top. Since right dominants are more suggestible than left dominants, the thumb test is also an indication of brain dominance. In other words, if your right thumb was on top, it indicates right-brain dominance; vice versa for the left thumb.

Question 33
Right dominants prefer visuals, charts, diagrams and maps; lefts like details in sequential order, analyses and written or verbal directions.

Question 34
Both left and right dominants have mood changes, but rights feel them more strongly and tend to moan and groan to be ecstatic about them. Lefts discipline themselves to sup-press and control these swings in temperament and end up with many fewer highs or lows.

Question 35
When listening, left dominants focus on words and the message, while rights take a more general approach that incorporates body signals, emotional tone, and other sub-tleties.

Question 36
Since left dominants analyze *everything*, they require sup-porting evidence before accepting new ideas. Furthermore, they love the structure of research.

THE TOTAL YOU

Your BPI indicates a general thought style that results in a fairly consistent pattern of behavior in all areas of your life. At times in your life, you are apt to vary from your natural style. When you are a footloose and fancy-free twenty-four-year-old you are more likely to show your right dominance than when you are forty-five, married, and financing college for two children.

Also keep in mind that two individuals might have the same BPI but behave quite differently because of early training or the circumstances surrounding an action. For example, you could be an extreme right dominant yet plan each project in detail as you were taught to do by parents and teachers. You might plan and carry out projects in a left-brained way only when a parental figure is observing your activities.

The answers of highly lateralized *and* mixed dominant people (double dominants) will be close to the middle of the BPI continuum when they are averaged. To determine whether you are highly lateralized or mixed dominant, look at your individual answers. If your answers are predominantly either 1's or 9's, you are highly lateralized; if your replies to the questions cluster toward midrange (4, 5 and 6), then you are a mixed dominant.

There is nothing good or bad about your BPI. It is simply a way of understanding your thinking style. Recognizing the components of your overall pattern allows you to evaluate which characteristics you enjoy as they are and which you may want to alter.

WHO NEEDS A 10?

What are you to divine from your Brain Preference Indicator? Is it better to be a 1, a 5 or 9? If you tried harder, could you be a 10? Would you want to be a 10?

Last question first: You definitely do not want to be a 10 *or* a 0! When you go off the continuum in either direction, you are unhappy. A 10 would be overwhelmed by emotions and ruled by the feelings of the moment. While the right brain is charming in its spontaneity and childlikeness, its dark side is emotionalism ranging from hysterical happiness to nagging suspicion and abysmal despair.

On the other hand, a 0 would be clinical and capable of recommending genocide to solve the population problem.

So you don't want to be a 10 or a 0, or anything else you're not. The benefit of knowing your BPI number is to understand why you do what you do and to make compensations when desirable.

Right-brained readers will be disappointed that their BPIs cannot be translated into colorful descriptions of their personalities and predictions about the future. The BPI is not a new kind of horoscope or biorhythm chart. Instead of such a gimmick, let's turn to *Monday Night Football* to clarify the differences between a 1, a 5 and a 9.

Even if you are not a football fan and you *never* watch TV, you have certainly heard of Howard Cosell. He is the articulate, logical announcer who analyzes each play and gives capsule lectures on the obscurities of football and the infallibility of his opinions. He is controversial because he is so difficult to contradict. A former lawyer, Cosell's verbal, rational skills make him a definite 1.

Cosell is complemented by Dandy Don Meredith, the color commentator who tells warm, humorous stories about his days as a Dallas Cowboys' quarterback. He describes how it feels to be tackled while your throwing arm is in the launch position. He shares his hunches about what the coach is thinking and which play will be called next. He occasionally sings a few bars from a down-home song and frequently drawls amusing comments about his fellow broadcasters. This "good-ol' boy" is a 9.

The third member of this trio is Frank Gifford, who combines the best of both and efficiently does the play-by-play in an intelligent, interesting style that pleases most everyone. He is a former running back for the New York Giants (right brain), who graduated from college with honors (left brain). He links fine verbal skills with a feel for what is tasteful and helpful to his audience. Obviously, Frank is a 5. He is that double dominant who combines two well-developed sides into a whole person.

If you are a Dandy Don, take a lesson from Frank Gifford and learn language skills, get more organized, but retain that great intuition and warmth. If you are a Howard Cosell,

THE SAD RIGHT, THE HAPPY LEFT

A variety of studies demonstrates how hemispheric specialization influences human emotions and attitudes.

The EEG (electroencephalogram) activity of ten-month-old infants was greater in the left frontal lobe when they viewed happy faces but greater in the right frontal lobe when they were shown pictures of sad faces. Adults react similarly.

Subjects who were contemplating doleful matters rolled their eyeballs leftward (driven by the right brain). Conversely, happy thoughts provided a rightward gaze.

Patients with left-brain damage are generally morose in their outlook on life, while those with right-brain damage are generally unrealistically positive.

Epileptics who have an inordinately high level of electrical activity in the left hemisphere laugh without meaning to and for no apparent cause. On the other hand, seizures that occur in the right brain produce sudden, unprovoked crying spells. These studies support the theory that the emotions of the right brain are generally melancholy, hysterical, and negative and the left is positive and cheerful but insensitive to nuances. Disconnected from or lacking a right hemisphere, the left behaves like the manic half of a manic-depressive, while a solo right emotes like the depressive side.[11]

select out the tasteful, feeling aspects of Giff's approach while retaining your brilliant linguistic ability and perseverance.

Obviously this is a very general description of the meaning and weight of three points on the BPI continuum. However, it will help you to get a picture of your range. As you read the other chapters in this book, you'll encounter other personalities with characteristics similar to your own. They'll be keyed with BPI numbers to help you make comparisons with yourself and learn work strategies suited to your style.

3

GETTING THE FEEL OF
RIGHT AND LEFT

Before you begin reading this chapter, be sure you have a pencil
and paper on hand and time to read the first portion at one
sitting (ten minutes).

It is 1990 and the long-threatened World War III has started
...this time on American soil. Considering the size of the
country and the years of preparation for war, it has been
sickeningly easy for troops from the Soviet Bloc armies to
permeate even the most remote areas of the United States.
All Army, Air Force, Navy and other military forces have
been mustered, and the President has announced that a million troops have been dispersed to strategic sites around the
country. The governor has announced that seventy thousand
well-trained reservists are in place around the state. A civil-
ian-defense warning siren went off about an hour ago and has
been wailing constantly since. Your office radio is tuned to
station KODE, and your staff is gathered around listening to
the mayor report what measures have been taken to protect

citizens, what strategies are to be used for evacuation. In midsentence, the broadcast is interrupted by loud thuds and muffled cries. Suddenly your office door bursts open and six enemy soldiers armed with machine guns and carbine rifles storm into the room. They shout orders and questions excitedly, shoving your staff members against the wall for body searches. One soldier drags the youngest of your file clerks out of the office. She screams as she is buffeted down the hall. You raise an arm in protest, automatically saying "Wait!" And you see a rifle butt coming down on you!

Please write the answers to these questions:

How many troops did the President command into battle around the country?_____

How many reservists did the governor call up?_70,000_

What were the call letters of the radio station your office was tuned to?_____

How many soldiers burst into the office?_6_

How were they armed?_machine guns, rifles_

Answers: a million, seventy thousand, KODE, six machine guns and carbine rifles.

If the World War III story was of compelling interest to you and you answered the questions immediately afterward, you just experienced a shift from your right brain to your left. The story is designed to set a malevolent scene and then focus it on you personally to move you to your emotional, visual hemisphere. Then the sudden switch to writing down facts and figures abruptly forces you left.

Did you feel the difference? Even a slight one? If you felt anything at all, focus on the process. Try to capture a notion of what it was like to be right, then left.

At first you may have been emotional, taking in the whole picture—seeing, hearing and feeling all at the same time. Then, when you were asked to recall figures, names and details, your state of mind probably was quite different.

The left-brained tasks focused your mind on the nonemotional aspects of the scene, and you probably calmed down quite a bit.

If a visual scene is particularly strong—whether pleasant or unpleasant—you may experience difficulty shifting brain modes. You might resist leaving the picture you were viewing or the emotions you are feeling. This resistance occurs because your body is experiencing the scene as reality with all the biochemical processes under way. Sometimes adrenaline rushes in and produces excitement or fear. In joyful situations, the brain's pleasure center releases endorphins and enkephalins, producing warm, fuzzy feelings.

On the other hand, if you have been working hard on a left-brain problem, you may become so engrossed with "the" solution or the next step in the plan that you are unable to shift right for a wider view. You know you're not getting anywhere, but you still feel irritation and resentment when someone suggests another tack or a broader view.

Just as some have difficulty switching modes, others shift too easily. Like a car with a bad transmission, some can't seem to stay in gear. They slip in and out of tasks, moods and thoughts so quickly and constantly that they have no perceivable point of view or direction. It is frustrating to deal with this type of person; it is frustrating to *be* this type of person. An awareness of your shifting patterns can help you overcome these and other thinking problems.

The sensation of shifting may at first elude you, but if you begin to pay attention to these feelings, you will come to know them. There *are* subtle, internal clues you can learn to identify. You can then use these to create and re-create specific body and mind reactions.

Yogis and other Eastern philosophers have been exercising this kind of internal control over so-called autonomic (automatic) body functions for centuries. Their breathing exercises have been shown to cause hemispheric shifts.

WHOLE-BRAIN THINKING

Research shows that by altering primary breathing from one nostril to the other, short-term hemispheric control is accomplished. (See Breathing Right [and Left].)

One swami was able to heat opposite sides of one of his palms to temperatures five to seven degrees apart through breathing and mental exercises. He noted that it had taken him twenty years of training to accomplish this, but biofeedback, called the "Yoga of the West," has enabled people to perform the same feat after several weeks of training.

Biofeedback uses sophisticated, electronic equipment to

BREATHING RIGHT (AND LEFT)

Ancient yogic techniques for changing mental or physiological states prescribed alternating one's breathing between the two nostrils. Research at the Davis Center for Behavioral Neurobiology, Salk Institute for Biological Studies, San Diego, indicates that the nose is more than a mere olfactory device; it is an instrument for altering brain activity. EEG tests show a consistent relationship between nasal airflow and cerebral dominance.

The researcher, David Shannahoff-Khalsa, feels that his work demonstrates "the individual's ability to noninvasively, selectively, and predictably alter cerebral activity and associated physiological processes" and also implies that humans need not be helpless victims of a given emotional state. "If you want to alter an unwanted state," he said, "just breathe through the more congested nostril."[12]

Dr. I. N. Riga, an ear, nose and throat specialist from Bucharest, Romania, discovered that surgically correcting nasal deformities had the simultaneous benefit of curing physical and emotional ills. Of four hundred patients with nasal obstructions due to deviated septums, those who had breathed through the left nostril suffered from stress-related diseases (89 percent left-nostril breathers versus 29 percent of right-nostril breathers). Once their right-nasal passages were open, these former left-nostril breathers were relieved of their stress illnesses. This concurs with other research that indicates that the right brain usually is the source of negative stress. (See Chapter 14, Stress.)[13]

---

measure such body responses as skin moisture, muscle tension, and electrical emissions of the brain. As brain waves shorten or lengthen and as temperature and muscle tension rise and fall, the biofeedback machine to which the person is attached signals these changes either visually or with sound. The person then devises internal strategies for achieving the desired body reaction.

Like the children's game of blindman's buff, as you get closer to the object, you receive verbal signals telling whether you are getting hot or cold. Then you change directions based on this feedback.

However, the biofeedback client has an advantage over the game player. A person who has developed a strategy for achieving warmer fingers or less muscle tension can perform the feat over and over again without further feedback.

Your feelings are *your* feedback, and by becoming sensitive to them, you will be able to shift and integrate your brain's activities as the situation demands. Like the person in biofeedback therapy who learns to control tension, perspiration, heartbeat, temperature and other responses, you can develop inner strategies for moving between your brain's hemispheres or integrating the thinking powers of both.

JOB SHIFTS

If you operate successfully on your job, the chances are that you shift sides well. But if there are times when you're not happy with your performance, try developing your awareness of shifting and what provokes it so that you can do it at will.

Shifting on the job:

- enables you to use more of your brainpower by consciously selecting the appropriate brain style.
- helps you to understand the behavior of others and alter or adapt to it.

- shows you ways to change or adapt to your job, resulting in higher performance and personal fulfillment.
- increases energy levels and releases creative abilities.

Some hypothetical job situations in which shifting hemispheres can help follow.

LAST-MINUTE JITTERS

You have just joined an advertising agency and are presenting a marketing proposal for a new account, a ski resort development project. It is the first project that is all yours. You've done the left-brain work; you have the facts, figures and conclusions.

As you enter the presentation room, your stomach flutters. Panic nearly constricts your throat. You have ten minutes before you're on. You know your stuff but your rightside fear is taking over.

At this point, you should turn your back to the group and write your key points on a chalkboard or flip chart. To overcome fear of "looking dumb," as you write on the chart or board, talk to yourself about how helpful it will be. You might want to recall a favorite teacher who wrote on the board. While talking to yourself, use positive, simple language because the right side is always listening and acting on the messages you send yourself. Speaking out loud is a left-brain activity that will help you clarify your message and calm your flutters.

If these crutches are not available, organize your notes and print *big key* words on a separate sheet of paper or five-by-seven file cards. Move around; if you feel comfortable with a member of the group you can review the main points of your materials one-to-one. Organizing, writing and clarifying are activities that move you to your left brain away from the panicky right. Printing key words is a drawing activity and provides a strong visual image for your right brain. Moving around and relating to a sympathetic person helps the right brain better comprehend the material. After moving your thinking left to allay fears, and your right to get a clear picture of your presentation, you integrate the two. The seemingly incredible result: a lucid grasp of what you are going to say and the confidence to articulate it.

Once you are under way, scan your audience for a sympathetic-looking person. Establish eye contact and check back frequently. This will continue to build up your confidence and enhance your communicative ability because you'll feel you're presenting your ideas to a supportive acquaintance. As the two of you become comfortable with this eye-to-eye communication, the person's physical reactions will provide subtle clues about the effectiveness of your presentation. You will automatically make adjustments, operating on intuition.

When you pick up signals from dissatisfied or "unfriendly" listeners, recognize their concerns. If they seem genuine, deal with them. Otherwise, focus on the supportive members of your group. Ignoring the negative members of the group and connecting with the positive ones can have another effect, too: The negatives will want their share of your smiles and glances and may modify their attitudes to gain them.

Your presentation has gained energy and liveliness! Dynamite!

THE BOREDOM FACTOR

You are attending the monthly staff meeting. The president of branch banking is conducting the meeting. Gad, she's hard to listen to—she is speaking in a monotone and keeps repeating her points. You find her boring, but you want to listen. You know when you're off somewhere, she can tell it—especially when you get that glazed look in your eyes. Here's the perfect time to practice using both sides of your brain. On the left, take brief notes or simply put check marks beside items she covers on the agenda. Does she follow an outline? What is the organization? Ask yourself

key questions: "Why does she see that as important?"
"Where did she get those statistics?" On the right, picture
the setting or the people she is talking about. Notice the
way she turns during her delivery, her expressions, and
how she smiles. Relate what she's saying to some other
subject or talk you've heard recently. Do you see any patterns emerging between the talk you heard on defense
spending, and this, on branch banking? Look for connections, and before you know it, you'll be listening intently.

ENIGMATIC ENGINEERS

As the director of the AMAX plant in Golden, Colorado,
you sometimes wonder if you should have stayed back in
engineering. Relating to those guys in Research & Development is frustrating. These so-called creative thinkers seem
to lose ideas that don't fit into a given concept. They tend
to rethink projects, reopening a dialogue that should have
ended once decisions were made. There appear to be no
boundaries or categories to their thinking. They have trouble expressing themselves in a logical fashion, and they
bring in irrelevant ideas.

Their heads are filled with images, fantasies and imag-
inings, their hearts with feelings, hopes and desires. But
they can't express themselves in objective or factual terms.
They change their minds for no apparent reason. They seem
to be inarticulate, uncooperative and do "fuzzy" thinking!

Here is the dilemma of a left-brained director dealing
with right-brained researchers: How do you manage them,
especially when they in turn see you as narrow, rigid and
one-track-minded?

For a change, use your right brain and open up to their
seemingly irrelevant speculations. Relax and see the picture a researcher is striving to paint. Fantasize what will
happen if this product brings riches and great fame to
AMAX. Try to bring order to the researchers' ramblings
by paraphrasing, summarizing and asking questions. Speed
the organizing process by asking for simple explanations,
using analogies and metaphors that appeal to both the left

and the right sides of the brain. The company will benefit from better communication and understanding. Its employees will gain new skills by using their less preferred brain hemispheres.

NOT FOR PLUMBERS ONLY

Recently John, the manager of a commercial art studio, commented that he felt blocked, tired and drained. The ideas that used to flow and overflow in his mind seemed to have dried up. As he discussed his work, two important aspects became apparent. First his clients became bigger and bigger, in dollars and prestige. (His current chief account was Bell Telephone.) Second, he has a great deal of pressure on his time from many administrative, political and social obligations that are tied into servicing the accounts.

Here is the case of a right-brained person who has shifted to the left. John needed to re-create the setting that allowed him to create so stunningly. In the past, daydreaming allowed fanciful ways of seeing concepts and data. Now with time constraints, he had eliminated daydreaming, and with it, the priceless insights. He had switched from cross-country skiing and bicycling to opening art shows and attending receptions. He had few solitary moments and absolutely no unscheduled time.

To overcome these blocks to creativity, he joined a health club where he can meditate while relaxing in the steam-room. He goes for long, contemplative walks on work breaks. At the art openings, he gazes at the pictures, avoiding chic talk.

He's having lots of success with his new behavior, winning the admiration of friends and associates. They're glad he's concerned about his health and has deepening interest in the arts. And at work, the ideas are flowing once again.

THINK HOW YOU THINK

You have noted that these four people used significant shifting between hemispheres and at times integration of the two. You also may have recognized the changes in behavior that precipitated these shifts. Just in case you're a BPI 9 who was totally absorbed in the vignettes and extracted few practical applications from them, pages 60–61 list the actions that produced shifts.

As in any dynamic situation, one change affects the others. Later in the communication chapters you will learn more about this interaction between or among workers,

LEFT TO RIGHT	RIGHT TO LEFT
1. visualizing, daydreaming	1. taking notes, writing on flip chart
2. discovering pattern, big picture, connections	2. organizing, setting priorities for notes, reviewing agenda
3. opening up to "irrelevancies"	3. evaluating, eliminating extraneous ideas, setting goals
4. responding to body language, tone of voice, hug, smile, laugh	4. analyzing body language, tone of voice
5. talking to yourself in a positive, supportive way; using colorful, playful, childlike language	5. practicing your rational opinions and presentations
6. seeing through others' eyes, trying to feel their point of view	6. taking practice run, comparing, judging
7. moving, exercising, recreating, experiencing, playing, enjoying	7. deciding, recalling, questioning, checking progress, goals, time

Here are some suggestions for providing shifts that are not mentioned in the previous examples or table:

LEFT TO RIGHT	RIGHT TO LEFT
1. shifting phone to your left ear (controlled by right brain) for *emphatic* listening	1. shifting phone to your right ear (controlled by left brain) for *analytic* listening
2. doodling, drawing, printing	2. writing, outlining, listing, working crossword puzzle, solving math problem
3. singing rounds, humming, recalling, joking, chuckling	3. asking questions, making puns
4. breathing deeply saying or thinking "maaaa" with each exhale; doing this until you feel relaxed; taking stroll to no place in particular	4. striding purposefully, touching toes or performing some other calisthenic activity, counting out loud until you have completed prescribed number
5. carrying a clipboard, notes or other comforting symbol	5. using dictating machine, picking up pointer or some symbol of authority
6. taking a minivacation at your desk; leaning back, relaxing, closing eyes, day-dreaming	6. going off alone, writing memo describing anger, concern, problem
7. visualizing green for freedom to glide, experience, enjoy, soar	7. thinking amber or yellow to slow down, considering consequences
8. making eye contact with others to feel their point of view	8. reporting experience to boss or spouse (preplan it with list)
9. relating to someone or something you know or have experienced	9. connecting with time, schedule, historic moment; looking at watch; mentally planning trip or day's activities
10. being aware of the colors, space, aromas, sounds, emotions around you.	10. estimating value of your precision, economies, foresight
11. seeing the whole situation, how each person and element is related	11. breaking problem into separate parts, revising policies until consistency prevails

whether they have similar or opposed hemispheric preferences. In addition, all occupations have right- or left-brain characteristics. How employees balance themselves is important to individual performance as well as to the group's.

Human beings are the only creatures who can think about how they think. But even for so thoughtful an animal, it is difficult to describe or even focus on.

But if you are to extend your brainpower, you must identify how it feels to be thinking in certain ways. You need to know how it feels to be processing thoughts primarily in your right or your left hemisphere. When you can identify these thinking experiences you can purposefully alter, re-create, heighten, or move between or among them. You do these things now by accident, not by design. In other words, you *can* think how you think.

Brain scientists have developed ways to measure specific thinking activities. The EEG (electroencephalogram) indicates which side of your brain is in primary use during specific thinking tasks. It is exciting to see quantification of your thought processes and evidence that a change of thought produces higher or lower readings on this biofeedback equipment.

For example, if you are wired to an EEG, which registers the electrical emissions from the left and right hemispheres of your brain, the voltage measured will change as you perform right or left hemispheric tasks. You can see the difference on charts or digital readouts. When you are expressing a personal opinion, your left brain emits different levels of electricity than when you are visualizing. In other words, you can see a physical record of your brain shifts.

The therapeutic purpose of biofeedback is to help clients control fine body functions, primarily to reduce the tension that causes such problems as headaches, irregular heartbeat, and high blood pressure.

The next six chapters discuss mind movers, exercises designed to help you experience and identify shifts between hemispheres. It is important that you understand and accept the feasibility of the concept before you go on. If you are unconvinced, you're probably a BPI 1 to 3 and should read the HOME BIOFEEDBACK box following this chapter for a list of simple, inexpensive biofeedback devices and exercises you can use at home to experience the control you can have over your body and thinking.

These mind movers are not difficult. In fact, you already have many of the basic skills and use them every day. For example, have you ever been out late at a concert or meeting and seen a group of tough-looking teenagers approaching you? You experience signals from your body that you are frightened; you feel a rush of adrenaline in your stomach, a prickly feeling on the back of your neck and an urge to run. (There are other, less apparent signals, such as muscle tension, increased heartbeat and blood pressure, and lowered finger temperature.) These are feelings you have come to identify with surprise and fear. And you have developed ways to quiet these body responses and avoid debilitating panic. You say logically to yourself:

"How many are there? Where's the nearest police station? The first step I learned in my self-defense class was..."

These and other thoughts are all the workings of your left brain and immediately calm your actions and appearance. They also help get the heartbeat, blood pressure, perspiration and temperature levels back to normal.

Years of experience with frightening situations have helped you identify body reactions and learn how to control them. Mind movers are designed to help you refine this control further so that you can cope consciously with thinking tasks that are now rather automatic or reactive.

In this chapter you have learned how, when and why to shift between hemispheres. You have a better understanding of the value of shifting—to you personally, to your job performance, and to everyone in your workworld. In Chapters 4, 5, 6, 7, 8 and 9 you will learn exactly how to refine your left- and right-brain skills.

WHOLE-BRAIN THINKING

Now you're ready for Chapter 4, which reveals a nifty shifting mind mover called internal brainstorming.

HOME BIOFEEDBACK

These items may already be in your home, if not, they are relatively inexpensive.

A *thermometer* that can be held by the mercury ball. Hold between index and thumb and get a reading.

Finger temperatures range from the mid-seventies to ninety-five degrees. Altering the temperature of a finger by several degrees in three to five minutes is considered noteworthy for beginners. Often you will produce results opposite to your intentions (lowering the temperature when you want to raise it) because you are under stress from trying too hard or because you are using the wrong inner strategy as you experiment.

Now try to raise and lower this temperature by relaxing (goes up ... gets warmer) or tensing up (goes down ... gets colder). Strategies for accomplishing this are:

• To make your fingertips warmer, see yourself in front of a fire, or on a warm, sandy beach. Visualize a complete scene of this sort and enjoy the comfortable, happy feeling that goes with it.
• To make your fingertips cool, think of a stressful, unhappy, dangerous scene. Fill in all the details and experience the negative emotions—fear, sadness, dread, anger, etc.

You might notice that it is easier to warm your dominant hand (the left if you are left-handed, and vice versa). The left-hand temperature fluctuates more than the right because it is controlled by the more emotional right brain. Women's hand temperatures tend to be colder than men's.

An interesting extension of this biofeedback experiment is to purchase two identical thermometers and learn to control each hand separately, making one go up and the other down. Home and outdoor thermometers may be purchased for $1.50 to $2.50 each at discount centers or hardware or variety stores. These thermometers are suggested because

(HOME BIOFEEDBACK, *cont.***)**

they are less expensive and sturdier than the regular medical thermometer, which has the advantage of better calibration.

A *child's lie-detector kit* measures moisture levels on the skin, which indicate stress level. Finger-warming strategies may be used to alter this body reaction also. As the stress level goes up, the body secretes more moisture on the fingertips, producing a higher tone on the lie detector. These kits are available at Radio Shack outlets and toy stores. They cost approximately $12 and require two batteries. Instructions describe other experiments which have biofeedback implications.

Two bathroom scales can help you develop an inner knowledge of how you distribute your body weight when standing. Place them side by side, with one foot on each. Take the readings on each side; then, with your eyes closed, develop an internal strategy for balancing your weight equally between the two. It does not matter whether the scales are the same; what is important is that you can learn to take a reading of both and re-create those readings with your eyes closed by becoming aware of how it feels to have your weight distributed in the same manner as when you took the reading. This same kind of biofeedback training helps individuals with leg paralysis walk again.[14]

MIND MOVERS

4

INTERNAL BRAINSTORMING

Our problem is to keep alive the powerful stimulant of individual thought at all levels and in every phase of our effort. Unless we do, we run the risk of making a displaced person out of the man with big ideas.

—Crawford H. Greenewalt

No idea is so outlandish that it should not be considered with a searching but at the same time with a steady eye.

—Winston Churchill

EVERY ACTION YOU TAKE, EVERY THOUGHT YOU THINK, every emotion you experience is routed through your brain. It is an amazing organ with potential far beyond the meager uses to which most people put it. It is this promise that inspires hope for the future of humankind and the goal toward which this book is directed.

It may be difficult for you to believe that you have the same basic mental equipment as Einstein or Madame Curie had, but it's true. There is little difference in size of brains— only in the ways we use them. (See BRAIN SIZE.) The advantage "great minds" have is an inclination to use both sides effectively while the rest of us dwell increasingly in the side that seems natural and comfortable.

BRAIN SIZE

The average human brain weighs approximately 3 lbs (60 ounces for men and about 55 for women). This difference should not be interpreted as proof of male superiority; the important factor within a species is the ratio of body size to brain weight. Einstein's brain was of average size, while Lord Byron's was huge (220 grams). As in other areas of human physique, it's not how big it is, but what you do with it that counts.[15]

Cro-Magnon Man had a brain 15 percent larger than that of contemporary human beings.
    The average brain has ten to twenty billion cells, 5 percent of which are developed.[16]

In comparing the sizes of brains between species of the same approximate size, it appears that there is a correlation between the size of the brain and distribution of food. For instance, species that live in trees have larger brains proportionately than ground animals. Therefore it seems that a complex challenge of attaining food stimulates brain growth.[17]

You can make better use of your mind. And it's not that difficult. It involves exercising both sides of your brain and relating the two. You go through variations of this process constantly. This does not mean that one side of your brain shuts down completely while the other one is active; it does mean that one side is active more than the other and that the shifts occur because of changes in activities or perception. To give you an idea how quickly and spontaneously this can happen, look at the following drawing:

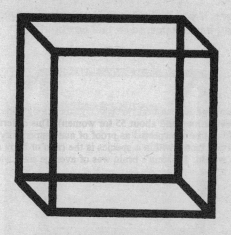

When you first viewed it, the top of the box probably appeared to be where the shaded area is, as in this example:

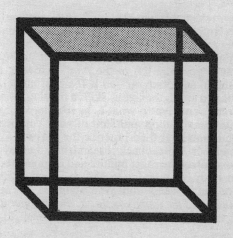

However, if you looked at it lingeringly, the opening of the box may have appeared in this position:

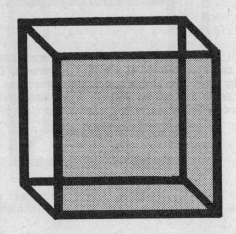

If you went through that shift, you changed your perception from the left brain to the right. The point is that it happens most easily when you are not trying. This is true with most hemispheric jumps, at least those involving movement *from* the left *to* the right. Allowing brain side-swapping to sneak up on you is the best tactic, but if you are trying to strengthen your skill in moving, it is important to become sensitive to what is happening so that you can replicate the situation and shift at will. You need to think how you think and then practice the moves.

Remember, biofeedback research and therapy prove that you can control the most minute and complicated functions of your body, so learning to shift between hemispheres at any moment is well within your abilities. *You have a powerful mind, and the more you flex it, the stronger it becomes.*

For the next few pages prepare yourself to be keenly

aware of what is happening inside your head. As you go through these brain shift exercises, try to note how you feel so that you can re-create that feeling and pattern of reaction again and again. This is how you will become adept at using both sides of your brain and selecting the more appropriate one for the task at hand.

The optical-illusion exercise is not really a true mind mover; it occurs so spontaneously and unpredictably that it really can't be counted as a willful movement. This does not denigrate its usefulness to heighten awareness of mind-moving or to strengthen your brain-shifting muscles. In other words, it is a warm-up, so as a warm-up look at all the optical illusions you can find. Here are a few:

As you shift from seeing the duck to the rabbit or the rabbit to the duck, you are shifting automatically.

This shift is less automatic. As you switch from seeing the young woman to the old hag, you must consciously move your eyes.

Whether you see a vase or profiles, the object you selected is in the foreground.

How many squares are in the figure below?

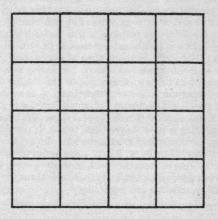

WHOLE-BRAIN THINKING

Your first answer, and the left-brain one, probably was 16, which you could compute by counting the small squares or by multiplying 4 down and 4 across. If you are keyed to the ways of testers, you might say 17 (the original 16 plus the outline of the total box). To see a total of 30, you must use persistent right-brained viewing, which would eventually allow you to perceive:

- The 4 quadrants of the large box;
- 5 more boxes of 4 (including 1 in the middle of the large box and 4 which are at the box edge and inset from the corners);
- And 4 boxes of nine small squares.
- Add these (5 + 4 + 4 = 13) to the original 17 and you have 30. (See MIND EXTENSION.)

MIND EXTENSION

Edward de Bono, a psychologist and a doctor of medicine, does research at Cambridge University on the behavior of biological systems. He spends much of his time lecturing on extending thinking through a specific approach he terms lateral, parallel, or inspired thinking—pushing yourself to look farther and in different ways. Through examples he explains the difference between lateral thinking and vertical thinking, which is traditional and logical. In vertical thinking, you proceed directly from one state of information to another state—like building a tower by placing one stone firmly on top of the preceding stone or like digging a hole by making deeper the hole you already have. A characteristic of vertical thinking is continuity; of lateral thinking, discontinuity. Vertical thinking is analytical (left brain); lateral thinking is provocative (right brain). In vertical thinking, the conclusion must come after the evidence, while in lateral-parallel thinking, it may come *before* the evidence. Lateral thinking is concerned with generating new ideas and approaches and with extending capabilities through imagination, intuition and inspiration.[18]

These warm-ups and optical illusions will heighten your awareness of how you think and how it feels to shift between hemispheres.

The first mind mover offered for your practice and use is also fairly familiar to you. Called internal brainstorming, it is based on regular brainstorming, that valuable group technique for discovering solutions and concepts. (See BRAINSTORMING.) Let's review its rules. A group gathers to create an idea or solve a problem. The purpose of the session is announced. Each person in the group is asked to voice any idea or solution that comes to mind, no matter how fragmented or impractical it might seem. There is one hard-and-fast rule in brainstorming: No one, not even the speaker, is allowed to criticize or comment on the ideas presented. Evaluation of the various ideas and selection of the most useful ones come later, but during the imaginative right-brained part of brainstorming, negatives are taboo.

BRAINSTORMING

There are four basic and unalterable rules to the group process of brainstorming that set it apart from other problem-solving procedures. They are:

1. Defer judgment on any idea that is expressed. This even includes encouraging comments to others or qualifying phrases attached to your own suggestions; for example, avoid "That's a good idea" or "My thought is probably irrelevant but here it is."
2. The session should be as freewheeling as possible, with each person voicing whatever ideas come to mind—no holds barred.
3. Participants are encouraged to hitchhike on the ideas of others. When one person's suggestion sparks an idea by another, it should be instantly expressed.
4. Quantity, not quality of ideas, is the goal of brainstorming. Evaluation and elimination can be accomplished later.[19]

WHOLE-BRAIN THINKING

Internal brainstorming is simply applying the same rules to your own thinking process. You need only a pencil, a piece of paper and some time to think. Write a sentence clarifying the object of your internal brainstorming session. Are you trying to find the money to send your youngest child to college in six months? To devise a marketing plan for a gadget you've just invented? To discover a theme for the party you're planning? In twenty-five words or less, state exactly what you want to do. Sometimes just defining the need or situation produces answers. (The process of definition is almost always the first step in any of the mind movers; therefore, options in problem-defining are offered in DEFINING A PROBLEM.)

Defining a Problem

There are many ways to define a problem and thus put yourself one step closer to a solution. Try these and see which ones work best for you.

1. Simply write out this statement and fill in the blank, using as few words as possible:
   I am dissatisfied with the present level of _____.
2. Push yourself into lateral thinking by forcing at least four additional definitions of your problem.
3. Ask yourself aloud again and again: "What do I *really* want from this situation/project/promotion/additional schooling, etc.?
4. Use "framing" to get a precise view first—as in a frame with boundaries—of what you have now, and then what you want. Compare these two views, and analyze the discrepancies, and you will understand more about the nature of the problem.
5. Minimize the problem by saying: "This is not so massive"; then the problem will be revealed in its simplest and most basic form.
6. Visualize the most pleasing outcome to the problem. This fantasy will contrast with the present situation, and the true problem will be clarified.

(Defining a Problem, *cont*.)

7. Write out this statement and fill in the blank in as few words as possible:
   The real problem is _____.
   Repeat this at least ten times, expecting a different answer with each repetition. This is a good technique to use when you suspect that the trouble is between people.
8. Break down the problem into subsituations and problems. This makes it more manageable and helps you know where to begin to find solutions.
9. Sometimes the problem is not really yours to define. It may not be your field of expertise or responsibility. To find out, view the situation from three points of view:
   a. I would like to talk to _____
      about this situation.
   b. I need a more expert opinion.
   c. I'd like to delegate this part of the problem to _____.

   If you get comforting responses to these statements, you will know that the problem is not really yours to solve.

Once the need is clearly delineated, keep your pencil in hand to jot down cue words for the ideas that come to mind. This frees you from worrying about remembering your ideas, and it helps you keep track of your thoughts without being committed to them.

If you are more comfortable with verbalizing and technological concepts (left brain), you might want to use a tape recorder to capture the rovings of your internal brainstorming. But writing out the problem is essential with either approach.

The next step is to make sure you are comfortable and in a quiet setting. You may wish to close your eyes. Lean back in your chair and let go. Now pose the problem to yourself. What answers do you hear, see, feel? Do words or pictures come to mind? If so, jot them down. If they are just fragments or glimpses of concepts, try to flesh them out a little. One idea will lead to another; some thoughts provoke several concepts or one whole solution. Keep going; let every idea come quickly, flowingly. Continue to write down cue words on your paper. Wherever they fall on the paper is fine; don't be concerned with order or sequence. If you find yourself slowing down, look at one of the cue words or concepts and go from there. After you've pursued this path for a while, look back at your notes and write down the first thought that comes to mind, starting over again, perhaps on a completely new pathway, perhaps retracing the same ground. When you retrace your steps, you will often discover some idea you sped by the first time. Continue this process for at least ten minutes. Sometimes you'll find many ideas rushing in all at once; at other times they will come more sporadically and singly. Just enjoy them as they come.

When you have finished (or ten to fifteen minutes have elapsed), think about how you feel and felt. Try to get a sense of how these ideas came to you. Did you see most of them in your mind's eye, in printed word form or as a picture? Did you hear your own voice or another one? Did they rush at you and dart from many directions, or did they come to you in a more orderly manner? Was it a stream-of-consciousness thought process, or did it have another feel about it? Try to identify the feeling you had about it. Was it comfortable and relaxing, or did you feel somewhat uncomfortable and forced? Did you proceed in fits and starts or as if your memory were unreeling? Once you have identified how the experience felt, hang on to the memory. The more effortlessly the ideas came, the more fully you were experiencing right-side thinking. If you frequently critiqued the ideas, you were engaging your left brain in the process. Practice internal brainstorming on other problems or needs until you can tune in the right-brain "free form" thinking process for ten minutes without leftward shift along the way. For an example of internal brainstorming see pages 74 and 75.

The question or problem was posed by a woman—to herself—about a young friend, Carol, who was trying to enroll in college. Her parents were divorced, her father was an alcoholic and her mother was just barely able to support herself and was very involved in a romance. The student had worked at two jobs for two years trying to save enough money to enroll in college full-time, but a series of misfortunes wiped out her meager savings.

This example demonstrates the way the right brain operates. Some of the flights of fancy might seem familiar to you. Notice that the first ideas were written in a sequence down the left side of the paper. They seemed to zigzag between the left and right brain. There are traditional and left-brained ideas like calling an educator-acquaintance, taking money out of the bank, getting her a better-paying restaurant job. Some of her rather impractical right-brained suggestions for Carol were: to rob a bank, to get married to her son, to drop out, and to become a prostitute. Some of those early speculations, such as to hold a bazaar and call the newspaper and TV, later produced a helpful plan. (Bazaar was misspelled—a right-brain mistake that this person would not make on the left side.) As the brainstorming continued to fill the other half of the page, a larger concept was forming: to hold some sort of money-raising affair, getting cooperation from the young woman's friends. The brainstorming culminated in a rather extensive plan for getting publicity for the fund raiser. It proved to be a workable plan, using almost all of the ideas mentioned in the internal brainstorming session.

The second half of internal brainstorming involves the left brain. Return to your internal brainstorm list and consider each idea separately. Cross out the negative, facetious and cynical thoughts. Most of us would not seriously consider calling the President or turning to prostitution. If your logical left and intuitive right both say no to an idea, then don't debate—just eliminate. If both sides of your brain react positively, then the decision is rational and emotionally acceptable. Jot down these viable alternatives. But what if you have a split decision—if your right and left sides disagree? List these ideas in a maybe column. Now

June 21

The problem I'm trying to solve:

How can I help Carol get enrolled at CSU this Fall?

Call John S.

Take the tuition out of my bank account.

Call Ch. 7 - Deal for Help

Ask friends for donations

hold a bazaar

rob a bank   call the president

Call the newspapers — [Joe D. human interest story - how students get by in hard times]

get her a better job = restaurant / computers? (Estes Park - Ed)

garage sale - / sell / Amway or Avon / body [prostitution]

mairy her to Jim

ADOPT HER.

Ask her employers for help — she deserves it — her folks should help.

run through them again. Often at this point a number of them fall into a pattern or form a whole solution.

In the example cited, the plan that evolved was:

I will invite Carol to have a garage sale at my house and

Make an appeal at breakfast
Club - fat cats - + business
people with $. She's will-
ing to work

Do nothing - <u>NO</u>

Will she give up? Why is she
doing this? - aptitude   Pray
                    test

Is she assertive enough? is she
the right field? scholarship.
                  grant.

Run an ad in the paper - sad
            story - or sell stuff

Got my stuff out to sell -

	rug	$50
who	books + pix	20
else	records	10
has	table	20
stuff	lawnmower	30
to sell?	desk?	—

will contribute some excess items worth about $150.00. I
will pay for an ad in the paper and put up signs. I will make
flyers and contact friends, especially conservatives who
don't believe in government handouts. This is their oppor-

WHOLE-BRAIN THINKING

INTERNAL BRAINSTORMING ANALYSIS		
Steps	**Process**	**Feelings**
I. Writing out the problem or need (*left brain*)	listing defining verbalizing delineating	efficient controlled focused
II. Brainstorming (*right brain*)	ideas, sounds, pictures and concepts appearing flowing production irrelevant and unrelated thoughts. defocused, blurry ideas	stream of consciousness relaxed, let go, time whisks by or stands still sense of expectancy, curiosity, wonder effortless thinking
III. Evaluation (*left brain*)	eliminate judge, scoff quantify ask 5 "W" questions (who? what? when? where? why?) apply to tangibles, practicalities	surprise at volume of ideas, track of thinking and value initially, the waste of time on silliness
(*right brain*)	eliminate repugnant ideas focus on attractive ideas	"I just couldn't" gut-level rebellion "Sounds like fun," exciting, etc. I had a hunch it would work
IV. Integration (*left brain and right brain*)	You see the whole solution or concept and fill in the details ... or they just "fall into place."	stimulated excited "aha" elated, powerful, self-confident "It'll be fun!"

tunity to show that they will contribute voluntarily if the government will "just get out of their pockets." I will call a friend in the media and suggest a feature story on how youngsters are working their way through college in spite of funding cutbacks. Carol will work the garage sale, get friends to help, including both her employers, and ask her parents for contributions to the sale. She should make enough money to get into the next semester of school and perhaps attract the attention of someone willing to sponsor an earnest, hardworking student.

Internal brainstorming involves four phases—with appropriate hemispheric shifts—as described in INTERNAL BRAINSTORMING ANALYSIS. But before you study it, consider these questions:

How did you feel when you were internally brainstorming? Between the time you wrote out the problem and when you started the actual brainstorming, did you feel any difference? Did you have a sense of timelessness, vagueness, or not caring intensely about the problem? Did some idea excite you? Then could you feel the shift back to the left brain when you did the evaluation? If you didn't feel anything, that's okay for now. As you use this technique, you will more and more experience these changes in feelings as you shift back and forth.

When you have a half hour to spare, propose another situation or problem and try the exercise again. Remember, the more exercise your brain gets, the better it works and the more keenly you will feel these shifts. When you have used internal brainstorming with some success, you have taken a very important step toward using your right brain and you have experienced the feel of shifting between hemispheres. You *know* that you can control the workings of your brain, and you're ready to focus on . . . CINEMATICS.

5

CINEMATICS

CINEMATICS, THE PROCESS OF SEEING PICTURES IN your mind's eye, is the second mind mover. In this chapter you will practice daydreaming and then discover how visualization can help you to solve problems and plan strategies as well as to learn and retrieve information.

FLASHBACKS/FLASHFORWARDS

The first level of cinematics is flashback/flashforward, more commonly known as daydreaming. You are probably familiar with the cinematic device of explaining a plot or character by showing scenes from the past. Your daydreams can flash back in the same way. Whether the occurrences were painful or pleasant, the more you feel the emotions of that memory, the more vivid your picture.

Flashbacks are shifts to the right brain because most visual and emotional activity is experienced there. Methodical and mechanical physical activities such as collating the latest mail, jogging or mopping can help you ease into this state. As the movement falls into a rhythm, you access the right brain and you see, feel and experience other moments, other worlds. Both sad and happy flashbacks can enhance your recall of details and put a past experience into current perspective.

"Thinking is when the picture is in your head with the sound turned off."

Your mind also flashes forward and imagines scenes in advance. Cartoons and comic strips illustrate this by showing an anticipated scene in a wispy balloon over a character's head. Flashforwards allow you to preview problem situations, savor your fondest hopes or test a plan of action.

Your flashbacks and flashforwards can become mini-vacations at your desk or work sessions for *both* sides of your brain. They are almost always pleasant, and you can snap back to reality in an instant. They are easy to come by and require no particular scheme or equipment. You can daydream anywhere, anytime, and on any topic *if* you give yourself permission. Enjoy them and use them!

A flashback could unfold in this manner:

> You're watching television and the heroine's face reminds you of your best friend, who moved to another state several years ago. "...should have answered her last letter...been busy. She takes her time about replying too. That's one of the strong points of our friendship...there's no guilt involved. I've had other comfortable relationships but none with this 'timeless' quality. She likes me as I am. It's the same acceptance I feel from relatives but better. Parents feel obligated to guide, criticize, evaluate. An Indian tribe somewhere had a tradition of leaving discipline to aunts and uncles so that the parent-child relationship was unmarred by negatives. The unpleasant aspects of parenting were delegated to an 'other authority' whose emotions were not so closely involved. Geezzz...what's happening with the TV program? I've lost the thread of the plot now."

See how easily flashbacks occur, how far-ranging they can be? They jump back and forth between abstract thoughts and strong visual images. They are filled with irrelevancies as well as nuggets of self-discovery.

Flashforwards have the same characteristics, and within one daydream you often set both processes in motion:

> You're driving to a ski lodge mountain cabin . . . and a red car nearly sideswipes you. Suddenly you are six years old again . . . your father is driving . . . and a red car almost forces you off the road. This scene comes back clearly, instantly and with all the emotions of the real experience. . . . As you continue the drive you flash forward to the three friends who'll be greeting you at the door. Have they been skiing yet? Is dinner ready? Are we eating in or out?

See how naturally you flash back and forth?

Try flashing now: Allow your mind to wander aimlessly, freely—forward or backward. See the images as clearly as you can, enjoying the many paths your daydreams explore. Just lean back for a moment and stare into space. Close your eyes or focus on some interesting object and G L I D E.

When you return to the here and now, make a mental note of where your daydream started and where it ended. You might even write down the beginning and ending points, but there's no need to record the entire daydream. It is fairly easy to recall the sequence of your daydreams. After all, they're *your* dreams, filled with your personal feelings and thoughts, each with special meaning for you. If your recall is not precise, that's okay too. The purpose of this exercise is to illustrate how easily you can daydream and to improve the quality of your flashbacks/flashforwards.

During the next few days, be aware of your daydreams and keep a record of them, using the above daydream log or a similiar system. Under "Locale," record where you were and what you were doing when the reverie started (work, home, shopping center, while typing, cleaning, staring, etc.). Under "Content," describe strong feelings. Under

DAY DREAM LOG

Day	Locale	Content	Flashback	Flashforward	Started	Finished
12-20-81 4 p.m.	I-70	Scared	6 yrs. old		see red car	as Copper comes into view
5 p.m.	Vail lodge	Uncertain		living room & front door	first lights of Vail	parking lot

"Started" and "Finished," note what topic the dream started on and what topic it ended with.

Identify the feelings you have during those dreams. Do you see incomplete, blurry images? Flashes of words? Do you hear sounds or voices? Do you flash forward more than backward? Is there a different feeling about each?

WHOLE-BRAIN THINKING

By recording your daydreams for a few days you will see a pattern. If you are right-brained, your daydreams will be highly fanciful and possibly purely escapist. If you are left-brained, they will probably be more down-to-earth and purposeful. Don't be concerned either way. Just reflect on how your hemispheric preference shows itself when flashing back and forward. Your abilities will increase as you become more relaxed, and your flashbacks/flashforwards will become more enjoyable and fruitful in producing helpful ideas. You'll be on your way to harnessing one of your brain's natural resources.

There is one pitfall to discourage in your daydream patterns—the dreaded worry habit. This scene describes it:

> You're in the dentist's waiting room a few minutes early for a filling. It's been a hectic day and you forego the dog-eared copies of *Time* and *Newsweek* in favor of a relaxing reverie. Suddenly you flash back to your last office visit. You can't remember whether you paid for it. You think you wrote out the check but can't recall mailing it. Surely when you called for this appointment, Mrs. Trent would have said something.

> "No . . . maybe not . . . she probably doesn't handle the money. Well, I must have mailed that letter . . . I'm very methodical about that sort of thing. On the other hand, I don't remember taking it out of the glove compartment."

> "I hate to walk in there and say 'hi' if I haven't paid it yet. What kind of jerk would he think I am?"

> "Oh, he probably doesn't keep track of that sort of thing."

> "Who are you kidding? He's got the first dollar he made after dental school. . . ."

> And so on . . .

In this kind of daydream, your left and right brains are arguing. You chew and rechew details, trying to digest them, but they remain tough and unpalatable.

Your flashback has just deteriorated into a worry session. And if you allow this to happen often, you're headed for habitual worrying—a worthless and draining practice.

To deal with these unhappy sidetracks from your daydreams, confront the problem and deal with it immediately whenever possible. Look in your glove compartment and see if the check is still there. Ask the receptionist to see if you've paid the bill. If you have, you can go back to your dream time. If you neglected to pay it, write a check on the spot or ask for another copy of the bill so that you can put a check in the mail. Even if you did neglect to mail the check, you'll feel better once you have expressed your concern.

You'll know you're on a worry-go-round when you start feeling physical symptoms of stress: furrowed brow, tense jaw and shoulders, queasy stomach or a generally discouraged feeling. If there's no clear action you can take to remedy the problem you are fretting over, interrupt your daydream-gone-sour. Get up, move around, drink a glass of water, eat an apple—whatever it takes to stop the worry cycle.

In spite of the multiple attributes of daydreams, there is a strong bias in our society against the practice. Many of us grew up believing that daydreaming was the eighth deadly sin:

"Marie does not apply herself and daydreams a great deal."

"Tommy . . . wake up and join the class."

"If you'd kept your mind on your work, you'd have finished the dishes by now."

Although it's true that focusing on a topic is an important skill, defocusing also has great merit.

Overcome the idea that daydreaming is a form of laziness or irresponsibility.

Daydreaming is more than just a pleasure you allow yourself occasionally. Those automatic shifts to the past and future are necessary for your health, happiness and creativity. Not only do they provide opportunities to defuse stress, but also you can use them to rehearse the emotions of a scene. In addition, you can flashback to relive your first romance or flash forward to punch your boss in the nose without facing the consequences of either scene.

Flashforwards also are indispensable to goal-setting, inventing and inspiration. During your seemingly aimless projections forward, you often see the full-blown results. Sometimes your vision is impossibly ideal and unattainable. You may not even want it realized, but that improbable leap forward expresses an original idea. You can act upon it, save it or discard it. The stories of inventors, artists and industrial tycoons fulfilling their daydreams are legion. (See DAYDREAM.)

DAYDREAM

In a series of studies, teachers, psychologists and many others found that daydreaming frequency and certain styles of daydreaming are linked to innovation of thought and to the tendency to seek novel experiences, at least at the level of imagination. Persons who show particular gifts in producing creative literary or artistic works (Goethe and Dickens were two of many cited), who are able to recall more of their night dreams and who excel in describing their own personalities are likely to do a great deal of daydreaming.[20]

Cinematics started off with daydreaming to *reacquaint* you with your ability to see with your mind's eye. Now you're ready for Step 2.

MEMORABLE MUNCHIES

Think of your favorite ice-cream cone. How many scoops does it have? What flavor or flavors? What colors are in the ice cream—pink for strawberry, tan for chocolate? What's in the ice cream—nuts and cherries, marshmallows and chocolate chips? What kind of cone is it—old-fashioned, golden-crusted or the green-and-pink-tinted kind? Or the latter-day sugar-frosted, chocolate-flavored cone? Is the cone pointed at the bottom or flat? Embossed with diamond shapes or circles?

What enables you to answer all these questions? Think about the mental process. A few readers might have seen the words "vanilla" or "rocky road," but most of you saw the whole ice-cream cone. As you answered questions about the cone's color and composition, the picture became clearer and clearer. There are many sensory experiences included in an early memory of an ice-cream cone: the feel of the cold ice cream on a summer afternoon, the pure joy of eating something rich and sweet (without concern for dieting or blood pressure) and the milky aroma of the dairy bar where you bought the cone.

The visual image is strong and clear, and that is why the ice-cream cone example is such a good one. It proves that you can and do visualize. Even those who think they are nonvisualizers can almost always picture the ice-cream cone because it was an early, pleasant emotional experience. Knowing you can see pictures in your mind is essential to Step 2 of Cinematics, directed visualization.

RECONSTRUCTING THE SCENE

Retrieval of past experience differs from the daydreaming flashback in that it is a conscious focusing on a previous occurrence. You choose to return to the scene using your right brain's visual prowess and to note the details and evaluate what happened with your left brain.

Sometimes when you're trying to retrieve a lost article or forgotten thought, you will reconstruct a scene in a response to a nagging notion that you're almost onto a clue:

"I remember having a funny feeling that something was amiss as I turned the door handle. Maybe that's when I put the . . . down and . . ."

This is the right brain's way of communicating a message. Without the verbal skills of the left brain, the right brain can only nudge you mutely. But as you begin to notice these feelings and give credence to them, they will become strong and reliable. You'll soon find it natural to replay that moment in time when you first felt uneasy . . . and *bingo* . . . the picture will fill in quickly.

To help you catch hold of those vague, fleeting sensations, replay the scene and jot down a few visual and sensory descriptions on the viewboard as shown. The vice-president of XYZ Corporation is scheduled to arrive at 1:00 P.M., and you can't find the XYZ file. Here's how directed visualization of the past (past viewing) can come to the rescue:

"Let's see . . . the last time I saw it was when I was . . . the phone rang, and I put it on the . . ."

The phrase "let's see" is more than a figure of speech. It triggers a mental activity similar to fine-tuning a television set. A picture comes to mind and you actually see yourself and the details of the situation. Focusing on the lost item in the location you last recall having it provides a focal point from which you can visually span out in all directions.

Who was on the phone? Was it morning or afternoon? Was it the yellow phone on your desk or the red one in the boss's office? Were you on your way to or from the file cabinet?

Notice that the right-brain side of the viewboard uses feelings, visuals, smells and sounds. Record these right-brain matters first. Once the picture is well in mind, shift hemispheres and allow your left brain to note the details of the image and determine the sequence of events that led to your mislaying the file.

In the left-brain column, list who, what, where, when, why and how for the scene. From this basic information, you will be able to deduce a great deal. As you review your actions and feelings through the viewboard, you will also become more aware of the difference between feeling a

VIEWBOARD

Left Brain information and details	Right Brain emotions and senses
WHO me	hassled nervous
WHAT phone & file	red phone big file in hand
WHERE his desk	phones ringing— irked — worried — cigar smoke
WHEN early a.m.	coffee cup in one hand steaming
WHY Boss wanted file NOW	he seemed tense
HOW I set it down and bobbled coffee	almost spilled it on new carpet

past experience and analyzing it. You'll know what it is like to be on the right side when you're viewing the memory picture, and on the left when you're critiquing it.

Eventually you will find yourself producing a clear picture and understanding its content. Now you are prepared for directed vision into the future, or *future viewing*.

In future viewing, you walk into the movie studio of your mind and say, "Take One." You choose the scene to be shot:

Pretend you are planning a dinner party for a mixture of business and personal friends. You have several goals: to have fun, to improve rapport with business friends, to return several invitations and to stimulate your social life.

You could be single or married, but just to make this example dramatically illustrative, say that you are a single male with minimal culinary skills and hosting experience. First visualize the table itself: Who will sit where? Which of your guests is left-handed? Should you serve buffet-style, or do you conceive of table-seating as the more appropriate arrangement? Do you need to change your guest list? Are they chatting amiably? Now see them eating and you serving. Should you get help? How is it progressing? Having fun?

Mentally answer those questions that come to mind when you view the scene, and make a few notes of your answers. At this point you are probably accomplished at directing your visualizations and can easily call up a future view. However, if you are having trouble, see VISUALIZING AIDS.

You may shoot and reshoot the scenario until you "get it right." Replay the scene in many different ways, testing each, incorporating the best into your final take. With each version, you may discover some new problem to be dealt with or another reservoir of resources.

The first time you view this upcoming scene you will want to focus on the main event—in this particular example, serving the meal. However, as you continue to work on the situation, you'll branch out in all directions—for example, greeting the guests at the door. Where will they put their wraps? How will cocktails be served? John arrives first; hall closet; teakwood tray.

Although it is sometimes desirable to repeat the future view several times to be certain you have anticipated all the likely requirements of the scene, don't become involved in endless speculations. Repetitions of your first view that do not produce new information are not helpful. Eventually you may end up losing control over them, and these future pictures can become the worry-go-round of daydreaming.

However, there is one last step in directed visualization that requires your retracing a previously viewed picture. Whether it is a visual directed to the past or the future, you need to replay it again for the emotional content.

ONCE MORE, WITH FEELING

This emotional aspect of cinematics is extremely important if you are to gain maximum understanding and help from the moving pictures of your mind. The right brain's input is constant; there's no getting away from the emotional flow, both negative and positive. So use it.

Here's an example of an instant replay of an emotional scene:

You're out jogging in the park with your eleven-year-old son. A couple is wandering by with their toddler and a dog. It is a large dog ... not on a leash. You feel a certain tension as you approach them because your son is deathly afraid of dogs since he was mauled by one at four years of age. All goes well until you are nearly past the dog, when suddenly it switches course and starts toward you.

Both you and your son are frozen in your tracks, your son ready to run in the other direction. The dog's owners look over their shoulders, nonchalantly smile, and call out: "Don't worry, he's just friendly."

Your son is terror-stricken and you say: "Please call your dog."

They glance back, looking annoyed, and mutter: "Just pet him ... he won't hurt you."

You grimly tell them that you don't pet strange dogs and that joggers should not have to fear for their lives in city parks. They scoff and say: "We told you he's just a friendly dog."

WHOLE-BRAIN THINKING

You lose your temper and shout: "But does *he* know that?" Then you threaten them with the leash law. They call the dog away. You and your son resume jogging, grumbling about inconsiderate dog-owners. You rehash how unreasonable they were and the righteousness of your case, but you have a gnawing feeling that it need not have been such a nasty encounter.

This is a perfect situation to review. By revisiting your exaggerated fears, feelings of protectiveness toward your son and indignation, you will discover how you could have defused the emotions of the scenario.

In this calmer view of those impassioned moments, you can more clearly empathize with feelings of the other humans in your dreams: a little guilt for having their dog unleashed, unwillingness to believe that anyone could really be afraid of their lovable dog and annoyance that your pettiness could mar their pleasant walk in the park. After all, your eleven-year-old must have looked pretty husky compared to their own two-year-old, who romps fearlessly with Rover.

To discover the emotional aspects of the situation, observe the body language and note the emotions you were feeling at the time. You can jot them down in this manner:

"I am *enjoying* the jog with my son when suddenly I feel *uneasy* as we approach the dog. I am *annoyed* that the dog's owners do not rein him in when I request that they do so. I am *concerned* for my son as he becomes frightened, and finally I am *outraged* at their discounting his fears. I am also somewhat *afraid* of the dog and feel *powerless* in protecting my son. Part of me is also *irritated* with my son for looking like a sissy as he stands there cowering."

You see how you can get to the nitty-gritty of your drama by replaying it. Just list the "I am feeling" words and you'll become aware of how the emotions of the scene develop: enjoying — uneasy — annoyed — concerned — outraged —afraid—powerless—irritated.

Now review the scene, observing the behavior of the other players. The young man and woman seemed to be *relaxed*, *happy*. They looked *annoyed* when you asked them to call their dog and then positively *hostile* when you shouted at them. They may have been feeling somewhat *guilty* that they were disobeying the leash law but *certain* that your fears were ridiculous. As they looked at your strapping eleven-year-old, they were probably *scornful* or *doubtful* that he could be afraid of their dog.

As you list the emotions you now discern in the other players in the drama, your left brain can ask: "What can I learn from this scene?" Through this appraisal, you may find that you really must help your son overcome his phobia. You may decide to call the animal-control center to ask for better enforcement of the leash law. Continue to replay the story until you discover a way of interrupting the deterioration of your enjoyable feelings in the park.

Whether you are aware of it or not, you have acted out the emotions of this scene many times before. You are accustomed to feeling defensive about your son's tender feelings. He has often heard the story of the mauling incident and knows he has a phobia about dogs. Both of you come to the situation with these scripts well rehearsed. Furthermore, others enter your drama with their own biases, problems and memories.

Repeating the scene with a focus on emotions will help you discover these scripts and adapt your final take in this way:

As you approach the dog, you look over at your son and say: "This dog looks very friendly. Sheepdogs are a gentle breed. Doesn't he look kind of silly with that hair hanging over his eyes? He must be that little baby's playmate. Let's rest for a moment so I can catch my breath." This calms your son's fears and possibly avoids attracting the dog's attention. Perhaps you'll strike up a conversation with the dog's owners.

There are numerous other ways of reviewing this scene for the emotional content, but since you are the director and main actor, you can produce a piece with an ending that satisfies you. In doing so, you can learn about yourself and others in addition to discovering practical strategies

---

VISUALIZING AIDS

This is a more detailed way of visualizing for those who have practiced all the steps of cinematics but are not satisfied with the quality of their visualizations.

Begin by *devising a title* for your future viewing or past viewing. It will help you exactly define the problem you are working on. In the dinner party scene of this chapter, the title could be: "Entertaining Twelve Business and Personal Friends in My Small Apartment with Limited Assistance and Finances." Not brimming with Madison Avenue pizazz, but certainly definitive!

Next, *list your characters* and then start with the main scene (remember, the main scene is not always the first one to happen). It is important to concentrate on this central picture first so that you know you are actually addressing your real concern. For instance, if you're asking the boss for a raise, you might get caught up in how you'll dress for the occasion and lose direction. Although proper attire is something you need to think about, save that until you set the tone of the scenario. Will it be in his office, on the golf course, at the conclusion of your latest successful project?

Once you see the main scene, *dwell on it* and *note or sketch* as many details as you comfortably can. Now *list the left-brain who, what, where, when, why and how.* Finally, *write out the right-brain "I am feeling/they are feeling" aspects* of the scene. Record all these aspects of your visualization on one page and *then sit back and review the entire record* of your findings. Now *close your eyes* and let all your observations—*both sensory and informational*—form a complete scene.

---

for coping with unpleasant or challenging situations.

If you're going to ask for a raise or announce to your spouse that you want to go to graduate school, viewing the scene with an awareness of the feelings involved will help ensure that you are better prepared for these important moments in your life.

The three steps of cinematics (daydreaming; visualization; and once more, with feeling) are designed to help you

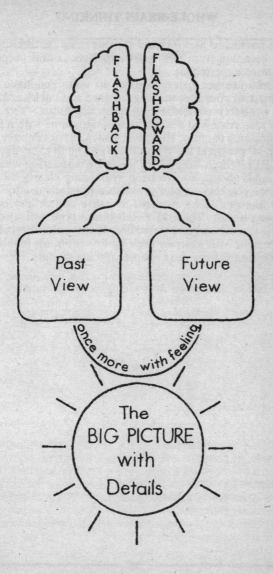

move backward and forward in your mind, extracting the most meaning from your past experiences and preparing for future experiences.

These are not new processes to you. You have daydreamed all your life, flashing forward and backward. You have probably envisioned the past and future. You have likely also reviewed and previewed situations with a focus on emotional content. However, you might never have realized how practical these processes can be in everyday life.

A BPI 9 (right-brain) type might be wondering what the fuss is all about. You've been visualizing clearly all your life. For you this chapter provides a practical use for your mind pictures and a moment to pause and reflect before charging ahead. The BPI 1 (left-brain) type will discover that he too can and does visualize. Right- or left-brain dominants alike will sharpen their inner vision, an invaluable preparation for the next chapter, on inside outs.

6

INSIDE OUTS

Break on through to the other side.
—Jim Morrison

Imagine a series of clear plastic domes, one within another. You can only see them from the outside. From the inside they are invisible. You become aware of an environment—one of those domes that surrounds you—only when you get outside of it. At that point you can see it, but you can't see the one which is now about you.

—Howard Gossage, *Ramparts*
(April 1966)

There is no ox so dumb as the orthodox.
—George Francis Gillette

Common sense is the collection of prejudices acquired by age eighteen.

—Albert Einstein

The contrary is also true.
—Groucho Marx

THE FIRST MIND MOVER, INTERNAL BRAINSTORMING, began with some optical illusions that helped you to recognize the feel of shifting your visual perception from one side of the brain to the other. These changing views allowed you to experience the physical difference between perceiving with your left brain and with your right brain. (See DRAWING ON THE RIGHT.)

Inside outs provoke a fresh and right-brain view of a particularly frustrating project, an irksome conflict, or any-

---

DRAWING ON THE RIGHT

In the book *Drawing on the Right Side of the Brain*, the author, Betty Edwards, explains and illustrates methods for shifting one's visual perception from left-brain viewing to the right, thus improving drawing ability. She explains that the reason most of us "can't draw flies" is that we perceive our subjects from a left-brain point of view; we are not drawing what we actually see but what we think we see.

She teaches the reader to view the subject with the right brain by such techniques as "looking at the negative space around the subject" and focusing on edges and contours.

Following these and other strategies suggested in the book cause an actual physical shift in perception and result in a dramatic improvement of art skills. Edwards' contribution lies not in the invention of these strategies (they are well known to artists) but in identifying the hemispheric processes involved and explaining them in lay terminology. Thousands of nonartists have been thrilled with the discovery that they can draw quite well simply by shifting hemispheres.

Inside outs are strategies for problem-solving and innovating by shifting one's perception of the subject from the left-brain approach to the right.[21]

---

thing else that has come to a mental dead end. Inside outs are methods for considering an abstract problem from a point of view that is just opposite of the norm, the obvious. They are especially helpful in solving a problem, creating a new idea, disarming an explosive situation or breathing new life into a hackneyed concept.

The first step required for all of them involves a left-brain definition of the situation. What is the problem? What needs to be done? What outcome do you desire? It is best to write down the problem or project in concrete, left-appealing form. Then as you look at it, try one or more of these inside outs. The examples provided with each are slanted toward on-the-job problem solving, innovation and conflict resolution.

1. *Visualize the extreme opposite of the situation.* Example: If you are trying to invent a gadget to open bottles, pretend you are trying to bond the bottle cap permanently to make it impenetrable. It will thus be easier to discover the weaknesses inherent in the current bottle caps and a way to get the substances that are inside, out—without resorting to the typical removable cap. You might invent a syringelike contraption that extracts the contents rather than beheading the package.

2. *Look at the space around the problem* rather than the problem itself. Example: You have an employee performing below capacity. Visualize all the physical surroundings of that employee: fellow workers, office space, tools and office procedures. Then analyze that employee in the context of the workworld. Is he a tall, athletic person crammed into a hot little cubicle? Is she a religious enthusiast trapped in an office ambience that is decidedly bawdy? Some simple alterations in the space around the employee might just do the trick.

3. *Reverse the objective.* Example: If you have high personnel turnover and are trying to reduce it, turn your goal upside down by asking: What can I do to *encour-*

INSIDE-OUT THINKERS

Inside-out thinking has produced some remarkably successful ideas. Fred Smith, president of Federal Express, conceived of his multimillion-dollar enterprise as a result of focusing on the outrageous proposition that the fastest route between any two places was through his hometown, Memphis, Tennessee. Starting with this reverse on apparent truth, he devised an overnight delivery system between any two points in the country. He assembled a team of hard-working, open-minded thinkers who made this inside-out idea a working model.

Sister Elizabeth Kenny, an Australian nurse, developed a singularly successful therapy for infantile paralysis before the polio vaccine was discovered. Instead of using the accepted medical practice of immobilizing affected limbs and joints, she massaged, manipulated and treated them with hot applications. In verified studies, six out of ten patients undergoing early treatment recovered within four to six weeks with no trace of the usually crippling ailment.

age turnover? You might find that high turnover is fiscally beneficial; it eliminates pay increments, pension fund costs and other expenses. If you're concerned that turnover leads to lack of continuity, consider breaking the work process into smaller activities that can be performed quickly with minimal training. Certainly high turnover averts inbreeding and gives you access to new ideas, a decided advantage in changing times.

4. *Assume that all of your information is wrong*—that nothing is as it appears to be, that fact is fiction and fiction is fact. Example: Your company has always used the most expensive beans in your coffee candy because "everybody knows" that's the way to get the best flavor. Assume "everybody" is wrong. Try the cheapest bean available. You might find that the taste is about the same or even better with the low-line bean. You could end up saving enough money the first year to buy that new equipment you've been needing.

5. *Do a "newie."* Example: Life on the job has become tedious and boring. Do something you've never done before—the more alien to you, your way of life, your work habits, your company procedures, the better. You may learn something from it and bring a fresh and stimulating perspective to work. Walk, ride a bike or hitchhike to work. Take a new route—ten blocks instead of your customary two. You'll see things you'd never have noticed before. Try a new food, a new kind of music or dance. Buy a magazine totally outside your normal interest range. Speak to strangers at crosswalks; see a wild or scary movie. Ask the custodian what he thinks of the new company product and tell your boss about your float trip down the Grand Canyon. A novel way a day keeps stagnation away.

6. *Brag, lie, exaggerate.* You might discover some hidden talents or desires by forgoing modesty and humility for a short period of time. Example: Saying "I'm a painter equal in ability to Grandma Moses" will help you recognize that you'd really like to try painting and will give you the courage to act on that desire.

   Lie to yourself about how many paintings you have sold; often your horizons will then be higher. Brag about your abilities; they're usually much greater than you allow yourself to believe. Friends, spouses and grandmothers will tolerate this kind of behavior best.

7. *If you always manage a stiff upper lip* or carry on cheerfully in face of all adversities, *change!* Example: You're worried sick about your projected income from investments. Admitting your concern will help others understand there is a problem. Making it worse than it is might excite you to do some creative problem-solving and to exert extra effort to save the day.

8. *Reverse the physical characteristics* of every object and person in the problem. Alter sizes, colors, density, capacity, purpose, weight, flexibility, priority. Example: Your company's storage space is limited and you have

no funds for expansion. You can reverse your perception of the problem in several ways. Visualize your building bending outward, upward and downward; for example, consider whether you can convert the roof to a warehouse by installing inexpensive plastic bins. Speculate that an unlimited amount of money is available from a benefactor or hidden resource until you hit upon a feasible solution. In fact, your special growth might justifiably warrant attention and a grant from some foundation. Reverse the size of the materials under storage. From books and catalogs, go to microfiche; from filing cabinets, convert to computer storage. Conjecture about hanging your lightweight, bulky items from the rafters with rope pulleys instead of stacking them on valuable floor space.

Once you become familiar with this approach, you'll find many ways to solve problems, especially those regarding space and procedures.

9. *Expect the unexpected.* Example: Your company is undercapitalized but desperately in need of first-class management. Fantasize about someone you'd like to work for you, no matter how famous or seemingly inaccessible. Focus on that state-of-the-art person. Then call or write your expert, asking him or her to manage your company for six months for a nominal salary. Expect a yes. Expect this person to be fascinated with the potential of your company and the challenge of making it an overnight success. With this attitude, you have a fifty-fifty possibility of getting an acceptance. Without it, you stand absolutely no chance. So what do you have to lose?

10. *Forget what you know.* Example: In planning your orientation program for new employees, block important details from your mind. Viewing company background and procedures from this naïve point of view will allow you to experience how the learner feels and to anticipate which bit of information should come next. Ser-

endipitously, you might find that some of the old ways can be improved or replaced.

11. *Be someone else*. Example: You have a fractious employee who is surly on the phone with clients but is extremely efficient in other areas. Conceiving of yourself in his or her body can help you correct the situation. Perhaps the employee is not a people person and needs to be assigned to work that doesn't involve public contact. Perhaps physical or emotional problems make the person grouchy. Even if you can't solve personal problems, you will gain information to help you make a rational decision about this situation.

FUN AND GAMES

Inside outs are the most lighthearted and playful of the mind movers. Whether your inside outs ever produce practical results or not, they still have value. They lead to humor and laughter, always a welcome release of tension and a pathway to camaraderie on the job. (See SPLIT-BRAIN JOKING.)

Indeed, humor is directly related to inside outs because it too is often based upon opposites. Jackie Gleason once said that most of his humorous characters showed adults behaving like children. Children acting like grown-ups also provoke a smile. It is surprising and charming to hear adult comments and questions issue from a small, innocent face.

Another amusing brain tickler is the paradox, which also involves opposites: absurdity and truth. What is apparent at first in a paradoxical statement is reversed at the second glance. Appreciation of a paradox involves a shift in your understanding of the statement.

For example: "One cannot understand the meaning of 'paradox' by its definition."

It seems flippant to say that a definition of a paradox cannot provide a better comprehension of it. But another interpretation of the statement reveals a semiprecious truth: You really need to experience a paradox to understand the term.

Try these:

> You have nothing to fear but fear itself.
> —Franklin D. Roosevelt

> .... technology is, by its nature, at the same time highly sophisticated and profoundly primitive.
> —Lewis Thomas

> A little pain never hurt anyone.
> —Anon.

At first glance these statements sound incredible or at least confused, but further thought reveals an inherent truth in each.

The absurdity of a paradox usually strikes first because most reading is done in a left-brained, analytical manner. Later input from the right brain helps in understanding the less obvious meaning of the statement. The overall view allows you to see the relationship between the two points of view.

A BPI 9 type might register the paradox from the latter viewpoint more quickly because he's not as committed to left-brain perception. In fact, this tendency to communicate from the right brain makes dominant rights attractive. When they express their view of a situation, art or music to us, they are tickling our imaginative faculties, entertaining us by showing us the right-brain illusion in contrast to the left-brain realism. We love the surprises that right-brained abstractions can reveal.

Irony is also often based on two contrasting perceptions. The appeal of Alfred Hitchcock's mystery movies and TV series is derived from such irony and surprise. The classic plot is the case of the proper English lady who kills her husband with a frozen leg of lamb. The absurdity of so mundane an item serving as a murder weapon is the first rib-tickler. Then when she invites the police inspector to

---

SPLIT-BRAIN JOKING

The two sides of the brain react or understand humor in two different ways, and to appreciate a joke fully, both sides must be in use. The left is quite literal in its interpretations of the joke and is especially drawn to wordplay. The right is more alert to the subleties and nuances.

A joke appreciated more by the left brain might be:

"The bigger the summer vacation, the harder the fall."

But the left alone might not be able to make the connection between "Siamese twins" and the punch line in this joke:

"A young man returns from a blind date with Siamese twins. His friend inquires: 'Did you have a good time?' The young man replied, 'Well, yes and no.'"

Patients with damage to the right hemisphere (especially when lesions occur in the frontal portions) are unable to see an overall pattern in the story and are therefore not attuned to the inconsistencies and absurdities that form the basis for the joke.

Furthermore, these patients cannot find the underlying theme of the story. Instead, each part stands alone. They also have trouble comprehending the emotional views of individual characters in the joke and so completely miss the byplay between them.

Therefore, a person with a damaged right brain could not understand or see any humor in the following story:

"One mother bragging to another: 'My son Freddy has a wonderful job. He's an investigator of food served in school lunchrooms. He goes from school to school, sampling the food they serve.'

"'What did he find out?' her friend asked.

"'It's all going to be in his report,' the proud mother replied.

"'When is the report coming out?'

"'As soon as he gets out of the hospital.'"

---

dine (on the lamb) and he ruminates verbally about the
nature and location of the murder weapon, ironies abound—
as does the entertainment. The inspector perceives the crime
and the leg of lamb from a strictly rational, logical point of
view. Meanwhile, the audience is privy to the absurd, irregular but also rational answer.

Hitchcock's surprising and usually humorous endings
rely heavily on leading the viewer through the logical, left-
brain facts of the situation and then suddenly revealing the
paradoxical, right-brain side of the story.

Similarly, inside outs are based on a different way of
looking at the usual. If you try just one and it produces a
good idea, you'll be sold. However, it often takes a number
of tries before you make a breakthrough.

In interviews, staff meetings and problem-solving groups,
individuals tend either to be talkative and full of ideas or
quiet and contemplative. In other words, they are known
as talkers or listeners. At the next such gathering, try an
inside out to reverse *your* style. Think about how you might
accomplish this with inside outs 1, 3, 6, 9 and 11 (space is
provided for you to record your ideas):

1. Visualize the extreme opposite of the situation:

3. Reverse the objective:

6. Brag, lie, exaggerate:

9. Expect the unexpected:

11. Be someone else:

If you got stuck on any of them, you might want to check the following examples to get you going again.

1. *Visualize* yourself talking and chatting and laughing nonstop if you are a listener, or visualize steel wires holding your mouth together—such as those used by people on diets—to stop you if you're a talker.

3. *Reverse your objective.* Resolve to be known as an animated contributor, a loquacious person, someone with whom others have to work to get a word in edgewise. Or set your objective to practice discipline by not speaking at all; imagine others pleading for your ideas and yourself deliberately withholding them.

6. *Try to brag, lie or exaggerate.* If you talk too much, exaggerate a possible outcome of your excesses. Fantasize a scene in which you blurted out your company's new marketing strategy and got fired for it.

   If you talk too little, brag to yourself about the importance of the comments you do make. Exaggerate positive reactions of others to things you say. This will give you some experience with feeling confident about speaking out.

9. *Expect the unexpected.* Expect to win your company's outstanding employee award for making a suggestion at a meeting if you're trying to be a talker. If, however, you want to tone down your verbal assertiveness, expect

that your next public comments will be met with icy stares, boos, hisses or a pie in the face. That's pretty strong medicine but a quick cure for garrulousness.

11. *Be someone else.* Actually be Johnny Carson, versatile, glib and charming if you're a listener. If you're a talker, be Clint Eastwood, stone-faced and taciturn.

So pick one, try it, see how much fun it is and what a sense of mastery you acquire. Then congratulate yourself for having the courage to experiment with something rather far out . . . to the right. Once you have produced a concept that saves time, money or effort, your left brain will be satisfied and your reversals in perception will become amusing, relaxing and productive.

7

SUSPENDERS

Focuser and analyzer that it is, the left brain must first pose the problem in specific, if often paradoxical, terms. It then must willingly withdraw, allowing the kinds of fluctuations required to synthesize new patterns. When the right brain flashes its ephemeral images, the left brain must vigilantly latch onto them. It must then give them verbal meaning.

> —Dudley Lynch, management consultant and editor of the Dallas-Fort Worth *Business Quarterly*, from *Management Review* (Feb. 1980)

IN CINEMATICS AND INSIDE OUTS YOU LEARNED TO access your right hemisphere by altering the way you perceive things. In this chapter you will learn to reach your right by suspending your left.

Most people already use one or two suspenders regularly: meditation, hypnosis, jogging, tranquilizers and the predinner cocktail. The first two are mental suspenders and the second three are physical.

Mental suspenders evade the left and access the right in two ways: by overloading the left with details or by starving the left for information until it falls into boredom.

Pretend you are a newspaper reporter covering a rally

against nuclear armament. Philosophically, you are opposed to this protest, but as a conscientious reporter you join the protesters in their half-day march across town. You are now standing on the state capitol steps watching the speakers array themselves on the landing above. It is cold and dark; you are tired and hungry. Beacons of light crisscross the sky. To blend in with the group, you join in chanting "no to nukes" in time with clapping and swaying. A feeling of togetherness overcomes you, and you feel a kinship with the earnest protesters. You listen to one speech after another, all basically saying the same thing. You are in a state of euphoria; everything seems to fit together, forming a great truth. Suddenly your rational objections are gone. Your left is suspended. Forgetting all the facts and figures of your point of view, you are drawn to the protesters' side.

A challenge can also suspend the left. When the challenge is overwhelming, the left is blocked and the right rushes in with feeble defenses and an outpouring of emotions.

This is similar to the strategy employed in Perry Mason trials, where the questions are pointed, relentless and require logical, immediate answers. The witness often blurts out the truth, the whole truth . . . as he feels it. The left brain has been inundated, and the guilty emotions of the right brain come tumbling out against all laws of self-preservation.

You might sympathize with this situation if you think of the times you've been questioned about why you proceeded as you did in a work project that failed. The logic of your planning and actions escapes you, and you sputter incoherently, sounding disorganized, ineffectual and apologetic.

As long as you control your suspenders, they are harmless—in fact, helpful. It is a valuable skill to be able to turn off that domineering left at times and allow your infantile side to play, to feel and to fantasize. However, there is a danger in allowing others to trigger these suspenders. When the con artist talks a mile a minute, staring you straight in the eye and draping an arm around your shoulder, you are not evaluating the message with your left brain but feeling with your right that the person is sincere, nice, honest, that you'd better hurry or you'll lose a good deal. The fast talking overloads your left and your right goes hook, line and sinker for the emotional message.

On the other hand, suspension of the left via deprivation can occur quite spontaneously without an external stimulus. If you are doing something monotonous such as driving down an empty highway or sorting nuts and bolts, your left soon becomes bored with the task and shuts down.

So mental suspenders derive from over- or understimulation of the left brain, which allows the right to take over, and the results can be helpful or harmful to you. At times you may seek out professional aid to help you suspend the left—a hypnotist, pastor or counselor who will guide you into another state of consciousness.

In a similar way, you allow television, theater, movies, reading, ballet, concerts and advertising to suspend your left. The producers of these media arts understand how to provoke this suspension of your left brain so that you can experience with your right. They may not be conversant with the split-brain mechanics of their crafts, but they employ techniques that move you right and make their fantasy your reality. The extent to which you feel the fantasy is a measure of their skill.

However, your preconceived attitude helps them pull you in. When you walk into a theater, you are prepared to suspend your knowledge that you are sitting in a physically limited environment. The visual, auditory and sensual experiences transport you beyond the theater and your body. The more right-brain-evoking the production, the more totally you will be absorbed by it.

Theater critics must find it confining to stay left-brained while they are watching a play. Presumably they love the art form they critique, but they cannot afford to allow themselves to move right and enjoy it on a personal level. Ah, well, it goes with the territory, and it may be a penalty to balance out the misery they inflict upon artists who are often forced left rather abruptly by the critics' negative evaluations.

Why and when would you ever want to suspend your left? For the same reasons you want to use your right brain:

• to change your perspective and solve a problem
• to relax and enjoy your playful side
• to help yourself do, or not do, something by suspending your belief that you can or cannot, must or must not do it

There are many techniques you can use to suspend your left, but most of them are expensive and involve some outside force or person activating the suspension.

Here is a generic suspender you can adapt to any occasion:

1. As usual, you need your left brain to get this off the ground. Starting on the left, define precisely what you are trying to accomplish. For example, say you have a problem with public speaking—you connect all words and sentences with an "uh." You might ponder for a few minutes why you use the "uhs." Understanding the reasons might speed the solution. Perhaps you are uncomfortable with silence; it makes you feel ill-prepared or inarticulate. Anyway, write out the problem as simply and succinctly as possible. "I say 'uh' between words and sentences when I speak publicly."

2. Your next step is to state in positive terms how you would like to speak—with authority, wit, flow and comfort.

3. Now convert your goal into four-year-old language. Remember, when you are addressing the right, your audience is the preschooler in you who accepts most readily words and suggestions that are colorful and active. Here's an example of the type of right-brain language to use: "When I speak in public I am funny, smooth,

happy, smart and friendly. When there are quiet times between words, I feel very strong because all eyes are on me. They listen to me and like me." (See MOMMY AND I ARE ONE.)

4. Memorize that childlike message and say it aloud several times.

All this work must be done before you suspend the left, or you will gain access to the right without purpose or direction. Even if you want to induce a relaxed or creative state, you still need to clarify your goal, because once the left is suspended, the right will wander aimlessly unless you have implanted the reason.

GENERIC SUSPENDER

Get as comfortable as possible in a setting where you will not be interrupted for ten to fifteen minutes.

MOMMY AND I ARE ONE

In trying to find the most effective subliminal message, Lloyd Silverman, research psychologist at the Veterans' Administration regional office in New York City, has tested many words, phrases, etc., and found the one that elicited the most pronounced results to be "Mommy and I are one." This sentence was helpful in calming the behavior of male schizophrenics. Females responded best to "Daddy and I are one."

Silverman tried this message at the suggestion of his wife, a psychotherapist, who had noted that schizophrenic patients often express a longing for symbiotic relationships, a merging or at-one-ness with a parental image. This same feeling is often experienced during meditation and jogging.

For dieters and individuals trying to quit smoking the "Mommy and I are one" message was more effective than such neutral messages as "People are walking."[22]

WHOLE-BRAIN THINKING

If the situation permits, close your eyes and roll your eyeballs upward. (This induces a state of Alpha—see BRAINWAVE LEVELS.) If you dare not close your eyes, then choose some point several feet above eye level and focus on it.

- While staring, focus on some rhythmic sound: the air conditioner, wheels turning on the bus, music.
- Breathe in time with that sound. If your left nostril is congested, then hold the right nostril shut until you can

---

BRAINWAVE LEVELS

Brainwave levels are described in terms of Hertzes, a quantification of the electric charges emitted by the brain and measured by an electroencephalogram. Following is a table indicating six ranges from the slowest, delta, to the most frequent waves of beta.

Hz.	Name of State	Characteristics
0.5–4	delta	Deeper states of sleep
4–8	theta	Drowsiness, dreaming, also occurs during such alert behaviors as sudden insight or recognition of event in memory. A trance state unless drug-induced. Used for *twilight learning*.
8–14	alpha	Relaxed wakefulness. Brain not actively engaged in any specific mental or emotional activity. Can be present when mental activity is habitual and does not require concentration; when focusing inward; when receptive, or conversely, when blocking emotional responsiveness. Neutral, resting, meditating. Achieved best with eyes closed.

(BRAINWAVE LEVELS, *cont.*)		
14–22	beta	Ordinary beta where alert behavior and concentrated mental activity occur. Also anxiety and apprehension.
22–23	high beta	Revving up, increased anxiety or hyper responses and thinking.
over 33	K-complex and unnamed	Short burst of high frequency occurring when short-term memory consolidation and problem-solving occur.

These ranges are approximate and vary among individuals because of differing response levels and location of specific parts of the brain. The matter is further complicated by the difficulty in measuring such minute amounts of electricity and screening out artifacts (interference from unrelated sound and movement).

breathe through the left. (See the discussion on breathing research in Chapter 3.) Deepen your breathing and slow its rhythm to every other beat of the sound you're hearing.
· Now tune out that sound and tune up the sound of your breathing until you hear only the rush of air in your lungs, filling, emptying, refilling. Let your jaw go, feel your heartbeat and the pull of your heavy hands and feet.
· Carry on with this scene as long as you have the time and find it pleasurable. Repeat it as many times as possible on your first project. Then, just before your next public speech, go through the process as close to presentation time as possible. You will find that you have eliminated the awkward pauses and made dramatic use of the silences.

This generic suspender can be altered for any situation. If you are tense, change the verbal message to your right brain to "calm, relaxed, peaceful." As you use the suspender more and more, it will take less and less time and energy to implement because you will have developed a reliable method for self-hypnosis. The reason the message must be prepared ahead of time is to guarantee that you will have a posthypnotic suggestion to implant at the beginning. Otherwise there is no outcome to the self-hypnosis other than the pleasant experience.

When you are hypnotized by someone else, you are led into a trance with such techniques as a swinging pendulum or monotonous voice and message to bore your left brain to sleep. Then the hypnotist sends a posthypnotic suggestion to the right brain. So the characteristics are the same, but with the generic suspender, you write your own program and pull your own strings.

If you are a dominant left, it may take work to use this or any other type of suspension of the left. Perhaps if you add up the dollars-and-cents value of suspending the left occasionally, you will be more motivated to work at it. Then too, remember that it gives you something free and useful to do when you're waiting at the airport. And you can move quickly in and out of suspension.

Dominant rights are usually easily hypnotized and sometimes are even affected when someone else is the subject. They get involved totally in any hypnagogic group situation (meetings where strongly accentuated singing, clapping, dancing and a message are involved). At times, rights will even undergo a suspension of the left due to rhythmic repetition of noises, marching or visual patterns.

If you are highly susceptible to suspension of the left, you might want to be alert to individuals and situations that tend to draw you in. It's pleasurable to be able to allow your mind to move right, but it is essential to be aware and in control of these shifts because they have both benefits and disadvantages for you.

Some of the same pluses and minuses can be attributed to the *physical* suspenders.

GETTING PHYSICAL

Physical suspenders, such as narcotics and the predinner cocktail, tranquilize the left brain. (See HOW THE BRAIN GETS DRUNK.) The first pill and the first drink arouse the right brain and quiet the judgment of the left. Suddenly it is easier to speak of emotions and illusions. That is why tongues loosen at cocktail parties, brilliant repartee is experienced (later forgotten) and instant relationships are established (also often quickly forgotten). If the drinking continues, the left is totally suspended, and the right can go on a real rampage, becoming peevish, obscene, violent, poetic or talkative.

During these periods of suspension of the left, the child in you is glimpsed. If the child is happy, these expressions will be sentimental, accepting and playful. If the child is unhappy, the picture will be morose, suspicious, and maudlin. Probably the office party so often produces disastrous

HOW THE BRAIN GETS DRUNK

Alcohol seems to attack the right brain with more force than the left, both initially and in long-term effects. The right brain gets drunk first, and this normally mute hemisphere intrudes upon the left's speech style. Therefore, speech loses precision. The drunkened right also loses its usually superior visual and motor functions.

This weakness for the spirits may account for a drunk's increased desire but diminished ability for sex; the "right" emotions are aroused but ability is decreased.

Chronic alcoholics have a more general degeneration of the right hemisphere cells and consequently often have loss of hearing in the left ear and poor left-hand coordination.

It was once thought that damage done to the brain by alcoholism is irreversible; however, CAT scans of recovered alcoholics show regeneration of some brain cells after just three weeks' abstinence.[23]

results because rights being rights together are uncompromisingly direct and natural. Perhaps the workworld is not yet ready for such honesty.

Other physical suspenders are such activities as jogging, swimming, dancing and running. These noncompetitive, rhythmic exercises lead to suspension of the left. The left becomes bored with the monotonous movement and paucity of intellectual stimulation. No wonder marathon runners report bursts of intuition and hallucinations, visual and emotional signs of right-brain thinking.

Usually a challenge to the left will snap it back into control. For instance, while you are absorbed in the rhythm of aerobics, the instructor may call out: "Everybody count in unison," and zap—your left has to respond.

You can use physical suspenders to help with your work projects. Do the left-brain work first by researching your project and accumulating the facts. Then while you are engaged in a repetitive physical activity, your right often will see an overall strategy or discover a helpful pattern.

Ed Stein, editorial cartoonist for the *Rocky Mountain News*, comments:

> Oftentimes I've analyzed the facts of a political situation and know what slant I want to take but just can't put it all together. Then, several days later, I'm wandering around, bumping into tables and cleaning my desk, when all of a sudden the cartoon, characters, actions and words all come to me full-blown in a clear picture in my head.

It seems his strategy is to lay the left-brain groundwork and then discover the overview while physical activity temporarily suspends the left. (For a summary of mental and physical suspenders, see FACTORS CONTRIBUTING TO SUSPENSION OF THE LEFT.)

One important suspender does not fit either of these categories, but it definitely causes suspension of the left. It is a suspender you already know. It is as easy as falling asleep. In fact, it *is* falling asleep and then *dreaming with a purpose*.

The dream state (REM [rapid eye movement] sleep) occurs approximately every ninety minutes throughout sleep. During those periods, the right brain is much more active than the left. (See THE DREAMY RIGHT BRAIN.) In addition to laboratory evidence that the right prevails during dreaming, a comparison of descriptions of right-brain functions and dreams demonstrates that they are the same: pictorial, emotional, hallucinatory, concrete, illogical and removed from reality.

FACTORS CONTRIBUTING TO SUSPENSION OF THE LEFT

1. Deprivation of food, sleep and/or sensory stimulation. These conditions literally starve the left and can produce an hallucinogenic state.
2. Overload of words, arguments or demands for concentration. These exhaust the left, which then allows a right-brain takeover.
3. Music, rhythm, cadence, marching, flashing lights, chanting, undulating movements and repetitious sounds can induce a trance.
4. Extreme physical comfort can allow you to glide to the sensate right; extreme physical *dis*comfort provokes you to flee there to avoid thinking about the pain.
5. An attitude of acceptance by the subject greatly aids suspension of the left. Probably dominant rights are more prone to be accepting because they are less analytical than lefts.

Politicians, teachers, preachers, military trainers and persuaders often encourage, by design or accident, a submissive attitude by exuding authority, confidence and paternalism. Obviously the style varies from role to role, but the dynamics are the same: Get the listener's allegiance by implying that the speaker knows best.

(Most of these factors are present in the rally against nuclear armament story at the beginning of this chapter.)

WHOLE-BRAIN THINKING

THE DREAMY RIGHT BRAIN

One of the earliest researchers to try to map the human brain was Wilder Penfield, a Canadian brain surgeon. He applied mild electrical current to the surface of the brain and found that stimulation of the right temporal lobe usually produces a dreamy state in which patients experience visual illusions and feelings of familiarity or strangeness. Probes of corresponding areas on the left hemisphere did not produce such responses.

Tests of electrical activity during sleep show much higher levels in the right hemisphere (in both man and other animals). The more deeply into REM (rapid eye movement) sleep, the greater the activity. Dreaming occurs during REM sleep.

As far back as 1844, a British physician, A. L. Wigan, theorized that sleep suspends the power of the left hemisphere, allowing the right to take over.[24]

Dreams can produce some of the same benefits as other moves to the right brain. For instance, they can solve problems and devise innovative concepts. Of course, a necessary precondition for *using* your dreams is the ability to recall them.

Some persons can remember every detail of several elaborate dreams a night, while others have no memory of dreams and often believe that they never dream. Extensive sleep research shows that everyone dreams and in fact that dreaming is essential to physical and mental health.

If you have difficulty remembering your dreams, try some ways devised by dream experts to enhance recall:

1. Keep a dream diary or journal so that you can start a dream-recording routine.
2. Have a tape recorder or a pad and pencil at bedside to record your dreams the instant you awaken.
3. Discuss your dreams with others to build your appreciation for and consciousness of dreaming.
4. Establish a cue for recall such as sipping from a glass

of water just as you doze off. When you awaken, take another sip of water and the dream will come flooding into your memory.

5. As you are falling asleep each night, suggest to yourself that you will pay careful attention to your dreams and recall them as you awaken.

6. Awaken gently—don't leap out of bed or sit up. While your eyes are still closed, review your dreams, then gingerly reach for your tape recorder or pad and pencil to record them.

7. Acknowledge the value of your right brain in bringing your dreams to you in vivid color, theme and action.

8. Find a dream partner with whom you can regularly discuss dreaming.

If practicing these methods does not improve the clarity of your remembrances, you might want to consult one of the many good books available on dreams. Now proceed to the next stage: devising a program for dreaming purposefully.

First, overcome the negative, fearful parts of your dreams by turning them into positives. If you have frightening dreams, suggest to yourself, just before you fall asleep, that you will convert them in this manner:

- "If I dream about falling, I will commence to fly, soaring anywhere I want to go, seeing anything I want to see."
- "If I dream I am dying, I will know that it is only an unwanted part of my personality dying."
- "If I dream about a monster, I will turn around and confront him. I will ask him why he's bothering me. I will ask for his help or how I can help him."

These messages might seem rather childish, but remember that the right brain does not mature emotionally beyond four or five years of age.

Once your dreams become less frightening, your recall will be better and you'll be ready for Stage 2, through which you will be able to direct your dreams toward specific purposes. Step 2 can be accomplished by giving yourself presleep suggestions.

You might pose a problem such as this:

"We're missing deadlines at the office. I don't know why or how to remedy it. Tonight I'll dream about the situation."

When first learning to work on a problem through dreams, you'll need to pose this kind of general situation. If your initial expectations are too specific or excessive, you may become disillusioned with the process and inhibit your right brain's talents. On the other hand, by appreciating the fantasies evoked, you can strengthen your dreaming skills. As you progress, you can be more specific in presleep setup. You might say something like this to yourself:

"I've sensed that John is unhappy in his work but I don't know why."

Dreams often dramatize behaviors you have observed subliminally in the daytime. If John shows up in your dreams threatening you with a pair of scissors, try to recall your last session with him. Did you "cut off" his thought in midsentence? Is he preparing to quit and "cut off" contact with you? Even if you do not have a clear interpretation, you can use the image as a conversation opener the next day. Tell him about it with a chuckle, and you might elicit the full story. It would be easier for him to express dissatisfaction about the job under these conditions than at the quarterly job review.

The final step in mobilizing your dreams for practical use is to program your right brain for a specific solution. Spend considerable time before falling asleep doing the left-brain work; analyze all aspects of the problem and define it. Then as you feel yourself dropping off, send a short, concrete suggestion to your right: "Tonight, I'm going to have an interesting dream about the best way to _____. I'll recall it in detail when I awaken."

Whatever you get for an answer and whenever you get it (midnight, fifteen minutes later or in the morning), write it down immediately. If you wake up in the middle of the dream or don't feel satisfied with it, go back to sleep with the suggestion that you will resume the dream with more revealing pictures.

Much of your self-esteem is vested in your work, and the nighttime review of your day's activities often expresses on-the-job concerns. Therefore, it makes sense to use those dreams for solving work problems while reaping the emotional benefits as well. It costs you nothing to dream, and the rewards are many.

In this chapter you have learned about left-brain suspension through physical, mental and dream methods. Now you are ready for the fifth mind mover, which is a triple-decker called hearing 1, hearing 2, and hearing extra.

TWILIGHT LEARNING

The suggestibility of the theta state has been used to develop a "Twilight Learner" by Thomas H. Budzynski, director of the Biofeedback Institute of Denver.

This equipment sends an auditory message as long as the client is in theta, that pleasant, highly suggestible state that occurs just before sleep. If the person is aroused into alpha or falls asleep (going into delta), the Twilight Learner's message ceases. Eventually the client can maintain theta for longer and longer periods and thus benefit from more extensive messages.

The Twilight Learning process has implications for educational purposes. No doubt, the sleep-teaching methods of the 1960s worked best when the learner was in theta, but since it is brief and irregular under normal circumstances, the absorption of information would be sporadic. If students could learn to induce and maintain theta for longer periods of time, learning could be enhanced. Educators who strive for a relaxed classroom environment may find support for their approach from the proponents of such techniques as Suggestology by Georgi Losanov, Superlearning by Sheila Ostrander and Lynn Schroeder and Kiddie QR (quieting response) by Liz Stroebel.[25]

8

HEARINGS: 1, 2 AND EXTRA

> And I heard a voice, such as I had never heard, ever before,
> saying, "From now on you need never await temporal attes-
> tation to your thought. You think the truth."
> —Buckminster Fuller

JUST AS YOU SEE PICTURES IN YOUR HEAD, YOU ALSO hear voices and sounds—the voices pertinent to another mind mover, hearings. The voices heard inside your head are verbal forms of what you're feeling and experiencing.

These thoughts are the incomplete, fleeting, multiple, incompatible, logical, illogical and irrational notions that congeal into the ideas that are expressions of your identity.

Hearings is a device to help you control those voices so that you can improve your concentration (through hearing 1), gain cogency and self-understanding (through hearing 2), and extract intuitive information from the words that play in your head (through hearing extra).

WHOLE-BRAIN THINKING

Although some persons have difficulty visualizing, it is unusual for a person not to hear voices and other sounds. (This is in the absence of any sight or hearing impairment.) In spite of the universality of the experience, the phenomenon of hearing voices in one's head usually has been construed negatively, possibly because very strong inner voices are symptomatic of several forms of mental illness. (See MULTIPLE PERSONALITIES.)

Rest assured that inner voices are normal and, what's more, that you can make use of them. The first step is to learn to operate all the sophisticated knobs on your inner player.

The primary knob is the volume control, and it is the easiest to regulate. Start with a voice or sound you'd like to rid yourself of, perhaps one of those jingles that keeps going through your head incessantly. How about turning down, then out, a television or radio commercial:

"You deserve a break today . . . at McDonald's."

Hear it full blown at first. Then hear only the music, allowing it to become very faint, as though you are moving farther and farther away from it until you are completely out of earshot.

MULTIPLE PERSONALITIES

EEG (electroencephalogram) patterns of individuals who have multiple personalities alter as their personalities change. Ten such patients were tested by psychiatrist Frank Putnam of the National Institute for Mental Health. He discovered that these differences in brainwaves were as great between personalities as between separate subjects.

In each patient he recorded EEG tests on four personalities: the core, an obsessive-compulsive type, the child and one other. He found the patterns to be similar to those of obsessive-compulsive persons, children, etc. Patients' most severely disturbed personalities would not emerge for testing.

Normal subjects tried to fake multiple personalities but could not alter brainwave patterns significantly.[26]

There are many times in this overstimulating society when you will want to get away from external sounds. You can erase them simply by turning down the volume and substituting a slightly altered message. Each time you make such a "correction," the original message becomes weaker and weaker. (See MEMORY PATHS.)

Sometimes you do it to yourself. You implant nonproductive and distracting ideas. Say you have misunderstood someone and have a misperception. You need to be able to turn off the voice that keeps repeating:

"Gary is the capital of Indiana" and replace it with a corrected version: "Indianapolis is the capital of Indiana."

HEARING 1: CONCENTRATION

This is basically how you can rid yourself of tiresome or incorrect hearings implanted by others or yourself. Once

---

MEMORY PATHS

Elizabeth F. Loftus reports that she has watched thousands of trial witnesses going from being unsure to positive through a variety of devices (positiveness of others, stress, insecurity of self, etc.) and that the opposite is also true—memory can go from clear and positive to doubt and fuzziness. It appears that new connections are formed between neurons as new learning takes place, and old ones start to diminish.[27]

Neurosurgeon George Ojemann and psychologist Harry Whitaker tested bilingual surgical patients with electrical stimulation and found that their first and second languages share some cortical area but also have some separate turf. The second language occupies more cortex than the first. They speculate that as the new language becomes familiar, the cortical area devoted to it becomes less.[28]

Psychologist Charles Furst, in *The Brain*, notes: "If the nerve impulses circle their selected pathways long enough, they leave an indelible memory trace."[29]

---

you are able to tune out what you don't want to hear, you are ready to turn up the volume and tune in the voices you do want to hear. Tuning out is a prelude to hearing 1, concentration, focusing on the thoughts you are hearing and sorting them. Eliminate the irrelevant, inconsistent hearings, then put the relevant ones in sequence. This constitutes the much-admired straight thinking. Here's how a hearing 1 might go for a rational BPI 3:

Left or Logical Voice

I've got to get that report finished by 11:00 A.M.

I'll need to get those charts from Ned and the computer data from Sally.
But first I'll outline the thing. . . . I can plug in their stuff later.

The first thing I need to do is define the problem. That's easy enough. . . .

"With the advent of three new high-tech companies being established in our region, competition is at an all-time high," etc.

Here's where I can plug in that stuff from Sally.

Then . . . I should have some alternative plans. . . . How many can I think of? . . .

We had that brainstorming session last week and quite a few of them came out. . . . I remember that Joe suggested . . .

Right or Feeling Voice

Ugh. If I don't get it ready, I'll have to answer to the old bear for it.

Maybe we could all have a cup of coffee. That would wake me up for sure.
Rats . . . I really wanted to have a cup . . . of . . .

. . . a doughnut . . . would . . . be . . . nice . . . too . . .

That was a helluva lot more fun than writing this report.

What was that he said?... Oh,
yes... it was something about
setting up a satellite office in
Banard's end of town....
That will be No. 3 on the list
because these alternatives
should be in order of expense
... and that satellite business
could be pretty costly.

I suppose the boss was really
impressed with Joe's creativity. I think he's a pain....

So No. 1 is...

You can see that even a dominant left is tempted from
the right but overcomes it by concentrating on left-brained
messages. (It's easy to understand the difficulty a dominant
right would have staying on track.)

Or you may be a third type: You have strong abilities
on the left and right and move to them without paying heed
to distractions from the other side. When you're left, you're
left; when you're right, you're right. (You are probably a
mixed dominant who is highly lateralized—typically a BPI
4½ to 6½.)

There is another kind of concentration, a physical kind
resting in the right brain. The athlete with good concentration is able to disconnect the left speaker and acknowledge only high-level performance messages. Lack of
concentration results in a scene like this:

Left-Brain Voice

That slope must be two hundred
feet straight up—a forty-five-
degree decline... phew...
sure could be dangerous....

I wonder if my insurance covers
skiing accidents....

My toes are a little cold... it's
probably eleven degrees
below....

Right-Brain Voice

The slopes are gorgeous today
... look at those drifts... that
one's all curled over like
Santa's beard....

Mmmmmmm... the air smells
so good... clean... makes
me feel alive... really alive
... and full of energy....

These new boots cost two hundred dollars and the buckles are too loose!

Oh-oh . . . which way does this trail go? . . . Gad . . . there are a lot of rocks. . . .

Let's see . . . the instructor said to bend my knees to the left when I . . .

Almost at the end of the tow now . . . hey, toes . . . squiggle . . . wake up, feet . . . we're about to get up. . . .

Poles are set . . . feet and ankles feel firm . . . here we go . . . ahhhhh . . . it's heavenly . . . feels so good . . . to just let go . . . and blend in with the slopes . . . just to flow in and out . . . lean this way and that . . . it's like I'm a part of the slope . . .

Wow, I'm flying!

So a right-brained task can be assisted or hindered by hearings. Simply being able to tune out the left-brained questions, demands, distractions and criticisms will help you concentrate on your right-brain task. People who perform mechanical, physical or perceptual jobs (operating machinery, performing as professional athletes or drafting) need hearing 1. So practice listening to the voice most needed for the task and you'll be able to concentrate effectively. Recognize both voices: Listen momentarily and then choose the side you are interested in. At the same time, acknowledge the other side because you don't want to lose its input. Then concentrate on the task at hand.

Hearing 1 is also the route to reading retention. Focusing on a voice within can be particularly helpful in understanding and remembering what you read. If you hear the words as you read, you'll grasp the meaning and retain much of the information. If you are distracted by another voice, comprehension is interrupted.

How many times have you been reading and suddenly find you're a million miles away? Your eyes are still looking at the words, but you have stopped listening to them.

This short-circuiting often occurs when reading difficult material or when reading for a long period of time. A help here is to pause at the end of each concept or chapter and rephrase it in your mind. This strengthens the neural connections in your brain that comprehend and store information (See USE SQ3R.)

Another technique is to establish a cue that will remind you to refocus. It can be tugging on your earlobe, drawing a circle on your note pad or taking a deep breath. Use this marker to get concentration back on track whether you're reading, talking or thinking.

Set a time limit: "I'll read two hours—it's a quiet time now—then I'll go down to the lounge for coffee." This satisfies the left brain's need for goals and certainty and the right's longing for a reward, so if you start to wander, both sides will nudge you to return to your task.

HEARING 2: LUCIDNESS AND SELF-UNDERSTANDING

There are times when you want to have the benefit of listening to several voices expressing various viewpoints. You want to hear the debate to form your opinion. If you are a right-brained judge, emotional arguments will be most

---

USE SQ3R

An effective study method should (1) be based on the strategies for effective learning, (2) help you identify and understand the important parts of the material, (3) help you remember these important parts, (4) be more efficient than merely reading the material over and over and (5) be easy to learn.

SQ3R is a classic, widely recommended study method that meets these criteria. SQ3R consists of five steps: survey, question, read, recite, review. SQ3R benefits both good and poor students. More extensive discussions of SQ3R are in books on study habits by Francis Robinson and by Clifford Morgan and James Deese.[30]

---

persuasive; if you are a left-brained judge, concrete evidence and logic will be most convincing. Whichever way the decision goes, you will be more capable of supporting it after having heard the debate.

Have you ever tried to describe a news story or repeat a joke that you haven't really thought about? If you haven't listened closely to the inner questions and responses, you have not formed a cogent sequence of thoughts. It's like giving your opinion on an issue before it is fully formed. You don't really know what you think. You don't really understand the news story or remember the joke because you have not listened to your own impressions, questions and feelings, which make the idea part of you. Once you have followed the voices back and forth in their internal debate, you can think and speak with one voice.

Ambivalence is the product of an unresolved discord between hearings. For example, you may understand intellectually that skin pigmentation is not the measure of a person, but the right-brained emotional message persists. To understand yourself, you need to know what the voices are saying and why they have such power over you. Then decide how you are going to integrate them.

A person who hears, "You can't do it, you're from the ghetto" just as she approaches success or a promotion may want to:

1. listen to the negative voice.
2. discover where it comes from (parents, teachers, husband, peers).
3. address it and ask questions: "Dear inner me, does a ghetto beginning really matter to this job?"
4. decide to tune that voice down and tune up a new voice exclaiming, "How exciting it is to be a manager!"

Some of those inner debates keep your values and motivation alive. There's always the tempting voice tugging at you ("The company will make it up") when you keep the extra five dollars the salesclerk mistakenly gave you. Listening to the pros and cons doesn't mean you'll always end up on the side of truth, honor and justice, but it does mean you'll have the benefit of several opinions. Similar dialogues help motivate you: "Call in sick" versus "If I get there at 8:00 A.M. I can finish the job by eleven." Listening and discovering where these voices come from and how they influence your life will be a significant step toward self-understanding.

HEARING EXTRA: INTUITION

In addition to those internal debaters that help you make balanced, seasoned judgments, there are other voices—more fleeting and less assertive. They are the faint, small hearings that whisper such things as:

- "Get in the other checkout lane; this one's slowing down."
- "Mr. Arno should be calling soon about the Q Report."
- "That location is going to be a hot piece of property very soon."
- "Twenty-eight thousand dollars seems like the winning bid to me."

Though these hearings might seem illogical and unsubstantiated, they are often correct.

It is difficult to measure the effects of intuition in work practices, but a study of executives who admitted to using such insights revealed that those who relied most on intuition had the highest profit records.[31]

Think about how and when such phenomena happen to you. They manifest themselves as inner voices, possibly accompanied by physical sensations, a funny feeling in your stomach or the hair standing up at the back of your neck.

Many psychics and psychologists declare that extrasensory perception is not extra at all, but rather available to all of us. Perhaps they are correct. Try listening to and acting upon those faint hearings. After all, you wouldn't want to neglect any of your talents.

To expand your hearing extras, grab onto those seemingly way-out flashes, those hunches and solutions that come to you while showering, shaving, bathing or driving. Many hearings seem to come when you are in connection with water, perhaps a momentary trip back to the womb, where anything was possible. So get back in that shower.

Often hearings are elusive, flashing in and out. The way they speak causes your left brain to say: "No! That's crazy . . . too risky . . . too wild," and so the voice fades away.

To cultivate hearings, pay attention to them—write them down, thank them for speaking. Be relaxed about the process but consider it important.

During the next week, be alert to any hunches. On the way to answering the phone, deliberately wonder who might be calling. If you guessed who it was, be sure to talk about it. If you missed, keep trying with telephone calls, ball scores and other guesses that can be confirmed soon.

As you give credence to your intuition, you will find the numbers of hearing extras increasing, the voices growing stronger and the information becoming more accurate. Eventually you will find them to be a valuable and reliable aid in your work.

However, becoming self-conscious of your talent may cause it to fade. Fred Silverman's so-called golden gut helped him program successfully for several television networks. He was phenomenal in shifting, scheduling and evaluating sit-coms, news programming approaches and detective series until his talent became the focus of public attention (cover story in *Time* magazine). Then he seemed to lose that effortless intuition. In other words, give credence to your ESP but don't force it.

HEARING EXTRAS—WORK FOR BUSINESS

In ancient times hearing extras were widely respected and used by traders, farmers and kings. If you wanted to know whether to expect floods, famines, assassins or happy marriages, you consulted with seers and prophets who were held in high regard and who often held ecclesiastical and governmental offices.

This high status for hearing extras continued even into the Industrial Age. Many of the earliest scions of industry consulted fortune tellers, psychics and clairvoyants as well as their own inner messages. Andrew Carnegie, John D. Rockefeller and Cornelius Vanderbilt founded and ran their businesses guided by hunches, guesses and feelings.

Scientific management emerged at the turn of the century and, as so often happens, the old ways were disavowed. During the 1950s, speaking of extrasensory methods in decision-making and information-gathering meant risking ridicule and loss of prestige.

A few self-made men who were in control of their own destinies relied on their intuition when it suited them. No one laughed at "Connie's hunches" (Conrad Hilton) because he used them adroitly to build the international Hilton hotel chain. Certain European and Eastern cultures have never lost their respect and reliance on intuition, ESP, astrology and other paranormal ways of forecasting and decision-making. Since the 1970s, skepticism of extrasensory phenomena in this country has softened, and there is real interest in encouraging intuition in the workplace. For example, intuitive development is part of the new Creativity in Business taught at Stanford University's Graduate School of Business. Similar courses are offered at a variety of institutions—from Southern Illinois University to California State University to Harvard. Police departments and insurance companies commonly call upon psychics to help them locate missing persons and property.

So try the hearing extras techniques. After you have some success with them, mention the topic obliquely at work to test the water. You may find that you are not alone in your attempt to develop extra mind-helpers. If others share your experiences, discussing your experiments and successes with them will increase frequency and clarity.

If you are alone, continue working on it. One day you

will make an outstanding improvement or anticipate an unpredictable occurrence. You will be asked to explain how you did it. Then you will have an opportunity to present your case and persuade a few others of the validity of hearing extras.

In this chapter you have discovered through hearing 1 how to magnify and diminish the volume of the voices you hear inside your head. This helps you gain better control over concentration, thereby improving your listening, reading and learning skills. You've learned from hearing 2 to sort out the multiple voices you hear so that you can achieve greater self-understanding and form opinions with greater clarity. Finally, you have discovered how to strengthen the erratic and faint voices that express gut feelings and intuition through hearing extras.

Now you are ready to go even farther, to exceed the ordinary avenues of knowing. Perhaps you'll be like the Dr. Seuss hero who touted his new, improved alphabet that went "on, beyond Z."

> So you see,
> there's no end to the things you might know
> —depending how far beyond *Zebra* you go![32]

9

UPRIGHTS

MOVING TO THE LEFT HEMISPHERE IS A COMMON experience for most of us because we operate in left-hemisphere-oriented families, schools and jobs. Few of us can cope without learning to access the left hemisphere, no matter what our BPI. Of course, it's much easier for BPI 1's to 3's to achieve that left-brain state in which one is alert, positive, optimistic, incisive, efficient and energetic. But if you are at the other end of the continuum and have only marginal left-hemisphere skills, you are at a great disadvantage in competing in the business world.

The manager of a major foundation found that she was not reaching the Board of Directors even though the meetings were pleasant and friendly. When she initiated a plan to present information in left-brained reports and statistics, they acted upon her suggestions immediately.

The right-brain mind movers so far were designed to help you overcome the constraints and biases the work-world has against moves to the right. However, left moves are imperative in your work setting, so five upright categories are described below. If you are a BPI 9, you'd better read and practice each one carefully; if you are a BPI 1, you can glance through to see if you have been neglecting any helpful approaches.

PHYSICAL UPRIGHTS

Look at yourself in the mirror. Do you *look* alert, positive, optimistic, incisive, efficient and energetic? Be honest, even brutally so. It's important. Your appearance is three quarters of the impression you make on others, and when reflected back in their attitude, influences how you feel.

So start by standing and sitting straight, getting a positive, pleasant look on your face, breathing deeply to exude energy and dynamism and paying attention to all the details of your appearance, from facial expressions to clothes.

Adjust your dressing style to a level just a little more conservative than is common in your workplace. If the accepted mode of dress is blue jeans and T-shirts, wear chino pants and a sports shirt; if it is slack suits and casual dresses, then go to skirted suits and tailored blouses. Upgrading your clothes will be a constant physical reminder to you that you are channeling your thoughts left and will help you focus attention on the matter at hand.

Make the physical adjustments in your body, face and appearance, and it will be easier for you to maintain the kind of alert attention helpful in reaching the left brain.

EYES LEFT

Start with your right-brain global view and fill in all the details of the picture. Focus on the fine points one by one, noticing the details of the details. Finally, put the details in some sort of order or sequence and record them.

A dress designer who managed her own small company complained that there were always gigantic snafus in the company's production and marketing procedures that diminished the success of her designs. She was encouraged to reverse her visualization powers and to write down every step she saw in the apparel's progress, from design through production and marketing. Then she filled in the deadlines for each phase and had a workable flow chart for the entire year.

FOCUS ON TIME, NUMBERS AND MONEY

Keep records of everything: your household belongings, golf game, car mileage and investments. Watch the clock, the stock market and the baseball standings. Simply heightening your awareness of time and the mathematics around you will increase your comfort with matters of the left brain.

BECOME A RESEARCHER

Whether you are planning a purchase or planting a garden, research the topic so that you know a great deal about it. Be methodical and scientific. Consult the best sources of information, weigh conflicting opinions and then draw a conclusion. Which computer is best for my office? Do the benefits of organic gardening supersede the convenience of using artificial fertilizer? You'll feel better about your desicion if you've done your homework, *and* you'll have opened more neutral pathways to your brain.

MAKE YOUR MIND DO PUSH-UPS

Try to learn something from everything you do. Extract meaning from everything you read: books, newspapers, magazines, your mail. Even junk mail can be informative if you analyze the meaning behind the message. Prepare a mental digest of books and articles and then record these summaries on three-by-five cards. Clip articles on matters that pique your interest and file them. Then commit yourself to remembering and using that information. Later, in Chapter 12, "Memory," you'll learn specific left- and right-brain strategies for accomplishing this.

ELIMINATE THE EXTRANEOUS

Don't hoard junk—physical or mental. If you can't use it or file it in a manageable way, then you don't need it. Eliminate the confusion in your daily life and you will find it easier to access your left brain. Periodically, analyze your daily, weekly, monthly and quarterly activities. Evaluate what is helpful and positive and then set about phasing out or minimizing unnecessary or confusing distractions.

SPEAK EASY

Speaking in public is a sure way to develop your left brain, so don't allow your right brain to help you avoid these occasions. Join social and professional groups in which you can hold office and perform speaking roles (chairing a committee, giving reports, participating in panel discussions). The discipline of making and following an outline, completing your sentences, and summarizing your rationale will give your left a real workout. Building your vocabulary, participating in theatrical productions, presenting book reviews and teaching adult-education courses are other excellent vehicles for public speaking. If this is extremely difficult for you, start with internal conversations. Write your own script, rehearse it until it is firm and clear in your mind and then enjoy the pleasure of articulating a point of view fluently. This rehearsal process has many work applications that will be discussed later in this book.

WILL / WILL NOT POWER

Set daily challenges for yourself: "I will clear my desk by four-thirty, allowing the next half hour for planning the next day's schedule." "I will skip lunch or coffee breaks three times this week." "I will return phone calls immediately, putting the less pleasant ones first." "I will not allow my mind to wander when I'm reading the president's report or listening to the stock market quotations." Most such exercises in self-discipline are simply a matter of paying attention to your attempt to alter behavior. It's not that difficult to deny yourself something or to persevere if you can remain in your logical left brain. You have all the supportive answers there: "The caffeine of coffee breaks upsets my nerves and my stomach." "The president's report always contains a few choice clues to the company's future plans." It is the right that plays siren to your good intentions and tempts you to act the child. Each time you are successful with a will/will not, your resolve and performance will be greater with the next commitment.

Uprights, the left-mind movers, need not be described and illustrated in detail because they are common, everyday procedures. It is important, however, to be aware of them so that you can achieve a daily balance of right- and left-brain activities. As a check on yourself, use the mind mover balance sheet one day a week until you get the hang of it. Here's how to evaluate the other mind movers:

WHOLE-BRAIN THINKING

MIND MOVER BALANCE SHEET

Internal brainstorming uses both left- and right-brain strategies. The open-ended, nonjudgmental stage of brainstorming is a free-wheeling, right-brain experience. The analyzing and evaluating of the ideas is a move to the left.

Cinematics leads you through progressive steps of visualization, taking you from spontaneous viewings to programmed mind pictures that serve specific purposes.

Inside Outs help you to solve problems by taking the facts of a situation and turning them inside out and upside down for completely fresh and, ultimately, practical solutions.

Suspenders move you to the right by overstimulating or boring the left and are helpful in overcoming blocks and altering behavior by accessing a suggestible state of mind.

Hearings help you move into either hemisphere depending upon what sort of task you undertake. A hearing 1, left-brained, works well in activities that require focus and concentration and hearing 2, mid-range on the BPI, for decision-making. Hearing extras encourages other spontaneous thoughts.

Uprights are everyday activities that shift you left. They help you be organized, positive and productive.

The ultimate goal in developing both sides of your brain is to perform your job more efficiently, more easily and more creatively. Once you are using a whole-brain approach, you will work in a more creative, satisfying way. A review of the steps of creativity verifies the natural need and use of left- and right-brain strategies. For example, consider the five stages noted authors on creativity* commonly use to describe the process.

*Silvano Arieti, M.D., author of *Creativity,* a 1977 winner of the National Book Award in Science; David Campbell, Ph.D., vice-president of the Center for Creative Leadership; Alex F. Osburn, M.D., author of *Applied Imagination*; Eugene Raudsepp, Ph.D., engineer, chemist and multiple author on creativity; and many others.

MIND MOVER BALANCE SHEET

Hearing 1	Uprights		Hearing 2 Internal Brainstorming	Cinematics	Suspenders	Inside Outs	Hearing Extra
read committee reports recall appt. time & agenda	plan day's schedule	"go get 'em tiger" while shaving revamped sales catalog	weighed merits of 2 computer programs IB'ed a personnel problem	saw CEO's announcement flashbacks, listen to car radio	went on relaxing mind trip while doing budget	ate lunch at generic Hamburger stand - got an idea on new low-line product	hunch about Bill during shower

Preparation—you gather information, study the main issues, define the problem and clarify goals. Sounds very leftish, doesn't it?

Concentration—you use discipline to tune out distractions and focus on your project. The left of discipline is soon supplemented by the right as both become absorbed and intrigued by your goal.

Incubation is the third stage—a time for mulling, stepping back and allowing all the material gained in the preparatory steps to mingle, merge and coalesce. This is a relatively unconscious process, which is actually inhibited by concentration and willing. It is, of course, the time when the right brain integrates the parts into a whole pattern. Relaxation, self-trust and enjoyment of the sense of freedom and discovery aid incubation. Several of the mind movers will get your there: suspenders, cinematics, hearing extras and inside outs.

Illumination generally comes rather spontaneously, often as the incubation period is winding down. The right brain is definitely in control here, using visuals, sounds, gut feelings and intuition to produce sudden insight.

Evaluation is the final step as you move left again to analyze that full-blown idea for its practicality. Then it will organize a sequence of steps for implementing your innovation.

Obviously, you need both sides of your brain to produce a viable concept—that is, to create.

So you see that creativity is not exclusive to the genius or artist. By choosing to balance your activities and thinking efforts, you are electing to perform your work in a way that will be more personally satisfying and most likely more productive and financially rewarding.

The remainder of this book targets the key areas of work which have major split-brain ramifications.

Each chapter concludes with real problems that have come to light in management seminars by Jacquelyn Wonder during eight years of consulting with major corporations throughout the country. Some cases are composites of many individual problems. These cases are designed to help you apply the mind movers in your own work and to demonstrate how others use this balanced approach to solve problems, stimulate innovation and rejuvenate their work. *Go through the processes yourself* so that your solutions will be tailor-made for your situation and so that you will develop the habit of using mind movers on the job.

WHOLE BRAIN ON THE JOB

10

COMMUNICATIONS: A MISS, A MESS OR A MESH

In order to see I have to be willing to be seen. If a man takes off his sunglasses I can hear him better.

—Hugh Prather

DEMENTIA PRAECOX

Since fear is all we have to fear,
      As F.D.R. was prone to say,
I launched my corporate career
      By casting all my fears away;
Speak up, speak out! and, most essential,
      Display your management potential!

So, in my best dynamic style,
      I shot my cuffs and banged the door;
And, with assured aggressive style,
      Walked tall across the boss's floor.
"Shut up, get out! I'm in a meeting!"
      Was all he said by way of greeting.

WHOLE-BRAIN THINKING

I set a later time to meet,
        Perhaps a modicum deflated;
And practised yoga in retreat,
        To get my psyche re-instated.
Breathe in, breathe out!—and off once more,
        Ambitious, through the boss's door!

"So, with respect Sir, I've concluded"
        (Was this my former, timid self?)
"Your whole damned strategy's deluded—
        I move you put it on the shelf!
You're in, you're out! Your profit's shrinking!
        You need some new, dynamic thinking!"

The silence which ensued was total,
        Though the thunder in his eyes,
Through the threatening bi-focals,
        Left but little to surmise.
Then up! and out!—his voice pursuing,
        With "What the hell d'you think
        you're doing!"

So now I nurse my injured id,
        And feel a somewhat chastened fool,
Who tried to climb the pyramid
        My first day out of business school!
But work! and wait!—that's tough for me,
        With 'A's in Corporate Strategy!

—Ralph Windle

A CASE OF MISDIRECTION

Pretend you are viewing the following conversation on a split-screen television. The person on the left screen is reading the morning paper and says to himself:

> Hmmm . . . the downtown building boom is moving this way. I wonder if our building is worth renovating. Now, who could give me an educated guess? Aaaah . . . R.S. [right-screen character] is an architectural consultant. . . . I think I'll give him a call.

L.S.: Hi! This is L.S. I was skimming the morning paper about all this building going on downtown, and you came to mind. You know, we haven't talked in a long time . . . too long. Why don't we have lunch today?

R.S.: Hey . . . that's fantastic. I'm free as a bird. I'd love to touch base with you. Where shall we go?

L.S.: Well . . . let me think. I have an appointment at ten-thirty that will probably go till eleven-fifteen at the latest. Why don't we meet at 11:30 and get a head start on the rush?

R.S.: Fine. Whaddya feel like today? Chinese . . . Italian . . . Mexican . . . deli?

L.S.: I really don't mind where . . . but the Inlander is about halfway between our offices, so we could walk and avoid that parking hassle.

R.S.: Sure . . . we could do that . . . but the Inlander is kind of old hat. Have you ever tried the Flambé or Roger's? Wait . . . wait . . . I just had a flash!!! How about the Winsmore? It's just been renovated, and they have a menu three feet long. Each room has a different decor based on some era in the state's history. I haven't been there since they redecorated it, but it sure sounds different.

L.S.: Uh . . . okay . . . but it's kind of a walk from here.

R.S.: Oh . . . that's right, it *is* a distance from you. Well, how about the Dunes? . . . Some of the folks here in the office went there yesterday and . . . let me ask how they liked it [pause; L.S. fidgets impatiently; R.S. leaves his desk to canvass the office]. Well, Bob says the food is good, but the service was lousy. Why don't I ask around and give you a call back in a few minutes?

L.S.: Look, maybe we'd better skip it this week. I'm on a fairly tight schedule and just wanted to grab a bite. I'll give you a ring when things loosen up a bit, and we can really do it up right.

R.S.: If you just wanted a quickie, we could try the . . . uh . . . what's the name of that place? . . . or maybe we should just go to the Inlander if . . .

L.S.: Listen . . . I've got a call hanging on the other line . . . I'll get back to you soon.

R.S.: Oh . . . all right . . . I'll be looking forward to it [he puts the phone down, looking hurt and puzzled]. [L.S. irritably hangs up, looks thoughtfully at the newspaper and then begins to do some paperwork.]

What happened here? L.S. started with a definite agenda for what he alleged was a social meeting. He might have

hired R.S. as a consultant for renovating the building he manages. R.S. was pleased and flattered to hear from L.S. and impulsively tried to convert a luncheon into a grand occasion. L.S. was not totally honest, and R.S. wasted time; but surely these are not fatal flaws.

You have witnessed a breakdown in communications—in this case, a verbal-auditory exchange involving spoken messages. You have no doubt detected that L.S. is a task-oriented, well-organized left brain (about a BPI 3½) and R.S. is a diffuse, emotional, dominant right (a BPI 7½). You can tell this by the language they use: temporal, deliberate and direct for L.S.; sensory, expansive and impulsive for R.S. Other clues are the ways they plan: L.S. with practicality and purpose; R.S. holistically and soliciting consensus. The direction of their interests also hints at differences: food and aesthetics for R.S. compared to information and efficiency for L.S.

If this scene were taped, you'd have noticed sound differences also. While he was relaxed, R.S. spoke slowly and expressively in a low, vibrant tone of voice. Toward the end of the telephone conversation, the tension of the breakdown in communication forced R.S.'s voice up, possibly to a whine. L.S. started with a cheerful, positive and forceful approach, but near the end his normally quick, spare speaking was sprinkled with evasions as he tried to extricate himself from a sticky situation. Lefts hate muddled, ambiguous involvements. As R.S. introduced more and more possibilities to the luncheon scenario, L.S. became more and more turned off. Neither adapted to the communication style of the other. Both are charged with criminal neglect.

You have seen the problems that can arise when opposite brain types are communicating. Later you'll witness how other pairings function and dysfunction. And you will learn how to solve these typical communication problems by adapting your style to others or by influencing others to adapt to yours.

IN THE BEGINNING WAS...

Animals communicate by barking, warbling or mooing. They also communicate through rituals and signals (baring fangs means "I'm dangerous," spreading tailfeathers intimates "I'm a real doll" and exuding odors warns "Stay away from me!").

Animals have keen senses of sight, hearing and touch. Humans have a sense of smell, but it's not very sharp. What's more, we're inept at interpreting the meaning of an odor. Can you tell whether a particular body odor indicates "You turn me on" or "Don't come near me, you creep"? Probably not, but you do have language, which enables you to communicate at a much more sophisticated level.

As humans progressed in communicating abstractions, most of the sensory abilities were neglected. Furthermore, many subtle physical signals have been masked by clothing, perfume and sunglasses.

Although gestures and body language are still parts of our communication, the word is our major means of transferring information and thoughts today, especially in the business world.

Although we can exchange vast amounts of information swiftly via satellites, word processors, central computers and copiers, our ability to communicate interpersonally has deteriorated. Technology itself may be in some part responsible. How much easier it is to turn on the telephone answering machine to deflect an unpleasant call than to explain to the caller that you are not yet ready for it.

To ferret out the inhibitors of true communication, one must understand the process. Communication goes through six phases and is circular and dynamic. When it is successful, energy for more and better communication is generated. For graphic-minded right-brainers, the process looks something like this:

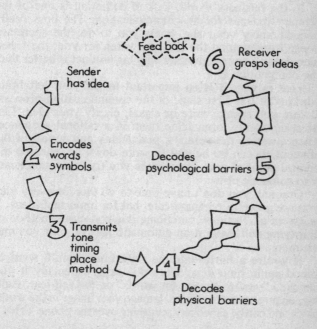

WHOLE-BRAIN THINKING

Whether communication takes place in a terse business letter, a marathon rap session or a lecture-discussion, the pattern prevails. Whether the message is greeted with open arms or a closed mind, the process is the same. Certainly, though, there are variables and barriers within each cycle.

I GET IDEAS...

If the sender hasn't clearly defined the idea, how can it be transmitted to the receiver? Whether the concept is good or bad, brilliant or stupid, germane or irrelevant, it cannot be understood by the receiver if it is not understood by the sender.

In the business world, lack of definition is one of the primary reasons for miscommunication: The boss really doesn't know what she wants you to do; the secretary doesn't understand the message taken for you; the salesman doesn't have a glimmer why his product is better than the competition's.

That is why it is so important to get your left brain working at this first stage of the communication process. Before you speak, write or signal, clarify your idea. List its components, organizing them in a rational sequence. Then question the veracity, practicality and appeal of the concept. It can be helpful to write down or rehearse the central point of your idea before you try to communicate it to someone else.

Granted, you don't have time to do this for every idea you are going to communicate, but for important ideas, it is essential. Besides, practicing this conscious method of clarifying will make it an automatic part of your communications.

If you're a fairly extreme right brain, you'll want to spend some time developing this skill, especially if you checked "yes" to "grope for words" on the self-test. Halting, unsure speech patterns damage your image in the workplace and can be especially punishing over the phone. (That's all the listener has to judge you by.) Dominant rights see the desired outcomes and assume they are communicating them to others. Unfortunately, they may describe the goal in glowing language, then drift off into unfinished sentences and vague words.

To improve your everyday speaking style, try these exercises:

1. Read aloud whenever possible: the newspaper to your spouse on car trips; the agenda at staff meetings. This practice will improve the volume, articulation and modulation of your voice.
2. Tape yourself explaining an opinion or bit of information. This rehearsal will help you understand how you sound to others and how well you express yourself.
3. Use a hearing 2 to clarify and organize your thoughts.
4. Rehearse your monologues in front of a mirror. Watch for irritating body language (pointing your finger aggressively), downcast or unsure glances, and attempts to muffle the message (hand covering the mouth). Look yourself in the eye, stand straight, speak confidently and *smile*.
5. Take on speaking roles at work and elsewhere. Volunteer to report back to work groups after you've attended a lecture, discussion or seminar. For public-speaking experiences, see the left-brain mind mover, uprights.

There are many other exercises that will help you become more articulate—many books, courses and other resources. But most essential is your recognition that better speaking abilities will make your work and private life more pleasant and successful.

ENCODING

The next step in the communications loop is encoding: translating the idea into some language or form appropriate to the message and receiver. A communication can be spoken: through radio, television, personal contact, a door-to-door campaign, a luncheon meeting, the phone. It can be written: as a letter, an ad, a billboard, skywriting or a computer printout. It can be signaled: by gestures, sign language, a barricade, a welcome mat, eye contact, touching or a contribution to your favorite charity.

Most kinds of communication include all three. The face-to-face model is the most intense and, usually, most productive, although some research indicates that voice-only communication seems to be best at revealing the true feelings of the speaker.

Your hemispheric preference exerts considerable influence on your communication skills and choice of modes. A BPI 2 type typically will prefer verbalizing over the phone, while the BPI 8 type usually will choose a face-to-face meeting.

It is ideal, of course, for the sender to be able to use the most comfortable methods, which are quite naturally the ones in which he or she is most skilled. But alas, we are often called upon to write letters and reports when we'd prefer to talk, or we must deliver speeches and instruct when we'd really rather shake hands or hug. For this reason, it is wise to work on the skills you least prefer because chances are you don't need practice in the others.

An important part of encoding is the actual language used. When the choice of words, topic and idiom are too disparate, sharing the same language will not bridge the gap. Gearing the language to the listener is an adjustment that seems to happen intuitively. Clues that you pick up help you avoid being condescending or overly intellectual, both of which score a definite miss with the listener. Sometimes your concepts and the receiver's are so different that you have a mess no matter how hard you try. The ideal, of course, is to produce a mesh, which produces understanding though not necessarily agreement.

TRANSMISSIONS

Whether the transmission is made by speaking, writing or gesturing, there are almost always two forms working at one time: the planned, conscious one and the unintentional, unconscious one. The first emanates from left-brain thinking, while the latter is right brain in origin. The tone of voice, sighs, phrasing and emphasis all send messages of which both sender and receiver may be unaware. Although these hidden clues may be subtle and non-verbal, they are part of the overall message. As a matter of fact, if the conscious and unconscious messages are contradictory, the receiver is more likely to rely on the subliminals. How many times have you witnessed the following scene?

The speaker is introduced, smiles broadly and says: "I can't tell you how good it is to be here today in your lovely city." As he makes this statement, his head wags from side to side in a negative way, and he clears his throat in mid-sentence.

Nodding "no" when he's saying "yes" gives him away. Clearing his throat during the first sentence indicates "I'd rather be in Philadelphia." Even the choice of words, "I can't tell you," is revealing.

Writing is a much more conscious method of transmission, although handwriting and word choice reveal unintended but real messages.

"Reading between the lines" is accomplished by using both sides of the brain. With the right, we sense that one message is heartfelt and guileless. With the left, we analyze the contextual meanings. If a report claims "Business is better than last year," the left brain will interject, "Was that the year your new design bombed?"

The transmission method most likely to be colored by the unconscious is physical gesturing. Trained orators are aware of body language and purposely include it in their presentations. However, the most effective communicators believe what they say. President Nixon's awkward gestures often did not coincide with his words. He rehearsed his movements and ideas to persuade others, but he could not convince himself. President Eisenhower, on the other hand, spoke sincerely and convincingly. Even when he lied publicly about the U-2 incident, he sounded truthful. No doubt, he persuaded himself first that the airborne surveillance was justifiable. In the manner of the method actor, he was able to match the conscious and unconscious sides of his speaking.

It is so difficult to fake gestures because they have been with us a long time. Anthropologists compare the facial expressions of animals with our eyebrow raisings, smiles and body posturing and show that they are derivative. We've toned them down a bit, but natural human behavior still is rife with them.

DECODING

After the message has been sent, it is the receiver's job to complete the communications loop. The listener translates the information for comprehension and then reacts. In turn, this reaction provides feedback, informing the speaker of the success of the communication. The process begins again with the idea altered, sometimes improved and sometimes not.

The first half of the loop included many possibilities for failure. If the speaker was not clear about the idea or had ineffectual communication skills or resources, the message could easily be lost or at least distorted. But the possibilities for miscommunication are even greater in the second half. The launched message looks pretty fragile to face these formidable barriers to listening:

1. *Physical*—bad seats, too cold, too hot, can't see, have to go to the bathroom, ill, can't hear, tired, in a drugged state, distractions, odors.
2. *Mental*—poorly informed, unaware of technology involved, inability to concentrate, lack of self-discipline.

"His logic certainly isn't my logic."

Drawing by Ross; © 1970 The New Yorker Magazine, Inc.

3. *Psychological*—prejudiced against the topic; biased
   against the speaker, I-centered and can't hear another's
   message, low emotional state.

Of these three groups, the third is the most difficult to
overcome because it involves poor listening skills, a problem that permeates the business world. In a communications situation, you listen about half the time but retain, at
the most, one fourth of what you've heard. Why? Certainly,
the sender who is boring, inaccurate or unfocused must
shoulder some of the responsibility for miscommunication.
But the receiver also has an obligation to be a ready recep-
tacle for the information. In the next chapter you will discover how to listen effectively to learn and remember
effectively, but for now, concentrate on the partnership role
of listening in communication.

Just as the sender is, for the most part, in control of
sending circumstances, the receiver can overcome physical, mental and psychological barriers to communication.

Your responsibilities as a listener are twofold: to listen as well as possible and to send feedback.

FEEDBACK

The power of the listener is enormous because the sender is greatly affected by the behavior, response and reaction of the receiver. The story is told of the psychology professor who paced incessantly across the front of the classroom. He was lecturing on behavior modification—a therapy that, in part, involves ignoring actions the therapist would like to extinguish from the client's pattern of behavior. In an after-class gripe session, some of the students decided to apply the method to the professor's distracting lecture style. They enlisted the cooperation of everyone in the class to look away, not respond—in short, *ignore*—the professor each time he left the lectern area to pace. No hands went up in response to his questions, no smiles rewarded his puns, no eye contact stoked his fires when he left the lectern. Within *one* forty-five-minute period, the professor's pacing habit had been extinguished permanently. This shows you how important and powerful feedback is.

The story illustrates several feedback methods: eye contact, smiling and replies. Asking questions, paraphrasing or getting pertinent material from the filing cabinet are all forms of feedback. It is interesting that whether the response is negative or positive, feedback keeps the communication process going. The sender might not be happy with a disagreeable listener but will at least know that a message has been received. No step in the communications loop is more important than feedback.

Each time L.S. spoke in the scenario that began this chapter, R.S. responded. The feedback from R.S. did not please L.S., however, and by the final loop, L.S. had tuned out R.S. by faking a call on the other line. In other words, L.S. stopped responding to R.S. and killed the communication. It is ironic that L.S. was irked by R.S.'s right-brain behavior, the very characteristic that prompted him to call in the first place. Of course, R.S. is not faultless. By ignoring the fine points of L.S.'s communication style, R.S. erred first. It was a needless loss to both, which could have been avoided if either had understood the other's communication style.

RIGHT OR LEFT?

How can you tell if someone is speaking from the right or the left? There are general differences in speaking and listening styles that can help you determine whether you are communicating with a right- or a left-brain type.

This chart shows typical speaking and listening styles for five different ratings on the BPI. Recognize yourself? Others?

BPI Rating	Sender	Receiver
1	Articulate, formal speaker who approaches subject logically if not warmly. Deals in facts and figures, uses unemotional, controlled language, precise terms. Opinions are strong and forcefully presented but without real passion in adult, almost condescending manner. Sparing, often awkward with gestures, keeps distance from listener both intellectually and physically.	Constantly evaluating speaker. Edits speaker's information and prepares a response. Dislikes emotional terms, inexact language. Ignores or does not understand body language.
3	Articulate and logical, uses facts and figures too but in more colorful terms. Ad-	Analyzes both the verbal and emotional message. Tries to separate heat from

BPI Rating	Sender	Receiver
	mires clarity but recognizes need for human elements. Relates suggestions to needs of the listener. Sometimes contrived and "parental" with listener. Withholds what "wouldn't be good" for listener. Language much warmer, entertains questions—at least the challenge of answering.	light. Likes to help speaker define real issues and terms. Likes to keep discussion on track.
5	Good speech skills but often seems in doubt of what he's saying. Inner debate elicits rewording, stuttering, equivocating. Occasionally ponderous because both sides must be expressed fairly. Changes sides or is on both sides at the same time. Erratic but uses real gestures.	Accepting of message but then reappraises *ad infinitum*. Must understand all the little points to be sure the two-way receiving set in his brain is satisfied. Picks up inconsistencies between the message and the intentions of the speaker.
7	Likes to tell people what they want to hear. Good use of emotional language but occasionally blocked by strong feelings. Forces self to stay on track. Colorful, active speaker who must train to present complex subjects. Studies hard to get handle on statistics and such. Automatically adjusts to needs and interests of listener. Expressive body language.	Sincerely wants to understand—open to speaker. Has flashes into the speaker's real self and meaning. Inclined to make erroneous assumptions, garble technical or unwanted emotional messages.
9	Disorganized, diffuse and wandering in speech.	Imputes bad motives to speaker. Can't hear mes-

BPI

Rating Sender	Receiver
Speaks best in emotional, colorful terms, metaphors. Self-indulgent; leads off topic to personalities and personal cases. "I am" is focus of talk. Seems childish and simplistic in speech, but honesty and openness are engaging. Often doesn't seem to understand what he is saying—just opens the mouth and out it comes. In a comfortable setting, might become lyrical, poetic in speech.	sages that upset his feelings and biases. Doesn't want to change mind. Easily threatened, exaggerates good and bad. Suspicious but doesn't know why. Defensive or sometimes gullible.

If you recognize yourself and your coworkers, you can understand how miscommunication can occur. In fact, you might wonder that humans communicate at all, considering the complex mixing of styles every time people interact. Before you proceed to the next chapter, reread the material for these five BPI ratings and try to relate them to conversations you have experienced at work. This will help to establish a feel for the pattern of communication used in your workplace and to see yourself communicating when you learn the right-brain and left-brain ways of speaking, writing and signaling.

This chapter began with a fictitious case of miscommunication. There are many real and more complicated examples in your workworld. The following is a typical problem that can arise when lefts, rights and double dominants work together:

THE BUSINESS OF SCHOOLS

I feel caught in a communications bind. I believe I was hired as superintendent by the school board for my business expertise. Now I find that the teachers, counselors and staff in the district resent my bottom-line, production-oriented attitudes. I scheduled a series of seminars to explain the parallels between good business practices and an effective educational program. My idea was to use Theory Z, quality circles and the corporate culture to introduce the best new management ideas into the educational setting. I thought that as educators, the group would support fresh, forward thinking. At my first seminar, I started on time, saying, "Time is money." Then I explained how individual departments might increase their productivity using these management practices. I requested feedback in the form of specific, written, measurable plans from each department by the end of the week. Two months later, I've receive nothing! Everyone is polite but distant. What do I do next?

Punt. Seriously, you've gotten off on the wrong foot (left, of course) with the entire group. Just as the punter does, you'll want to adjust your kick to the receiver's style. Unlike the punter, you'll want to kick to the receiver instead of away. It might be wise to establish a rapport with one or two individuals until you can get a new game plan.

Next, take a cinematics trip back to a time when you were assigned a new boss to shake up the system and get things back on course. How did you feel about it? About the new boss? Have you ever had a working experience in which you were scolded about wasting time, money or materials? Visualize how that looked, felt, was.

Now analyze the way you presented your program and consider how it might have seemed to your faculty and

"I'm sorry, but I can't carry on an intelligent conversation. I'm visual."

Drawing by Weber; © 1979 The New Yorker Magazine, Inc.

staff. Perhaps they don't really resent your practical ideas, only the way you present them.

Try a little internal brainstorming on the ways you might adjust your program to appeal to both right- and left-brain people. In a group this size, you're sure to have both.

In the meantime, ask your left-brain confederates to help you compile a brief, easy-to-complete questionnaire that would elicit ideas and suggestions from the group. Include some incentives for these contributions: recognition, money, time off, progress reports.

Now that you have your front four in place, try a new offensive. Use some razzle-dazzle plays to execute your game plan: films, coffee and croissants, role-playing, group brainstorming, buzz groups, games and participation.

Scout out the most like-minded members (three or four) of the faculty group. You know from reading this book that your bias is a left-brain one and that fellow left-brain people will have certain characteristics. Seek out their impressions of your program. Discover what practices have been followed in the past and which of your plans are feasible in the immediate future.

If you utilize the language your team likes and understands, you'll find the key to team spirit.

This situation illustrates the problem that can arise when a left-brain bottom-liner must enlist the cooperation of left-*and* right-brain workers. (Did you notice that the answer was written in football terminology? This is a surefire method of irritating the left-brain questioner. Football is a physical, emotional game preferred by right-brain people. If you found the style annoying, consider how it feels to be inundated with information via a method *you* dislike.)

SPEAKING TO ONE OR ONE HUNDRED

Speaking effectively required a fine balance between the left and right sides of the brain. Next time you attend a lecture, notice how it is structured. Are both right and left approaches included? Can you detect a pattern in the way the speaker moves from left-brain to right-brain approaches?

If you find yourself following the lecturer every step of the way, chances are that the speaker is shifting from side to side, alternating between precise, logical speech in rapid, crisp style and some personal comment, a joke or a dramatic experience in an animated expressive style.

Good speakers and teachers have a sense of pacing. They feel when the audience is with them and present the facts quickly and clearly. Then they release the tension with some right-brain gesturing, intonation and drama. An audience can remain spellbound for long periods if this alternating speech style is followed. (See LISTENING FOR STYLE.)

However, if either style is sustained beyond four or five minutes, attention wanes or tension builds and finally breaks the listener's concentration. The same one-sidedness can occur in conversations.

Consider, for example, these hypothetical situations. During a coffee break at a business seminar you are trapped by a geologist who has just completed a study on erosion

Listening for Style

Research conducted during a twenty-year period by a psychological testing group under the direction of Drs. David Merrill and Roger Reid, founders of Tracom Corporation and PPR (Performance Prediction Results) tests, found that to be effective, speakers must be aware of at least four different styles of listeners. To their chart, we have added BPI's, which neatly correlate with their description of listener characteristics.

BPI 1–3	BPI 3–5	BPI 5–7	BPI 7–9
Analytical	Driver	Amiable	Expressive
While listening sometimes looks puzzled, questioning, thoughtful, skeptical. Rubs chin or brow. Is evaluating, critiquing.	Result-oriented, wants action. Asks, "How can I use it now?" "What's practical?" "What's the point?" Is impatient.	Cares for speaker as well as participants. May look concerned, worried if someone is ignored, or smiles to encourage speaker or others.	Likes to be involved. Easily bored with technical data, becoming fidgety or "class clown." Has good intuition.

To appeal to and hold the interest of this broad spectrum of listeners, a speaker must balance many elements of speaking, providing enough technical data to please analyticals but not so much that expressives will be bored; showing openness and comfort to allow for amiable's questions, yet moving fast enough to satisfy goal-oriented driver. It takes constant tuning of the presentation to reach the total audience.

levels at opposite ends of your city. Even if you have a smidgen of interest in the study, it will soon perish as the research is described down to the gram difference between erosion on the west side and that on the east side. As you try to follow the intricate and tedious data, you feel yourself tightening up from the bottom of your feet to the top of your head. If you can't escape soon, you will surely shoot straight up through the ceiling.

The other extreme is the general enthusiast (right-brained) who jumps from topic to topic, never finishing any thought but always sure that the entire experience is a peak moment for both of you. With much hugging, wet-eyed staring and deep sighing, this person moves around the room, smothering conversations with oozing emotionalism.

Whether public speaking is part of your job or not, you will want to analyze your habits to see whether you use left- and right-brain appeal in balance. Here are some excesses you may perpetrate, depending upon where you fall in the BPI scale:

Extreme Left Dominants Tend to	Extreme Right Dominants Tend to
focus on dry, detailed facts	ramble from topic to topic based on opinions and feelings
be inflexible, become confused and annoyed by interruptions in line of thought; return to beginning and review after each distraction. When asked questions off the topic, will postpone answer until "we get to that part of the presentation" (by then, the listener may not care)	be easily led away from the point; often have great gaps in line of thought because of an inclination to leap to the end; the overall effect is similar to a cartoon strip with several panels missing—the ending is there, but the reader can't always fill in the blanks.
delivery is monotonous; the more academic the material, the more cold and expressionless speech becomes	the mere process of thinking "right" (visually, emotionally) can produce imprecise vocabulary and speaking style with slang, swearing, grunts and groans; speaking with musical or rhythmic background can produce emotionally charged language

It is not difficult to tell when you have been on the left side too long. Your listener's eyes will glaze over, or the person will remember some urgent piece of business away from your voice's reach. Staying right too long is less apparent from the listener's behavior, unless the person is assertive enough to ask: "Where is this going?" "What's the bottom line?" or "What do you want of me?"

When lecturing or presenting a speech, your awareness of time limitations will nudge you leftward, but in conversation or business transactions, it is more difficult to avoid wandering off, especially if the listener is someone you relate to easily.

This is often a problem in the workplace. You become fond of a co-worker whose interests and personality are compatible with yours, and any exchange of information can develop into a marathon conversation not related to work. In other words, you overcommunicate because of a match in communications styles. A certain amount of this can be justified if these meanderings result in productive ideas. Brainstorming sessions and think tanks were invented to induce this sort of freewheeling talking. The most productive teams usually include people from all points on the BPI scale; the interaction produces multiple viewpoints.

PRODUCTIVE GOSSIP

One of the most important communication modes in the workworld is gossip, a practice so maligned that we claim to get involved in it only infrequently and accidentally (as with reading the *National Inquirer* or watching TV).

Why do you suppose gossiping is so irresistable? Because it allows us to relish right-brain experience for its own sake. When we gossip, we talk about how we feel and what we think other people feel. Perhaps there is so little outlet for right-brain thoughts in the workplace that when the floodgates open, gossip rushes through in torrents. After indulging, we feel guilty and try to rationalize:

"The office grapevine bears valuable fruits."

"The 'good-ol'-boy/girl' network is okay because it features cooperation and hearty, sincere information exchange."

There should be no need to launder these gossip forums. Gossip is legitimate communication. When it can be confined to facts instead of conjecture, gossip is a valuable part of workworld communication. Of course, without some gut feelings and imagination, it would be less insightful.

Here is a model for gossiping productively:

1. *Choose your partner with care*. Select someone who will not telegraph your conversation to the entire world. Pick someone who has access to information and a handle on reality. If your source does not understand the material or habitually perceives facts subjectively, then your confidential speculations will likely resurface elsewhere and in a distorted form.
2. *Find your opposite on the BPI scale*, since such a combination promises an even outcome to the conversation. This balancing act seems to occur quite naturally in gossip coalitions.
3. *Limit your gossip* to topics that really matter to your workworld. Gossiping about personal matters is a luxury you cannot afford. However, information on serious personal problems is essential to understanding the behavior of fellow employees, and often gossip is the only opportunity for discovering them.

If you can set these left-brain parameters for your gossiping and stay within them, you'll find that it can be a satisfying, helpful addition to your workworld communication.

AND THE WORD WAS WRITTEN

Once committed to paper, a computer disc or microfiche, an idea has been set into permanent form. Therefore, the weight of each written word is greater than the spoken word. The love note is often treasured long after "I love you" is said. The verbal contract, as Sam Goldwyn said, "isn't worth the paper it's written on."

It is the complaint of employers everywhere that nobody can write a decent letter, memo, report—even sentence—anymore.

On the other hand, teachers in creative-writing courses claim that if you can talk, you can write. Apparently there are two different kinds of writing. To quote Peter Elbow in *Writing with Power*:

> Either creativity has won out and produced writers who are rich but undisciplined, who can turn out lots of stuff with good bits in it, but who are poor at evaluating, pruning, and shaping. Or else critical thinking has won out and produced writers who are careful but cramped.

The first is right-brained and designed to tell a story or to describe something real or imagined. The second is left-brained and for the purposes of record-keeping and exchanging information. Both aspire to influence the reader.

Nowhere in this book's workworld applications of the split-brain theory is the difference between left and right thinking clearer. Nowhere else is it more important to integrate the two. Written business communication would not be so difficult to compose or to understand if its writers used a whole-brain approach.

Kurt Vonnegut once said that there are two kinds of writers: swoopers and bashers. He considers himself a swooper, who flies over the scene and swoops in for vignettes and details. The basher drives straight ahead, taking things in sequence. He could have been making the distinction between right- and left-brain ways of writing. By combining the two, you can produce logical yet readable business memos, proposals and reports. Here's how to do it.

WHOLE-BRAIN THINKING

1. *Make a list* of all the ingredients this composition will need: enclosures, a sales pitch, a description of property, confirmation of an appointment. Make this list in no particular order, as it comes to mind. If you are a basher, it probably will be in perfect sequence with every step noted. The swooper probably will have a few parts missing and include some irrelevant points. But no matter; it will all be cleaned up later.
2. *Define the purpose of the communication.* Is it to get information? Give it? Persuade the reader? Assert an opinion? All of the preceding?

Notice that the first two steps are left-brain actions. This will help the swooper limit horizons to manageable proportions and the basher to feel righteous enough to indulge in the next, right-brain step.

3. *Visualize the person or persons to whom the communication is addressed.* Give it the full cinematics treatment so that you can see the entire body of the Democratic National Convention if your message is addressed to them. Ask them questions. See and hear their responses. If you have trouble getting started, you might want to try your favorite suspender: a meditation or relaxation method designed for the workplace. Once you have recorded all the thoughts that have come to mind, you'll need to shift left again.
4. *Write, type or dictate* the ideas that come to mind. You might hear them if your bias is auditory (a hearings 1 or 2). You might see the written words or a scene if you are visually oriented (a "cinematico"). And sometimes you may not be conscious of either one, and the words will seem to flow from your fingertips to the typewriter keys or through your voice (hearing extras). This automatic approach is pure pleasure. Do you recognize it for what it is? But do not analyze what you are doing, why or how—just let it happen. There are differences in how you compose your material when writing with

your left or your right side in control. The basher is likely to be making a deadline, getting the facts, covering the points. The swooper usually is soaring, gliding, jumping in and out of the picture, floating.

5. *Compare the list* you compiled in the first two steps to be sure you covered all areas. Anything extra you come up with, set aside for further consideration.

6. *Rearrange the ideas in a logical order* (simply number the paragraphs). Now reread what you have written and pretend that you are presenting the material in person. Watch the listeners' reactions. Do you feel comfortable with the language you're using, with the message you're sending? Are the listeners responding favorably? Do they understand what you're saying? If the answer is "no" to any of these questions, rewrite the offending parts.

7. *Produce an edited copy* of this piece with thoughts properly sequenced and with spelling and grammar corrected. Check for such details as overuse of certain phrases or words, inconsistencies, redundancies and verbosity. This cut-and-slash step can be fun even for a right-brain person if it is seen as a purely mechanical step in polishing prose.

8. *Get a second opinion.* Have someone else read it to make sure it exactly conveys the meaning you intended.

Granted, you cannot take the time to follow these eight steps with every missive you compose at work. So start with a major written communication for which you have several weeks' lead time (for example, a proposal for future company directions, a summary of the professional conference you attended, an evaluation of the school district's reading program). If you feel the project is important, you will make the effort to work your way through each step carefully. Each time you apply the system, it will seem more natural. Later you can abbreviate it and adapt it to your own needs.

MAKING MISSES MESH

In the following cases, you will see how problems arise in written and spoken communication between individuals at all points on the BPI scale and during all five steps in the communication loop. You will also discover how an understanding of brain-styles and a facility with mind movers can help bridge these gaps.

I am the project manager for and a partner in an architectural design office in Denver. I am concerned about the decline in the number of our clients during the past year. The economy is poor, but I feel something more is wrong.

When a customer proposes to build in a certain location, or renovate a particular office building, or whatever, I try to keep my ideas open and flexible. I avoid defining ideas for fear that this will preclude innovative thinking.

I question clients to discover the nuances in their design and their unexpressed concerns. I like to look at the psychological as well as structural aspects of the building.

As the meetings start in my office, I am occasionally still talking on the phone or trying to clear items off my desk, I suppose more than occasionally. I must admit that I am often late simply because I have so many projects that I find it difficult to tear myself away from one.

I sometimes miss beginning comments of the meeting because I am fascinated by people. I observe their overall appearance, whether the colors they're wearing suit them, and interactions between them, such as subtle put-downs and flirty glances.

If I hear a particularly interesting call coming in to my secretary, I may be distracted.

In presiding over meetings, I try to come to a consensus in order to use everyone's ideas. I deliberately go back and probe each member further. I express myself in sensual, colorful words, descriptive adjectives, feeling terms. But sometimes people don't respond to my most provocative statements! I like to make physical contact with people, shaking hands, hugging and touching because I feel it promotes a sense of closeness.

In my letters, I often use the words "love," "care," "hugs" and "concern." I am an emotional person who gets angry at times when someone is clearly trying to stay in a rigid, narrow path. I've even pounded my fists and shouted on occasion.

At the meeting's conclusion, I ask everyone for feelings about the plan, for their gut reaction. Speaking of gut reactions, hours go by and I've hardly noticed that we have had no lunch.

When everyone leaves, I sometimes feel vague over just what I said I would do next or when I will do it. But I tell myself, "Well, we'll clarify that later."

I love people; I love life; I love my work. Why is my business declining when I put so much into it—my time, my heart, my soul?

You are a flaming right-brainer. You're adorable, talented, interesting...and aggravating as all get-out. Furthermore, you're kidding yourself with this "I don't know what to do" bit. You are so intuitive you know exactly how to right things, but you can't bring yourself to do it because it involves all those left-brain things you despise: defining, planning, assigning priorities, listing, limiting, judging, analyzing, reporting and reviewing. You know you must stay on schedule, on budget, on the point and on the plan.

Before you become morose and withdrawn, here are a few positive strokes to ease your pain. Without such people concern, open mind and insatiable appetite for the new as yours, the world would be a dull place.

Another thought that might make the situation tolerable is that you can play the left game the right way—that is, perform all the left-brain tasks expected of you in a right-brain manner.

Take your business meetings. Reconsider the questions and problems you just posed, pretending that you are one of your clients. Visualize how the client sees those scenes. Get a clear picture of how you look and act. See yourself as they see you: bizarre, thoughtless and willful, rather than the intriguing, spontaneous person you always thought you were.

Ask yourself: Is it helpful, reassuring or even polite to be unprepared or late for a meeting? Of course not. You could force yourself to be ready and organized by keeping a calendar—embellished with cartoons and doodles if it pleases you. Perhaps as you are concluding the meeting, you could check it off your calendar by filling in the date block with scrolls and other embellishments.

To help you stay on track, have an agenda ready for your meeting. This is something you can have someone else do. From notes, jottings and records, a left-brain assistant will love compiling a logical, sequential agenda for you. Now commit yourself to that agenda. After all, you wouldn't want to disappoint your helper, who worked on it so loyally. Here again, as each item is completed, you can blot it out with floral designs and doodles.

To create a tangible close for the meeting, take graphic notes, placing the important issues at the bottom of the page and sketching a foundation under them if you like. Then, to assign responsibilities, draw nameplates of employees in each of the foundation's building blocks. Get it? You're composing a picture of the meeting, and you'll be able to use its organization and clarity to remember what happened, who suggested what ideas, what the outcomes were.

To eliminate office distractions and stress from your meeting, hold it on the building site or include an investigative tour. The movement will be a physical activity (for

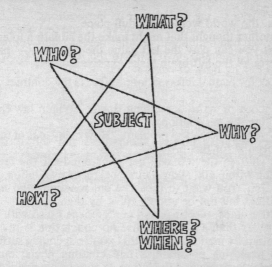

your right brain) and provide concrete items and events to relate to the discussion. Another good tension reliever is a snack break. Movement, social pleasantries and change of pace and focus help make meetings interesting and relaxing. Remember, the most left-brained person in your group still has a four-year-old right brain that loves variety, surprises and "doing things."

To improve your concentration, pretend you are a secret agent who must remember every word spoken, every nuance shown. Recording the behavioral subtleties will be no problem for you, since your sensory right brain soaks them up like a sponge. But don't be distracted by them—save them for amusing replays on your own time. Your mission: to concentrate on the words.

Rather than merely reverberating to the vibes of others, look for practical applications of your sensitivity. If you pick up the impression of a tiff between two clients, analyze it—see if it relates to the business between your companies. If not, discard the information as your would excess baggage. However, if it seems to have some bearing upon your business, try to discover its implications.

As for your emotional outbursts: If you feel one coming on or see one building in another person, shift yourself or the other potential obstructor to the left. You know how to do this by now, of course:

Ask for factual information: "What is the contract deadline?"

Record or write something down: "Which law firm is handling the negotiations?"

Pose a mathematical problem: "How many tons of cement are needed for this project?"

A shift to the left will get your mind off the feelings welling within and allow a more balanced evaluation of the situation. You want to preserve gut reactions and understandings but not be unduly ruled by them.

Oftentimes, meetings and conferences finish with a fizzle rather than a bang because no conclusion is reached, no summary made. It seems that you're spending sufficient time exploring possibilities and creating plans, but not enough clarifying and finalizing. When the agenda is being set, pencil in time for each segment of the meeting and an adjournment goal. Clarify in advance with the clients just how long the meeting will last. Left brains will love the efficiency, and right brains will feel more eager to attend if they know a definite end is in sight (right brains don't like to be hemmed in).

You are wise to be investigating the root of your problems: the lack of structure and organization. You have the talent to do a good job and need only left-brain touches to reassure your clients. This is a small toll when you consider the rewards of your job. You are able to pursue creative work with interesting individuals and challenging projects. So structure and rejoice!

> I am a female engineer and I have wanted a raise for the past two years. I certainly deserve it and am offended that I had to ask for it. I feel outstanding work should be rewarded! Recently I had several new job offers. I then learned that the three

male engineers in our department make $100 to $250 a month more than I do.

I decided: "Now is the time!" I made an appointment and prepared my facts and figures on the income I personally produce for the organization. Armed with letters of recommendation from satisfied clients, the knowledge that my male counterparts made more and a statistical brief, I went to my meeting. I am normally rather emotional, but for this encounter I was well prepared and was determined to be calm, factual, direct and assertive.

I presented my file and a request that I be given a commission that would bring my income nearer to the male engineers' salaries. After glancing briefly at the file, my boss tossed it back across the desk as though it were of no interest or importance.

He said coldly: "If I had all those other job offers, I'd take one of them."

I was crushed.

I humbly acquiesced; I did not want to leave. I have four years' seniority, I live within a convenient drive of the plant and I dread starting a new job when I feel comfortable here. I told him I would take whatever he offered.

How could he be so unreasonable? What could I have done differently? Is there any way to recover my losses?

This example illustrates too well that extreme switches in communication style can create serious problems.

The two of you have been communicating on a surface level, and your direct, left-brained method was too much, too fast, for your boss to accept. Co-workers come to depend upon certain behavioral styles that they expect from others; the more left-brained they are, the more difficult it is for them to accept anything but the anticipated conduct.

Normally, if you present a left-brain person with a well-defined, factual case and a reasonable proposal, everything turns out fine for you. But apparently other factors are at work here. Perhaps he is a dominant right or mixed dominant in left clothing—either type would respond emotionally to your perfectly legitimate complaints and request. Maybe he felt guilty about the unequal treatment he'd given you. Perhaps, all along, he sensed your unspoken grievance and was irritated when you finally voiced it. Perhaps he feels that women engineers can never be as good as men no matter what statistics indicate.

Another possibility is that he is an extreme left dominant who will take advantage of your nonassertiveness for as long as possible and then discard you at the first protest. The cold, calculating rationale may be that you'd never be as valuable to the company once you'd made this assertiveness breakthrough.

Whatever the situation, your sudden change of behavior upset him. He reacted like a stone wall, and you capitulated completely—a typical right-brain reaction to bullying. Where do you go from here?

Under the circumstances, perhaps your best bet is to take one of the other jobs. He sounds intractable, and you sound humiliated. It will be difficult to overcome this emotional defeat. Also, is there another department to which you could transfer?

If these are not alternatives, then here is a plan of action that could work if you have the energy to exert self-control and the patience to endure.

Through cinematics, review the "new assertive you." Just because he couldn't adjust to your change of behavior doesn't mean you were on the wrong track. It might simply mean he needs more time to adapt to your renovated personality. However, since you gave in to his tantrum, it will be difficult now to convince him.

You need to reinforce your own perception of what you want and why you are entitled to it. You can accomplish this by visualizing several times a day the role you want to fill in your organization—now and in the future. If you have plans to rise, then see yourself managing, attending management-level meetings, making and articulating decisions.

You might take a close look at your appearance and demeanor. Do you dress in a professional manner? Is your behavior appropriate? Are you pleasant, efficient and consistent? Do you voice self-doubts or fear of responsibility? Right-brain people are more apt to prefer nontraditional clothing and behavior and to express themselves in self-deprecating terms. From this time forward, behave in a dignified, serious, organized manner.

These are your adaptations to the situation. Now, how can you give the boss a new perception of you—and perhaps of himself?

No matter how unreasonable he seems, he still wants to think well of himself. Possibly he reacted vehemently because he caught a flash of himself being unfair to you. Perhaps he would really like to change that perception of himself. In our communication, we project how we see others. To help him be fair, honest and even-handed, visualize him that way. If you can focus on this perception, your attitude will change and he will change—perhaps only slightly, but remember, any move in the right direction should be rewarded. It need not be directly for the improved behavior but should be given immediately following it.

A less direct but highly effective reward is to describe some insight you had based on one of his pet theories. Another is to bring in a newspaper article supporting a point he made.

He will be more open to feelings, fairness, changes and you if you can shift him right occasionally. Help foster his right-brain expressions by commenting on the comfortable way he arranges his office furniture or his layout for the monthly newsletter.

Use some right-brain language with him, drawing visual scenes rather than conclusions. Suggest alternatives instead of solutions. This will give his right brain a little exercise and his spirit a little freedom to choose.

When the memory of your unpleasant encounter has dimmed a little and he has overcome his most extreme biases, have another go at getting your raise. Rather than proposing a commission to bring your pay to the level of the male engineers, ask for a simple raise in salary. After all, you are equal; the pay should be on an equal basis rather than by special arrangement.

In your new campaign, discard that emotional baggage between you. Start fresh. Include the statistical information, but forget the other job offers. It smacks of blackmail to mention them and invites the cruel comment he made. Possibly it riles up a resentment against women, his own lack of job offers or other submerged issues.

Is there a project or new responsibility you'd like to undertake that would enhance the company's standing? If so, describe it briefly, enthusiastically and colorfully to him.

This example illustrates a mixed-dominant person confronting a mixed but predominantly left-brain manager. On the one hand, she was unable to articulate issues under stress (she ended up sulking over not automatically receiving raises on her merit). On the other hand, she is a proficient engineer, her talent for this dependent on left-brain mathematical and analytical abilities. She moved into a left strategy to confront the manager, which proves that two lefts don't necessarily make a right. The engineer is highly lateralized—well developed in hemisphere-appropriate skills—but is not in control of her shifts. When she saw that her left-brain approach was not working, she might have used some right-brain language and gestures to move the boss into right-brain territory and then softened him with an emotional pitch. Eliciting guilt, sympathy or altruism would most likely have reduced him to a malleable mass of caring. After all, even lefts have their right sides.

I'm the administrative officer of the trust division of a large bank. Luckily, I intercepted a letter from one of our serious young estate officers to a client who has recently been widowed and is embroiled in a nasty quarrel over the estate with members of her husband's family. The following is only the *introduction* to a four-page, single-spaced report our employee was sending her.

Dear Mrs. Thorn:
During your recent visit to Denver, you contacted our offices regarding the contractual litigations ensuing from the demise of your spouse, Mr. Thorn. A team of specialists with our firm has gathered the following data and set forth five proposals for disposing of this problem.

Copies are being forwarded to all parties concerned. It is hoped that you will carefully consider each alternative proposal weighing all considerations and then communicate your preferences to this firm with all due haste as time is of the essence in this matter.

The following is how I reworded it. I know this is better, but not 100 percent. I still feel we're not serving well clients who are befuddled by legalese and already suffering from emotional trauma.

Dear Mrs. Thorn:
During your recent visit to Denver, we told you and Amy that we would propose a course of action in the dispute with Mrs. Raines. This letter sets forth our recommendations. Copies are being sent to Gil Shatz, Amy and James. We urge all of you to discuss these proposals and communicate your decision as soon as possible.

You were quite right in rewording that letter. It was cold and unclear. You corrected two problems via left-brain techniques by eliminating the unnecessary jargon and by rearranging thoughts in logical sequence.

Here's how some right-brain color and warmth could be added:

Dear Agatha:
It was good to see you and Amy looking so well when you visited the office last week. You are coping with the legal

matters resulting from Mr. Thorn's death with great courage.

Hank Smith and I brainstormed your case and came up with a number of plans, which we've outlined in the attached report. When you and Amy have had a chance to consider these choices, please call me, and we can discuss their merits.

Once you tell us which way you want to go, we will proceed immediately. I am looking forward to speaking with you soon.

This version is designed to allay Mrs. Thorn's fears about the complexity of the situation and her ability to handle them. The informal language and personal references might seem inappropriate to your firm's policy, but the rewards in client response will prove valuable in the long run.

Perhaps you could test this style in a rather scientific way by asking an estate officer to prepare all communications in this way for six months; then compare case progress with others at the firm. You'll want to evaluate such factors as complaints, payment of bills, referrals to new clients, clients staying with their decisions, and overall efficiency.

If you try this plan, select an estate officer who seems fairly right-brained (you might use this book's test). Suggest following the eight steps for written communication. The visualizing step is especially important in dealing with clients who are depressed or confused. Recalling a personal experience about a death in the family and reliving it through cinematics will help the writer compose a truly considerate and supportive letter.

To be sure, visualizing happy scenes can evoke warmth too: Future uses and enjoyment of inheritances and family heirlooms can be visualized.

Once you have found a good letter writer, you might ask the person to provide a few hours of training to other employees with letter-writing responsibilities.

If you prefer a more direct approach, have a meeting of all those involved in this process and explain your concerns. You could show them the three examples, explain the eight steps in writing a well-balanced letter and then offer to help edit their letters until they get the hang of it.

You sound like a clear, logical writer who will easily adopt this system.

The boss in this case probably is a mixed dominant who possesses good managerial skills but still listens to those gut feelings that are so important in detecting communication problems. The letter writer seems to be a total left who is fresh out of school and determined to show how much was learned there. A need to prove oneself and inexperience with "the school of hard knocks" can lead to a lack of sensitivity. But experience and brain balancing can work wonders with this sort of problem.

Worlds Within Worlds

Your working environment is a microcosm of a world that depends more and more on the exchange of information or communication. Is your workworld spinning smoothly in an efficient orbit? If there's a wobble here and there, you can bet that miscommunication is the basic problem—someone is not sending or receiving well.

The split-brain paradigm can help you identify and solve communication inefficiencies. So stand back and get a view of that world: Whether you're the boss or an underling, whether you're in a multibillion-dollar operation or a half-time home industry, evaluate your communication problems.

The split-brain strategies suggested in this chapter are just a few of the ones that can solve your problems. Others may be better for your situation, especially if they are designed by you to fit your needs. So start using those mind movers now and discover your own solutions.

11

IS ANYBODY LISTENING? CAN ANYBODY HEAR ME OUT THERE?

THINK OF THE PERSONS WITH WHOM YOU MOST ENJOY talking. List them below:

_____

_____

_____

_____

Now, put a "1" before the best, most congenial communicator on your list. Then number the next three.

WHOLE-BRAIN THINKING

© 1980 United Features Syndicate, Inc.

Think about each person on that list and how he or she looks and acts when listening to you. Which ones do you feel really understand you? Compare No. 1 with Nos. 2, 3 and 4. Compare No. 1 with acquaintances not on your list. Write down the single characteristic which all four have in common that separates them from acquaintances *not* on your list: _____.

Most people respond, "They're good listeners, they're interested in what I have to say." Yes, listening is a vital skill in communication.

Perhaps you're thinking, "I don't need to listen; I need to tune out all the unnecessary trivia I'm exposed to day in and day out."

Or maybe you're feeling, "Listening is inborn. You either have it or you don't."

You do need to protect yourself from too much sound, and skillful listening does come naturally to certain gifted individuals. But you can learn how to tune in and out the sounds around you.

First you need to evaluate your own listening habits. Start by checking the following phrases that pertain to you. After each characteristic, place an "O" if you feel it applies to your behavior occasionally; put an "F" for frequently. Don't agonize over this; just list your first response.

1. *Physical*
   I appear attentive _____, focused _____, alert _____, interested _____; maintain eye contact _____; lean forward

___; smile ___; nod agreement ___; pat hand or shoulder in support ___; respond naturally ___, spontaneously ___, impulsively ___; am distracted by noises ___, others ___, physical discomfort ___, own thoughts ___; make notes ___; check calendar ___; check watch ___; locate relevant materials ___.

2. *Verbal*

I answer others' statements with such expressions as "Really" ___, "Oh" ___, "I see" ___, "Good thinking" ___; praise others out of proportion to reality ___, realistically ___; reply by moralizing ___, condescending ___, threatening ___, name calling ___, ridiculing ___; when in disagreement I find positives in others' statements ___; interrupt ___, have ready a response before they've completed their thoughts ___.

3. *Sensitivity*

I sense others' physical discomfort ___; notice their underlying doubts and irritations ___; seem impatient for them to finish ___; reject expressions of strong feelings by minimizing them ("You'll feel better in the morning—it can't be that bad") ___; point out the logic of their fears or anger ___; postpone comment on what they've said ("Let's wait till we hear from the lawyer") ___; move to another topic without reaching a satisfactory conclusion ___, divert attention ___; introduce irrelevant matters ___; compare others to someone else ("Your case is exactly like my cousin's") ___.

4. *Interpretation*

I jump to conclusions about others' statements ___, diagnose situations and prescribe solutions ___, impute motives that don't exist ___, ask pertinent questions ___, ask questions that demonstrate my knowledge rather than real interest ___, ask hostile questions ___, question relentlessly ___, accurately paraphrase what they've said ___, guide discussion toward a broader understanding of the subject ___, introduce related information ___, suggest helpful resources ___, summarize the progress of the conversation ____, express opinion of the topic in an open way ____, rush the speaker to go faster than his/her comfort level ____, abruptly force close of the subject ____.

Now think about your overall perception of yourself as a listener. Are you comfortable with it? Did you discover behaviors you'd like to discard? If you found yourself not being sure about these various characteristics, you might want to get an objective opinion. Enlist the help of several individuals who are familiar with your listening habits. Ask them to answer these same questions about you. When you have several points of view, including your own, you'll have a general idea of your listening behavior.

How does your overall listening portrait look? Do you seem to be a skillful listener? Do you see a consistent pattern of qualities and flaws throughout the four categories? Following is a discussion of each area, with suggestions for improvement.

1. *Physical*. The listener who leans forward, reacts with animation, maintains eye contact and seems genuinely interested encourages the speaker to pursue the topic thoroughly and candidly. The listener whose attention is easily wooed away by sounds, physical discomfort, clock-watching and other distractions is a real drain on the speaker's energy and confidence. A disinterested, bored, tired, edgy, restless audience defies the most polished presenter.

Other supportive physical responses include comforting touches, making brief notes, helping to locate such resources as the phone book, files and maps and mirroring back what has been said.

Left dominants tend to be less physically demonstrative than rights but show more energy and concentration. Rights tend to show more emotional support but are often distracted and less disciplined in their listening habits than lefts.

Wherever you are on the BPI scale, you can improve

your attentiveness by developing left-brain skills if you are a right dominant, and right-brain skills if you are left-oriented.

More specific suggestions include: (a) Use cinematics to see the speaker as a powerful, fascinating person and the topic as important and useful; (b) try a suspender to shift your focus to one aspect of the speaker's appearance. Concentrating on the eyes helps you penetrate the outward appearance and look directly into the real person; and (c) "pace" your responses by matching your behavior to the speaker's. In other words, if he tilts his head, tilt yours slightly. If he leans forward, you lean forward. A subtle mirroring of behavior establishes a feeling of support and comfort. (See NEUROLINGUISTIC PROGRAMMING.)

2. *Verbal.* Supportive verbal expressions such as "right," "interesting," "nice" and "fine" help the speaker know you are listening and you care. If they reflect honest interest, such noises are valuable, but a forced or incessant stream of "ummm" and "yes" becomes irritating and suspect. Constant compliments and praise might lead the speaker to believe that you are insincere or have poor judgment.

Interrupting the speaker casts a pall over the communication and is justified only when dealing with insensitive, nonstop talkers. A method that works well here is to withdraw all your physical and verbal responses from the marathon talker. Break eye contact, lean away, fidget, remain silent. Usually the talker will run out of gas in a few moments.

Having a response ready before the speaker is finished is frequently criticized by communication experts, because you've judged their message before they've completed it. But with practice, it is possible to use both sides of your brain during listening and have an articulate response ready when the speaker stops. However, this requires a fine balance between hemispheres. If the right brain isn't tuned into the silent messages, then the

---

NEUROLINGUISTIC PROGRAMMING

Neurolinguistic programming is a technology that teaches how to reach people's internal processes by identifying their language patterns and observing nonverbal behavior in order to utilize these processes. Persuasive and successful communication then becomes a conscious choice rather than an unconscious accident. A neurolinguistic programmer is much like a master clockmaker who can study the inner workings of any clock to determine exactly which adjustments will make it function more effectively. This is a systematic and practical model—a behavioral technology that makes explicit a set of procedures for encouraging personal and professional excellence. This technology allows you to model and learn any useful and worthwhile behavior. It was developed by Richard Bandler and John Grinder.[33]

---

left brain's finely drawn response might be off the topic or inappropriate. If the left is concerned about time, worried about money or simply irritated with the speaker's message, then the response often will be snappish, abrasive and disruptive.

To avoid either possibility, approach the listening situation as relaxed as possible. Get physically comfortable, open yourself to the speaker, commit your time and attention to listening. Tell yourself you will enjoy the encounter. These steps put both the right and left brain in the mood really to focus on the conversation.

3. *Sensitivity.* The listener who can interpret nuances of the speaker's behavior and message is able to send back sensitive responses. Without these insights, the listener may run roughshod over the speaker's message—minimizing, distorting or circumventing it. Seemingly irrelevant words dropped during the conversation are cries for further explorations. Anger, giggling or constant smiles indicate moods, as do a slumped body, a drooped head, or the continual clicking of a pen. Hearing the underlying message is largely the work of the right brain.

To develop your sensitivity, challenge your left brain's need for staying on track by asserting: "To get what I want, I must understand this person. I want to figure out this puzzle." Then remind yourself that tuning in to that person is the best way to make a sale, end the conflict or understand where the marketing department is really headed.

Now, with your right brain, empathize with the speaker. Try to experience his sense of reality under his skin—feel your blood flowing along with his; feel his anxiety, nervousness, anger. Suddenly you will be on the same wavelength. You will really be interested, and it will show. You will be listening to the whole person with your whole brain.

4. *Interpretation.* Clearly acknowledging your understanding of the speaker and the message is a boon to communication. It is feedback of the most valuable kind. It tells speakers what you have heard and helps them gain a better understanding of what they have said. When your responses display a misunderstanding, immediately explore to get an accurate perception. A well-phrased question will help both of you reach a better understanding of the topic and each other, but beware of prosecutorial or cynical questions. They sometimes make the speaker feel that personal accuracy or honesty are in question. Then the speaker is apt to respond only at an emotional level. Occasionally this happens quite innocently because the listener is avidly interested in the topic and the speaker is not well versed in it. So be careful of making relentless requests for specifics.

Be aware of personal biases that might distort your understanding. If you dislike math and a speaker is relying largely on facts and figures, recognize the value of information and don't allow a prejudice to color your impression of the presentation, the speaker's company or product.

Another incompatibility can manifest itself through differing conceptions of humor. For full appreciation of a joke, metaphor or paradox, both sides of the brain must be engaged. If you do not think someone's jokes are funny, they may be one-sided and incomplete—or your perception may be limited to right- or left-brain hearing. If you are concentrating on left-brain material or are inundated by right-brain feelings, you cannot appreciate both sides of the joke; it is the contrast between right and left views that provokes laughter. Humor exclusive to either brain hemisphere tends to be shallow. The right brain interprets subtleties and loves novelty and fun. Look for the odd twist, the paradox or pattern. Information presented through a joke or a puzzle is understood and retained long after stark facts vanish from memory. The stuffiest speaker has some humor within, and your supportive chuckle will help bring some of it out.

A left-brain aid to interpretation is to expand your knowledge of the topic as well as your vocabulary of technical and emotional words. As you learn more, you have a better chance of finding words that have a meaningful connotation for both of you.

Another left-brain responsibility in listening is to enforce discipline. Stop yourself, be patient, let the speaker explain. Make yourself listen even though you want to talk. It's like doing three more push-ups when you're tired. Each time you push, you get stronger.

If you become angry or scared while listening and find yourself unable to hear the message, shift left by taking notes, paraphrasing, or checking statistical data (the budget, the grade book, the specs). When you become impatient or bored, shift right by empathically aligning yourself with the speaker and choosing to listen.

As you listen creatively and have new and varied responses, you involve your whole brain. You'll then listen to the facts and logic of the message as well as simultaneously understand the speaker's commitment to them.

WHAT'S IT TO YOU?

Up to this point your listening skills have been discussed mostly in relation to how they aid the person with whom you are communicating. In other words: How supportive is your listening style to the communication loop? But there are corollary benefits to polishing these listening skills. The higher the quality of communication the more information you will gather from it, the better you will remember it and the more comfortable you will be communicating.

The techniques used face-to-face are needed even more in communicating by telecable, teleconferencing and the telephone, because there are fewer clues to help you understand the message. Researchers at the Center for Advancement of Creative Persons and University Associates in California and the Synectics Institute of Massachusetts have found that we receive a mere 8 percent of a message from the words; 37 percent comes from the tone and 55 percent from nonverbal or body language. When dealing with strictly technical data, the percentage gained from words shifts higher.

Not only is understanding affected when there is no visual feedback, but also the stress of listening more intently can be extremely tiring. If your job entails a great deal of time on the telephone, you can reduce the tension by visualizing the person on the other end of the line, stretching and moving, asking questions and looking at material related to the conversation. If you're listening for facts, put the receiver to your right ear (connected to the left brain), and when you're trying to comprehend the emotional message, shift to your left ear. Dichotic listening research shows that the left ear prefers emotional, musical, restful sounds, while the right is biased toward information. (See DICHOTIC LISTENING.)

Developing supersensitive tonal listening will help you understand more of what you hear in one medium. Some ways to inculcate tonal listening skills are:

DICHOTIC LISTENING

Musical, emotional messages appeal to the right brain via the left ear, while the right ear prefers informational, language input. D. Kimura found that when competing verbal material is presented to both ears, the right ear (left brain) has a clear superiority in response accuracy and reaction time.

Other researchers tested many aspects of this phenomenon, which is called "dichotic listening." They have based therapies on it. For example, in trying to improve a client's self-image and overcome depression:

the right ear hears a straightforward lecture in a nearly expressionless voice. The left ear is presented a tape which has the sounds of gentle ocean waves with a very faint and occasional message which says "I am so happy . . . I feel good all over . . . I am loved." The listener is not aware of the latter but does experience a feeling of euphoria and well-being.

This approach can be adapted to a therapy for altering behaviors. For dieters, the lecture can be on calorie counting while the right brain hears, "I feel full . . . I have a small appetite. . . . I am very comfortable and happy."

The most effective messages to the right brain are short, simple, positive and in the present tense.[34]

- Concentrate on the pitch of the voice, pauses, breathing, tenor of the "ummmm" and "ohhh" sounds. (See BREATH-ING RIGHT [and LEFT] box in Chapter 3.)
- Listen for words used repeatedly ("the board," "the box," "my wife," etc.) and the *emphasis* each gets.
- Watch for personal references that may have hidden significance. "I've missed several days' work this week" might mean that a person is behind in preparing the report promised or is interviewing for another job.
- Notice when and how the speaker laughs. Keep track of likes and dislikes. What time of day does she prefer to call? Is music playing in the background? Other noises? Dead silence?

Tonal listening is especially helpful in another one-way listening situation. When you are attending a lecture or program, tuning into the auditory subtleties will help you stay interested in the topic and to understand the information because it provides an exercise for your mind. You are physically restricted, but you can keep your body alert with isometric exercises. Tighten your shoulders or buttocks, shift positions or circle your feet.

You can also conjure up exaggerated comical versions of the topic or speaker to keep yourself alert. Another helpful tactic is to form a question you would like to ask the speaker and then see yourself asking it. If the scene is real enough to you, you'll get the rush of adrenaline that usually precedes public speaking, and you will become physically perked up. This sort of mental exercise benefits understanding, too. As you experience a hearing 2 or a hearing extra, the issues will become clearer.

LISTENING LEADS

So far in this chapter, you've looked at yourself as a listener, you've learned physical, verbal, sensory and interpretative listening skills and you've heard how they can help you in two-way and one-way communication. In addition, the split-brain aspects of listening have been explained. Now you need to know how to apply this information and these techniques in real life. Following are questions most frequently voiced in Wonder listening skills classes.

> I'm a new City Court judge and find myself exhausted and unable to listen well after about four or five hours on the bench. It's even worse when the lawyers are slow or the subject very boring. What can I do?

This is certainly a common complaint from persons in professions that entail listening for long periods. Following are suggestions gleaned from interviews with judges on ways they cope with this problem. (See LISTENING SKILLS).

"Having an overview of the case and its direction helps. I take notes in two columns. In the left, I record important facts, statistics, and questions I'd like to ask. In the right, I jot down words or statements that seem contradictory, hunches and emotions I feel and little human-interest scenes I observe."

"From time to time I lift my legs, make circles with my feet or tighten my muscles back there under my robe. No one can see!"

"I watch the jury and call for a break if several jurors seem restless. Occasionally I ask a question for clarification and to break up the monotony of listening to one voice. I listen for humor, observe mannerisms and styles. During recess, I drink tea or coffee or take a brisk walk. In off-hours, I exercise to build stamina, and I constantly remind myself that I am an able professional performing a much-needed and valuable service."

> I've just become a practicing therapist after teaching for some years. I'm sad to say I'm having great difficulty listening to my patients. Sometimes I'm concerned that I won't remember an important point they've made. At other times I find myself incredibly bored or impatient. These listening problems affect my ability as a therapist. Help!

You're allowing your left brain to insist on perfection. This concern for high standards probably is one of the reasons you decided to become a therapist in the first place. However, you'll find you can have better access to sympathetic right-brain listening through relaxation. When you shift, you'll easily hear the changing pace of the voice, the intensity or lack of it, the musical or nonmusical qualities. The themes will come together in a whole mosaic of understanding, much more helpful than simple details.

As for your boredom and impatience, ask yourself: "Why is he boring me?" "What's behind that dull repetition?" Or,

IS ANYBODY LISTENING?

LISTENING SKILLS

From 1979 to 1982, two of my associates and I interviewed 54 city, county, district and federal judges, 120 counselors and a variety of salespeople, investment analysts, etc. We used a short questionnaire, with the first question being, "When do you find it most difficult to listen?"

The judges found that the physical barriers of hot and stuffy rooms or loud noises—"When police cars go by outside with sirens and horns and I can't hear myself think"—make it very difficult to listen. However, the No. 1 listening barrier, mentioned again and again, was the tedium of listening to a disorganized, boring case—"When the lawyer drones on and on and I believe he is wasting my time." Judge John Kane stated, "When a lawyer uses a phrase such as 'There's a lot less here than meets the eye' or 'You'd better sit down while you're behind,' it makes listening a joy and clings to my memory."

Some psychologists yearned for structures, but those content in their profession found few times when it was difficult to listen. Michael Solomon summed up the responses of many: "When I am bored listening, I ask myself, Why am I bored? What is it I don't want to hear—or why is he/she boring me? What are they covering up?"

Salesclerks, analysts, etc., found it most difficult to listen to irate customers or clients relentlessly questioning and attacking them.

In summary, the judges often felt exhausted at the end of the day. They constantly pushed themselves "left," watching for substantiating facts and a logical progression. The counselors, able to listen to the ebb and flow of a conversation—the rhythm, the intensity—were not as tired from a day of listening; and the salesclerks and analysts found listening easier if they had a specific technique for deflecting anger and criticism.

—Jacquelyn Wonder

"Why am I bored? Is there something I don't want to hear?" Analyzing your own reactions may reveal some unrealized information about yourself—surely the fulfillment of a therapist's dream.

WHOLE-BRAIN THINKING

During dictation when my boss talks off the top of his head, I must frequently request him to repeat his words. When I don't have an overview of the topic, I can't develop a feel for what he's saying.

Taking dictation is a propitious time to suspend that left brain and allow your hand to do the work. Analyzing the meaning of the letter adds an unnecessary burden to your thinking process. The object is to hear the words clearly (focusing on one word at a time) and allow your brain to signal directly to your hand which word to write. It's similar to the skill of typing.

Once you have recorded your boss's message and you are reading it back or typing it up, you can ask for clarification. Besides, it's the dictator's responsiblity to make sense. Disavow responsibility for the tone and logic of the letter, and you will not be distracted.

While answering the phone, I feel overloaded if the caller rattles off name and company and message. I stop listening and seconds later can't remember any of it when I speak to my boss.

Your anxiety and stress excite your right brain, which then overwhelms your left. To move left again, set a manageable listening goal. Resolve to remember the names of eight out of ten callers or their companies or their questions. You don't have to recall everything. A realistic expectation will allow you to relax and listen better. Make the most of what you do hear by saying:

"Mr. Jones, what was your company again?" "That was the XYZ Company?" "Would you please spell your name, sir?" The caller will know you heard part of the message and might even realize that the pace was poor. Meanwhile, you'll have the essential information for your boss.

I have trouble listening when I am preoccupied with a personal concern.

On rare occasions such as the death of a loved one or a grave financial crisis, this is to be expected. However, if you find that personal concerns interfere often you'll want to change, and you can. Decide to switch left and put your emotions on hold.

Allow yourself a limited amount of time to mull over the problem. Force yourself to concentrate totally for that length of time. Don't allow wanderings. Then when the time is up, say to yourself, "I've given that problem enough attention for today." If this distraction does creep up again, shake your head and say, "I'm not going to acknowledge this now."

Focus on the facts, names and dates of your work to keep your listening on track.

I just can't hang in there with slow speakers.

You are in the company of most other listeners. The human brain is capable of listening at rates up to a thousand words per minute, but most of us speak at a hundred words per minute. So a slow speaker seems really boring. You are actually suspending your left brain and shifting right. Fight back. Pretend that you have a fast-forward device that is doubling the pace of speech. Or do busy work with the information given you: Outline it, draw graphics, relate it to an abstraction, embellish the concept with jokes, puns and related facts. You might even do an inside out with the message and come upon an original, important idea. To provide a physical response, lean forward, smile and nod in agreement when the speaker shows any sign of speeding up.

Many listeners have the opposite problem: They can't cope with rapid speakers. The best approach here is to relax, move right and attempt to capture the whole message. By opening up to the speaker's overall appearance, gestures, words and message, you will get the holistic picture. Face it: You can't capture the details anyway. Try to summarize the essential information in a sentence or two immediately after the speaker stops. Usually this is an accurate interpretation of what has been said.

> I get angry easily about redundant procedures in the office and simply can't listen. For example, my office manager reminds me to make a general-file copy each time she dictates a letter—she's probably told me fifty times this year!

Perhaps your anger reinforces a perception of the office manager that you are an emotional person who needs to be told and retold as a child would. So resolve to give up the anger, which may be making the situation worse.

Analyze the interaction: perhaps there is a need for these instructions that you might not understand. Discuss this with your office manager. She might reveal that she repeats instructions to remind herself or to stay on course.

Or you might realize that you resent these repetitions because they remind you of taking unwanted orders as a child. Understanding and discussing the emotions will help you accept the manager's need to tell.

Dealing with another's anger also is a frequent listening complaint. Often the left brain is so busy preparing a defense that the right completely takes over, leaving you in no condition to deal with the angry person, as this situation illustrates:

> My desk is in a heavily trafficked area of a large government agency. People who are angry with what they call "bureaucratic runaround" often stop and ask me for help. Many times, their problems aren't even related to my department's function. I try to be as helpful as possible but find it difficult to understand their complaints and maintain a pleasant tone when I am the object of undeserved anger. Many of them rant and rave, making no sense at all and discounting every suggestion I give them.

Move left immediately by asking for facts and figures, analyzing the problem and even writing it down. Usually these questions will calm both of you and dispel the anger, especially if the complainant sees the root of the problem. Remind yourself that the other person doesn't know whether the problem is your department's fault or not.

If you still feel your anger rising, disassociate yourself from it and the situation by taking a deep breath and flashing on a cool, green scene. Then suggest a walk to the water cooler or reference book across the room. You might even want to move the discussion to a nearby empty room. The process of physical activity helps alleviate the rush of brain chemicals produced when you are preparing your defenses.

Now maybe you are ready to listen with an open mind and a whole train to the angry person's complaint, and the person to you.

> I'm overly enthusiastic about things. My mind races ahead, intent upon some problem or plan. I even decide on a solution or an answer before I hear the whole story, so I don't really listen all the way. Sometimes my lapses are really embarrassing and costly.

You need some left-brain balance to your right-brain responses. Your right brain wants to show how quick and smart and pleasing it can be. Here's what to do.

Promise yourself you will save your impulsive solutions and opinions until you've heard the whole story. Commit yourself to remaining quiet throughout. Then review what has been said and compare it with your inspiration.

To avoid a rush to judgment, analyze the message in detail. Try to discover any signs of propagandizing that might lead you to an unwise decision. Did the speaker drop names or imply an untrue endorsement? Use ambiguities, half truths or name-calling to distort the message? Make sweeping generalizations or just out-and-out lies to sway you? You may find it tiring and not your style to be rational in such situations, but you'll feel better knowing that you are arriving at decisions on the basis of facts rather than your desire to please and to seem quick-witted.

> I am distracted by criticism, especially when I fear that someone else might overhear it. I don't really recognize the mistakes I've made because I'm in such turmoil.

Even in its mildest form, criticism tends to get the adrenaline going. To protect yourself from this reaction, realize that emotion-provoking words are, after all, only words. You might select the ones that really bother you and look them up in the dictionary. View them intellectually and then visualize them bouncing off you just as though they were hollow rubber balls encountering a durable, strong surface.

When you are being evaluated (a euphemism for "getting chewed out"), ask your boss to move to a more private place so that you can concentrate on learning from the comments. Simply walking will pacify your scared right brain.

To help yourself through the critique, picture the scene bathed in the yellow color of a traffic light. See the critique as a necessary warning that a change is coming; then the message will be regarded as wanted and needed information. After all, you don't want to be in a collision. If traffic scenes don't appeal to you, visualize a gauge or indicator providing you with feedback that will benefit your future actions.

Thinking of the criticism in this manner will help you listen. And when you hear yourself thanking the evaluator for the information, you'll know you're in control and using whole-brain listening.

> When I go in to talk to my manager, he continues to sort through papers and sign letters without looking at me. Without eye contact, I don't listen. The effort of trying to reach him becomes para-

mount; I miss the point and most of the conversation.

First, analyze how you present your message. Timing is important here. Is he trying to complete a project or clear his desk to go home? If so, save your breath. Also, have you thought that your sending style might be wrong for his receiving style? Are you giving reports and data to a right-brained boss? Do you ramble and take a lot of time?

If you are sure you are approaching him at the optimum time and in the optimum manner, then you can start looking elsewhere for a solution. You might just level with him. Say that a great deal more could be accomplished if he would just focus on the topic for a set amount of time. You might ask him what style of information he prefers (written reports, oral presentations, charts, etc.) and for suggestions to improve your communication.

Whether these strategies help or not, decide that you will listen to him, with or without eye contact. Always have a pad and pencil with you, and look down to take notes. This will be an effective alternative to eye-to-eye communication.

> Sometimes I am provided with too much information at one time and simply can't absorb it. I have no chance to ask questions or put the information to use, so my mind wanders. How can I listen effectively in these marathon sessions?

Try all the mental and physical tricks of the trade mentioned earlier in this chapter. Invent your own stimulants. Shift positions, take notes, find a pattern to the information and diagram it, use hearings to formulate questions and comments even though you can't voice them. Use a marker or cue where questions come to mind.

Organize your listening for this occasion as carefully as you would a speech you're making. Brief yourself ahead on the jargon, decide on your goal in listening and then listen with a purpose.

WHOLE-BRAIN THINKING

If these sessions end with an evaluation, suggest strongly that meetings with no chance for interaction are difficult for both senders and receivers.

> When I receive directions over the phone or even in person, I feel I understand, but then I end up late and lost.

Miscommunication thrives on directions—even when like-minded persons are involved. Often they are given ineffectively or in a style that does not suit the listener. Just as frequently, the listener distorts the information or does not really listen. "It's over by the dam that almost broke several years ago. You go quite a way down Highway 34; there is a restaurant on the left..." is a typical right-brain set of directions. Although it is comforting to know the general location, traveling *down* a highway and turning *left* are inexact expressions in this context. Once you are lost, they mean nothing.

Just as inadequate is: "Take Highway 34 south for three miles; turn west to the fourth building on the north, No. 306, Suite 452." Even if you have all that written down, you still have a problem demarcating each step of the way. If only you had a few landmarks to assure you along the way. To save yourself from such misdirections, write the directions in two separate left- and right-brain sections to be sure you have covered both kinds. Even if you suddenly see a flash of the site being described and feel you know exactly where it is, listen carefully for the whole story.

When you must rely strictly on verbal instructions, get input from both sides and then repeat the left-brain details to the direction giver. (In Chapter 12, "Memory," you are given guidelines for enhancing this type of short-term memory.)

These same principles apply when you are listening to directions of any kind, but you might need to question more thoroughly. Most persons who are explaining the company filing system or the videotape machine are so familiar with them that they leave out details or use inexact descriptions. You might ask them if they discovered an easy method when they were learning the system. This would remind them that it wasn't always simple for them, and they just might have a surefire trick to share with you.

When you've elicited their best information, review and record the steps from a left-brain point of view. Then get a right-brain overview: Are the files color-coded and symmetrically arranged? Does the tape look like a "S" as it feeds into the machine?

> I work for a pension trust fund as a telephone operator. Most of the calls are problems and complaints. The callers are constantly negative, hostile or dejected. I feel very heavy in my heart when I even think of work. It is torture to listen to the callers, and when I get home, I just want silence.

Studies show that persons in your type of work can handle the stress for an average of three years before experiencing burnout—a crucial need for balance. While in this job, you'll want to use all the left-brain aids you can to minimize the drain on your energy. Confine your questions and comments to the facts to avoid becoming emotionally involved. This might seem callous, but survival is the name of the game.

In your work and private life, whenever possible avoid dumpers, individuals who unload their miseries on you. Your job is demanding enough in this respect, and you can't take everyone's troubles to heart. Seek out fun-loving, optimistic friends and activities. Involve yourself in fascinating subjects that can completely absorb you when you're not on the job.

Discuss with your boss the possibility of alternating your tasks half days with someone who might need work diversity too.

If you have no prospects of moving out of this position, make a concerted effort to revitalize yourself. Humans don't irretrievably burn out like a light bulb. With brain balancing, you can restore those overworked filaments in your head and find new challenges and enjoyment in your work and life.

> I'm not the only one with this problem. At staff meetings, the other engineers and I felt we were listening carefully, but then when the assignments were made, we blanked out. I certainly didn't hear mine.

You may have done this purposely to avoid the assignment. Sometimes that childish right brain has devious ways of helping you play hooky.

During ordinary communication with no active listening aids, we retain only one fourth of the information given— and that for only thirty seconds! That is why it is so important to be an effective sender and receiver. Your boss may have noticed that you were glassy-eyed and made the assignments as a form of warning or punishment.

At any rate, tell your colleagues about the listening strategies you've learned. If all of you put them to use, surely someone will understand the assignments.

KEEP THE FAITH

Don't be discouraged if you have difficulty listening. It really is hard work. As you start applying the techniques and tactics described in this chapter, you will find that you are gathering, sorting and remembering more of what you hear. You will notice a dramatic change in the quality of your listening and, therefore, of your communication. Keep in mind that the more you use them, the easier they become and the more benefits you reap from communication.

Now resolve to adopt and adapt to your own way of listening these tenets of whole-brain listening:

Is Anybody Listening?

- Positively, not negatively
- Confidently, not timidly
- Helpfully, not grudgingly
- Analytically, not skeptically
- Passionately, not indifferently
- Thoughtfully, not dogmatically
- Patiently, not irritably
- Actively, not passively

Put these all together and you'll listen *creatively*.

12

MEMORY

I can't memorize the words by themselves. I have to memorize the feelings.

—Marilyn Monroe

New patient: "Doctor, I don't know what to do. You've got to help me; I just can't remember a thing. I've no memory at all. I hear something one minute, and the next minute I forget it. Tell me, what should I do?"

Doctor: "Pay in advance!"

Depend upon it, Sir, when a man knows he is to be hanged in a fortnight, it concentrates his mind wonderfully.

—Samuel Johnson

"SHE'S SPACEY."

"He's losing his marbles . . . must be getting senile."

"She's a snob—passed me right up and never said 'hi.'"

"If he ever makes it to an appointment, you can bet he'll be late. I don't know if he's overcommitted or should be committed. Anyway, you can't believe anything he says."

How well your memory functions affects your image in many ways: age, intelligence, common sense, competence, reliability, friendliness and even honesty. If you forget appointments, facts and figures, names and faces, you are thought to be not as capable as someone who has a reliable memory. Although it is not necessarily a true reflection of your intelligence and abilities, your memory *is* a crucial aspect of how others view you.

An efficient memory requires both the left and right sides of your brain. An accurate, facile memory does not automatically translate into understanding and knowledge, but it certainly is an essential part of learning. Being able to learn new information quickly and effortlessly is the keystone to superior work performance. With the information explosion, improved learning and memory skills are sorely needed by everyone.

Most of us meekly accept the memory we have in the belief that a good memory is inherited. Although some individuals *are* born with superior memories, that does not mean that you cannot strengthen yours *significantly.*

Improving your memory involves the same methods as improving your tennis game or sales approach. It requires:

• a knowledge of various techniques
• the discovery of a method or style that works for you
• *practice*

You can learn to use the full potential of your memory by choosing to follow these three steps. Through this chapter you'll acquire a knowledge of techniques that use both the right and the left brains to improve memory. They have been employed successfully by individuals with ordinary memories who committed themselves to remembering more to make their lives easier and to improve their job performance.

For example, a new bank president wanted to be able to recall the many details that were a crucial part of his job. He did his memory homework and was then able to remember a long list of his principle clients. Could you recall all fifteen with just one read-through? Try it. Read the list and see how well you do:

    Hamil Feedlot
    Royal Petroleum

Celestial Seasonings
Corn Construction
Mountain Resorts
Adolph Coors Company
Wild West Disco
Flairmont Furniture
Western Sling Manufacturing
Colorado Fuel and Iron Steel Corporation
Advanced Building Systems
D & F Tower Condo/Office Building
Winter Park Ski Area
Writer Corporation
Gates Rubber Corporation

Most persons with no memory training can recall about six or seven, but even if you got all fifteen, you can make remembering easier and more fun by trying the following technique.

Set a goal. If you remembered six clients initially, vow to improve to ten, twelve or fifteen. Write that number down.

Now look at each company, close your eyes and relax. Allow whimsical images of the industry to come to your mind. You might visualize a sick hog (Hamil) gorging at a trough (Feedlot) in the middle of an oil field owned by Princess Diana (Royal Petroleum). Actually see this. Get a picture in your mind.

Next, you might see the princess sprinkling heavenly spices (Celestial Seasonings) onto rows of corn houses (Corn Construction). These houses are in the mountains (Mountain Resorts), where mountaineers are drinking Adolph Coors Company beer and dancing country-and-western style (Wild West Disco). The dances become so wild one woman's skirt flares out onto the furniture (Flairmont Furniture). One woman is wearing a bra with a fringe on it (Western Sling Manufacturing). As you approach her, steam spews from her head. Her arms are colored red and are as hard as iron (Colorado Fuel and Iron Steel Corporation). She lifts her steel arms to the heavens and becomes part of Advanced Building Systems to use in erecting a monument to Princess *D*iana and her *F*riends. Then you see this group actually constructing the tower. (*D & F* Tower Condo/Office Building). When it's finished, it is wintertime, and they ski down the building (Winter Park Ski Area). As they ski, they are composing a book about their recent experiences (Writer Corporation). Suddenly they see a huge gate ahead and ski right through it into a rubber plantation (Gates Rubber Corporation).

Now try to recall all fifteen by reviewing your pictorial drama. How did you do?

You just employed a whole-brain approach to memory—goal-setting from the left brain, visualization and fantasy from the right.

YOURS TO REASON WHY

Before proceeding further, it would be wise to think through just how good a memory you will want and why. It might seem that anyone would want to improve recall, but that's not necessarily so. Some persons enjoy a poor memory. There can be payoffs for *not* remembering. Absentminded professors are not expected to have good memories; the effect is supposed to be lovably eccentric. Executives don't have a mind for details because they are so burdened with *important* matters. And Marilyn Monroe's spacey, late-for-everything behavior added great charm and mystique to her public image.

However, if you are a mere mortal who is embarrassed by missed appointments and frustrated by lost keys, it is in your best interest to improve your memory. Consider what kind you have now and how much you want to improve it. Then check these levels and set your goal.

Level 1 is a subsistence memory. It is minimal to expect to remember such essentials as where you parked your car and the time and date of your next meeting.

It is nearly impossible to hold a job involving any respon-

sibility without operating at this subsistence level unless you are self-employed as an artist or poet or held in affectionate regard as the office scatterbrain.

Level 2 is a maintenance level. At this stage you should be capable of retaining subsistence-level skills plus more intricate memories evoked by such questions as: "Why am I on this elevator with the third-floor button punched?" "At which hotel did I make reservations for the chairman of the board?"

At *level 3* you should be able to add something that will help you get ahead in life: remembering names and faces.

You do not need to remember all names and faces, especially if you meet many people in a casual, fleeting manner. Simply decide to remember half of the names of people you are introduced to at the office or on the phone, plus their careers or main interests.

At *level 4* you should raise your goal to remembering

proposals, appointments, phone numbers, names of three quarters of the people you meet professionally and, say, 50 percent of those in your social life.

At *level 5,* in addition to level 4 accomplishments, you should remember all the main ideas in books and articles, television broadcasts, and conversations with VIP's at staff meetings. You should also be able to paraphrase these well at the optimum moment.

This level enables you to use information you acquire from your daily reading and experience. Although this achievement takes considerable effort, the memory habits you have acquired at the other levels will help enormously.

Level 6 adds a touch of elegance to the first five. At this point you don't even need to look up telephone numbers, zip codes or tool specifications—you simply commit them to memory as a matter of course. You can utilize the number strategies described later to achieve this level.

Level 7 is for the champions. It is for superachieving stockbrokers, teachers and presidents who are organized, on time, considerate (they remember names and details about those they meet), compassionate (they remember that your granny died six months ago) and brilliant (they quote *The Wall Street Journal* and Henry Wadsworth Longfellow verbatim).

It is understandable if you quit before getting to this level. Not all people want to acquire such a sophisticated talent, but it is within your grasp if you want it. As you work at increasing your memory, you'll find that the techniques that expand memory also open additional circuits in the mind. You become more aware and mentally alert as your memory improves.

The ability to remember past events and experiences is crucial in our everyday activities. Whether we consciously recognize it or not, memory gets us safely from home to work in the morning, allows us to perform our jobs effectively and enables us to relate in depth to our friends and business associates.

In the next few pages you'll learn techniques to help

you reach the memory level you've chosen. These are not new methods. In the field of mnemonics (the science or art of aiding the memory) there is truly nothing new under the sun. What is new about them is the conscious use of both sides of your brain.

Mnemonics developed in tandem with the changing needs of humans for remembering and grew from the simple to the more complex. Following is a description of these methods, starting with the easiest and most natural and moving to the most complicated.

Visualizing was probably the first mnemonic method because primitive humans were so visually oriented. (See VISUAL PRIMITIVES.) They needed to remember the location of stars to anticipate changes of season. When they saw the Great Bear in the sky, they knew it was time to move south.

Organization was least important to early people because they automatically responded to natural occurrences for a few million years before noticing that nature is organized. But each time they figured out that one thing led to another, they were organizing thoughts, helping themselves to remember and setting the foundation for future generations to develop mnemonic tactics.

From those early beginnings we have categories for all things in existence: animal, vegetable and mineral. We have the libraries' Dewey decimal system based on two older

---

VISUAL PRIMITIVES

Based on recent laboratory studies of the brain and a close reading of the archaeological evidence, psychologist Julian Jaynes shows us how ancient peoples from Mesopotamia to Peru could not "think" as we do today. Unable to introspect, they experienced auditory hallucinations—voices of gods, actually heard as in the Old Testament or *The Iliad* or "visions" such as the burning bush and other miraculous signs recorded in the Bible. These voices and visions, coming from a person's right hemisphere, told a person what to do in circumstances of novelty or stress.[35]

---

strategies: the alphabet and consecutive numbering. We have colors and careers, geography and music, computers and countries—all systems for organizing information and enhancing memory. We learn these categories starting in infancy, and we reshuffle them endlessly into pairs and trios of memory aides.

If you find this hard to believe, try to recall the names of all the states in the United States. Rather than attempting to name them at random, you will no doubt choose one of these approaches: alphabetically, geographically (northeastern states first, midwestern states second, etc.), chronologically (according to their entrance into the Union, with the thirteen original states first) or by size (Rhode Island first or last; Alaska at the opposite end). You might try to name the continental states first, working your way to the coastal and border states. If you've visited all or most of the states, you might re-create your itinerary.

All the while as you're using one of these approaches, you'll be ticking off the names of the states on your fingers or writing them down so that you know when you've made it to fifty. In any case, you will use an organizational system that works for you personally rather than recalling them randomly. Methods vary in their appeal to right- or left-brain people, but you can be sure you will choose the one that is natural to your brain dominance.

You will also note that the more consciously you organize, the easier the material is to retrieve. If you set up the filing system, you will remember where things are. If you prepare the agenda, you'll recall more of the meeting. If you organize your airline tickets or your keys by putting them in one spot, you'll find them.

PATTERNS

Looking for patterns utilizes both visualization and organizational skills. You can use this technique to remember where you parked the car by saying to yourself: "My car is in parking space D-3."

The left-brain person might jot down this designation on a small notebook carried for just such purposes, or associate it with some calendar event—for example, December 3. The right-brain person will visualize three guard dogs protecting his car from thieves (D-3 equals three dogs).

To use both sides of the brain, snap a mental photo of the entire parking lot: Is it a rectangle, trapezoid or shaped like a piece of Mom's apple pie? Now note the car's location. Seeing a pattern is a right-brain function, but adding details draws on the cooperation of the left.

Building a pattern into the material works especially well with numbers. It is nearly impossible to memorize a series of numbers without patterning because they are abstract. For example, you might analyze the phone number 375-2553 as follows: 3 into 75 equals 25 followed by another 5, which makes two 5's and ending with the same number you started with: 3. If you are more right-brained, you might prefer looking at a phone number such as 273-1821 and relating it to yourself in a personal context. "I'm now 30 (sum of first two and third numbers, 27 + 3). At 18 I was allowed to drink beer and at 21—liquor!" Or with 755-6516 you may use this approach: "My father is 75 plus 5, and I'm closer to 65 than 16." The idea is to look at the numbers and pair them with something that has meaning to you, the more personal the better. A related strategy is association.

ASSOCIATION—THAT REMINDS ME

Before human beings had written language they maintained their accumulated knowledge through oral history. They would recite everything that had happened to their forefathers chronologically by relating each incident to the previous one. These recitations would take days to complete and covered hundreds of years of experiences. They were able to accomplish these memory feats by using association, connecting new information to the old.

Relating the material you want to learn to something you already know is achieved with analogies, metaphors, comparisons, contrasts, paraphrases and paradoxes.

For example, one way to remember the difference in the spelling between "principle" and "principal" is to think of your high school principal as a pal. To remember the difference between "port" and "starboard" you can associate "port" with "left" because they both have four letters. If you can't tell a stalactite from a stalagmite, remember that stalactites grow from the ceiling and stalagmites grow from the ground.

When you open your Swiss bank account to squirrel away millions, use the numbers of your birthday (7–26–1955)—plus the total (1988) for a whopper number you can easily recall: 72619551988.

These examples illustrate the principle of associating something you want to remember with something you already know.

William James, the nineteenth-century Harvard professor, educational philosopher and psychologist, described this process vividly:

> The more other facts a fact is associated with in the mind, the better possession of it our memory retains. Each of its associates becomes a hook to which it hangs, a means to fish it up by when sunk beneath the surface. Together, they form a network of attachments by which it is woven into the entire tissue of our thought. The "secret of a good memory" is thus the secret of forming diverse and multiple associations with every fact we care to retain.

It is not entirely an accident that William James also was a proponent of a liberal education. The broader the spectrum of information you can relate to new learning, the better the chance that you'll have a particular fact to associate with it.

THE LOCI OR LOCATION

In the Roman Empire mnemonic methods were formalized when the loci method was developed. According to a story told by Cicero, a poet named Simonides was speaking at a banquet when a messenger called him outside for a moment. In Simonides' absence, the roof of the banquet hall collapsed, crushing the occupants beyond recognition. Simonides was able to identify the bodies by remembering the places at which the guests had been sitting. Noting that it was his memory of the places where the guests were sitting that had enabled him to indentify them, Simonides inferred that memory can be improved by associating mental images of the matter to be recalled to their location.

Loci is the Latin plural of locus, which means "place or location." Thus, the loci is the system that uses places or locations. Greek and Roman orators could speak at great length without notes by visualizing objects that represented the topics to be covered. They mentally placed these objects in different locations, usually parts of a building. As they spoke, they saw themselves moving from room to room, retrieving the object images along the way. This practice may be the origin of the expression "in the first place."

The loci system involves organization, visualization and association. To experience it yourself, try to recall a sequence of events or items by placing them visually in your office.

As you walk through the doorway, you see the purchase orders lying on the receptionist's desk, your marketing plan straddled atop the water cooler, and the file of the new major client, Petry-Vappi Construction, squeezed in the tray of the copier machine . . . and so on through the list of files you want to take with you to a meeting. Then, when you want to recall the list, just pretend you are walking through the office doorway, and each item will pop out at you. It is quite easy to visualize when using the loci method because you have something concrete (the location) to which you pair the idea or object.

Dr. Dugan Mahoney of Strong Memorial Hospital in Rochester, New York, explains that physicians use a modified form of loci—chronology—to remember and structure patient interviews:

"When interviewing a patient concerning his illness, I find it very useful to structure my interview in a rigid chronology by asking questions such as, 'When did it all begin?' 'When did you develop chest pain?' 'How long has it been going on?' Then I quickly summarize the patient's story, highlighting points that are important or that I am not clear on. Using this format, I usually don't need to take notes, even with very complicated histories."

Both loci and chronology are handy ways to remember where you put things. You simply return to the scene of the crime and go through your actions step by step.

If your memory is tied to an emotion, it will be even easier to recall. (See FLASHBULB MEMORY.)

MEDIATORS

A mediator is a convenient device in which you pair the idea you want to remember with a dramatic alteration in your surroundings or behavior. When your grandfather tied a string around his finger as a reminder, he was using a mediator. The process is the same in this situation: You are driving to work and realize you need to make an airline reservation. Move your pen from your shirt pocket to your slacks. Then, when you get to the office and your pen is out of its usual place, you say, "Ahaaa, I must call the airline." Similarly, you could move your watch from one wrist to another or kick off a shoe.

Mediators can be time savers. Have you ever forgotten to turn off your lights at the parking lot after you left for work in the dark, early-morning hours? If so, try pulling down the visor on the passenger side of your car to remind you to turn off the lights when you arrive. As you select

---

FLASHBULB MEMORY

The stunningly clear memories connected with emotional events are described by this researcher:

> It is as if our nervous system took a multimedia snapshot of the sounds, sights, smells, weather, emotional climate, even the body postures we experience at certain moments.[36]

What is the physical process involved? Here's one explanation:

> As an individual's state of emotion or arousal arises, substances are released into the fluid that tend to encourage memory fixation. The fluid reaches many receptors and the synapses that are currently or recently active immediately store.[37]

---

your mediator, connect it visually to the item or concept to be recalled.

Mediators typically differ from other methods in that they are *physical* cues. They are primarily right-brained because they rely on visualization, physical experiences or startling, incongruent cues. However, the next method, chunking, requires a more left-brained approach.

CHUNKING

The human brain has trouble remembering more than six or seven items, numbers or letters at one time; three is the usual number. To overcome this "seven limit," memory experts have contrived a grouping system called chunking. Your Social Security number is a good example. Instead of trying to make you remember this mind-boggler, 294637612, they have inserted two hyphens, thus providing three memory-manageable chunks: 294–63–7612.

Take this list of unrelated items on the office shipping

list: paper clips, balance sheets, felt-tip markers, budget forms, *Fortune* magazine, pencils, briefcase, letterheads, binders and plants. See if you can discover the hidden characteristic of the list that makes it ideal for chunking.

It is much easier to remember if you recognize that there is one "l," two "f's," three "p's" and four "b's" than as a random list.

The purpose of chunking is to reduce memory material to manageable bits of information and/or provide a key for yourself when there are no meaningful connections among items.

ACRONYMS AND ACROSTICS

Chunking requires analyzing how items might be divided. A refined method of chunking is the acronym, a group of letters that forms one word, assuring easy recall.

New organizations spend time and effort devising a name with initials forming a pronounceable and meaningful word, an acronym. For instance, a group organized to promote the replanting of trees in the outback would project a clearer image with the name Restore Our Outback Trees (ROOT) than the Society for the Reforestation of Deciduous and Nondeciduous Trees in the Outback (SDRNTO).

Research has found two additional benefits to acronyms. They chunk the information so that you need remember *only* one word instead of many. The acronym also provides cues to each word by listing the first letter of each word in the acronym.

A closely related strategy for making something meaningful is the acrostic, which is a series of words, lines or verses in which the first or last letters form a word, a phrase or a sentence. "Every Good Boy Does Fine" has been used to teach many generations of youngsters the lines of the treble clef on a musical scale: EGBDF.

Engineers at IBM, Storage Technology and other high-tech firms use the following acrostic to help them remember the color code for their computer resistors.

Acrostic	Resistor Color	Resistor Code No.
Bad	Black	0
Boys	Brown	1
Rape	Red	2
Our	Orange	3
Young	Yellow	4
Girls	Green	5
But	Blue	6
Violet	Violet	7
Gives	Gray	8
Willingly	White	9
Get	Gold	
Some	and	00
Now	Silver	

By relating the first letters of the resistor colors to the words in the naughty acrostic, engineers can easily remember the code number. For example, Orange is paired with Our and is the third word (using zero as the starting digit). Another resistor was developed later, with gold and silver intertwined. The engineers' fertile minds added: "Get Some Now," which means Gold and Silver None or 00.

RHYME TIME

Rhyming is a method that appeals to the ear rather than to visual or analytical faculties. Think how much easier it is to memorize "The boy stood on the burning deck" than the Gettysburg Address. Even into adulthood, we remain dependent upon the mnemonic jingles learned so early in life that it seems we always knew them:

> ABCDEFG
> HI-JK-LMNOP
> QRS and TUV
> WX, Y and Z

Now I've said my ABC's
Tell me what you think of me.

Thirty days hath September,
April, June and November,
All the rest have thirty-one,
Save February, with twenty-eight.

Rhymes and jingles are stored in the right brain and paraded before the left for review. The left actually extracts the meaning by saying: "Let's see—thirty days hath September, April, June and November . . . and this is April . . . so this month has thirty days."

DIRECTED VISUALIZATION—ASOE

Most likely, you use visualization every day to help you remember how to perform such mundane tasks as replacing your typewriter ribbon, loading the stapler or assembling the filing cabinet. You see how it is to be done.

The picture-making abilities you developed in cinematics will serve you well in creating and reviewing human scenes. But mnemonics' visualization requires a much sharper focus because you are dealing with abstractions. Therefore, add the ASOE (ah-so) method to your cinematics when you are visualizing for memory:

A   *A*ction—get drama, adventure, movement in there!
S   *S*ubstitute—pair your items with substitutes. If you're connecting a man to a nail, see him smoking a nail instead of a cigarette.
O   *O*ut of proportion—giant tears on a tiny elephant's cheek.
E   *E*xaggerate everything—see millions of plants in your reception area.

The more absurd, ridiculous, action-packed, sexual, bizarre the picture, the more vivid your memory will be.

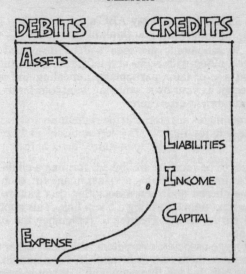

If you were reared in a restrained atmosphere, you might need to put yourself through some silly sessions until you get the hang of it. Lock yourself in the den (if you're inhibited) or free-associate with an amusing friend...but let yourself go. Don't allow the left brain to criticize the visuals of the right. Squelch such left-brain messages as: "This is stupid...or not wild enough...or embarrassing," etc. Accept what comes. The right brain gets stalled by negatives.

Now actually see the picture in your mind and hold it for a moment.

Bow McLean, vice-president, Colorado National Bank, uses a visualization to help employees remember how to differentiate between debits and credits. He points out that in a general ledger there are only five categories: *A*ssets, *L*iabilities, *I*ncome, *C*apital and *E*xpenses. Then he draws this clever visual for them and says: "Just remember, ALICE is a pregnant lady!"

Modern mnemonic systems are much more formal than

those developed earlier. Many of these modern systems have been the subject of memory books; thus these latter additions to mnemonic methods will be described only briefly here, along with right- and left-brain connotations. If you find one of them particularly appealing and would like to adopt it as your own, you may want to refer to more thorough treatment elsewhere.

THE LINK SYSTEM

The objects to be recalled are linked, forming a chain. The link system involves forming a visual image for each item to be remembered and then associating this picture with one of the next items, forming a chain link. This approach was used earlier in this chapter to remember the bank's main clients.

Do not try to associate every item with every other item; rather, connect them two at a time. If, for example, you are giving a talk that has five main points, it would be easier to underline a key word for each of the thoughts and then form a visual chain. If your speech is to cover *unemployment*, *inflation*, *agriculture*, *defense spending* and *Social Security*, link the first two, unemployment and inflation, by seeing a bunch of hobos sprawled under a bridge and inflating big balloons. Now pair balloons and agriculture— see the balloons bursting and all sorts of carrots, corn, wheat, hay, milk, etc., blowing out and spilling all over. Get the action in—let your mind go wild. For agriculture and defense spending, see tanks, missiles and soldiers with guns stationed around a farm field. Next, link defense spending and Social Security by making an image of a huge dollar bill being pulled and torn apart by all the soldiers on one side and millions of poor, elderly, handicapped people on the other side. Now you have the main ideas for your talk linked together.

You've used both sides of your brain—the left to find the key words and put them in a chronological order, and the right to construct visual images. By using your whole brain, you'll find it easy to remember all the points you want to cover.

PEG O' YOUR HEART

Related to the link and loci systems is the peg system, which was developed to help with abstractions, more difficult to remember than the tangible and concrete. The peg also gives you an immediate image, but in addition it facilitates recalling items out of order.

It works in this way: You picture in your mind the peg word for each phonetic sound and its associated number, which conveniently rhymes. These ten pairs will illustrate the concept:

1. gun
2. shoe
3. tree
4. oar or door
5. dive
6. sticks
7. kettle
8. gate
9. wine
10. hen

Practice these peg words backward and forward until you can recall them instantly and automatically. Now you are ready to apply them to difficult situations. For example, if you want to memorize the names of the Canadian provinces, you can associate them in this way to your pegs:

1. gun	Nova Scotia
2. shoe	New Brunswick
3. tree	Newfoundland
4. oar or door	Prince Edward Island
5. dive	Saskatchewan
6. sticks	Manitoba

7. kettle   Ontario
8. gate   Alberta
9. wine   Quebec
10. hen   British Columbia

Start by seeing a Nova Scotia salmon with a smoking gun in its mouth (one-gun–Nova Scotia salmon). Now try the rest. You can retrieve any of the items (Manitoba) without starting at the beginning of your scenario because the peg pairs rhyme (6—sticks) and you connected them visually to the idea to be recalled (see a sobbing man stuck in the bell of an ice-cold tuba with a sharp stick piercing his scalp).

A method for remembering numbers is the phonetic system.

THE PHONETIC SYSTEM

This approach also uses association and visualization. By changing numbers, which are difficult to remember, to letters and using them as words or codes, recall is facilitated.

You begin by memorizing pairs of words to numbers and then converting the numbers into letters. Here is a list of ten pairs with consonants (vowels are easily inferred from the context):

1—t
2—n
3—m
4—r
5—l
6—jsh or ch
7—k or hard c
8—f, g
9—p, b or d
0—z or s

Once you have memorized this code, you can convert these pairings into phrases or sentences such as this one:

Dow Jones Prices Rampage
9   6   9   4

(The number 9694 is the code number for an IBM computer part on a ticker tape.) This sentence will be much easier to remember if you see mountains of ticker tapes strangling the brokers! Because it conjures up a picture in your mind, you'll remember it.

Memorizing the list of ten will be easy to accomplish if you keep this explanation in mind.

1 will automatically become a "t" sound because they are similar in appearance and have one downstroke.

2 will be an "n" becuase it has two downward strokes.

3 will be the "m" sound because it has three downward strokes.

4 is an "r" sound because it ends with an "r."

5 stands for the "l" sound because the Roman numeral 50 (L) begins with 5; also, the five fingers of your hand easily make an L.

6 j, ch, sh and soft g—the letter "j" turned around is almost like "6."

7 is "k" or hard "c" because "k" is two 7's back to back.

8 is the "f" and "g" sound because when written, they use double loops.

9 is the "p," "b" or "d" sound becuase they all look like 9's in various positions.

0 stands for zero because of the end sound and for "s" because "s" and "z" are similar.

If you have trouble remembering part numbers, route or license numbers, try making the numbers into letters and then into words by adding vowels (a, e, i, o or u) between them.

License #ZG <u>7 2 9 9</u> Ziggy has KNoBB knees!
        KNBB

Part Number <u>3 8 5 2</u> MaG LaNe or
              MaFaLaNa
    <u>MGLN</u>
     or
     F

Another use for the phonetic system is code pricing by retail stores. Suppose a dress shop has eight dollars invested in a garment that sells for thirty-six dollars. The price tag will be coded with an F or a G to denote the eight-dollar investment. Then when a salesperson has a customer who wants to haggle over price or it's clearance sale time, the code tells him how to reduce the price and still make an acceptable profit on that garment.

This method works equally well with proposal numbers, new catalog systems and identification procedures. These natural associations can easily convert into sounds, then words or sentences. Comparing or translating associations into "way out" words and phrases requires creativity—a left- and right-brain skill. Although the phonetic system is difficult for most persons to master, others love it and use it with ease.

DIFFERENT KINDS FOR DIFFERENT MINDS

We are all different, and we all have different workworlds with different memory needs. Therefore, you must decide which mnemonic methods serve you best. What worked for the memory students previously described in this chapter might require a slight twist to adapt to your particular situation. The following cases focus on the concerns most frequently voiced by students in the Wonder memory classes and demonstrate how mnemonics can be altered to specific jobs and individuals.

I'm a loan analyst for a large mortgage company and often visit the site of an organization applying for a loan. I need to remember pertinent information told to me as I walk through the building. I've found that if I take notes, it is distracting and unnerving to my clients.

Use the loci system. Visualize some specific item, bit of information or person at each location along the way. For example, in the entry or reception area, ask when the company's operation first began. In the main hall (or personnel office), inquire about the number of employees on payroll, the turnover rate and the annual outlay for employee benefits. As you pass the marketing department, direct your questions to market shares, sales and future products. In the warehouse you can ask about inventory, storage, source of materials, supplies and stock on hand. At the finance office you can check on loans, line of credit and interest rates. Upon leaving, you may want to know the number of days for deliveries, billing dates and payment procedures. Careful focus on these items at each site, a few brief notes on such matters as comparison ratios or unusual company policies, plus a short written summary at the end of your tour will provide you with a clear recall of your visit.

I'm the vice-president of marketing for a large midwestern manufacturing company and have twelve district managers. They complain of varying difficulties with remembering names. Some can recall only the names of VIP's or senior customers. Others have trouble with foreign names, or remembering customers' names when they meet ten or twelve at one time.

Knowing their own BPI rating will help them choose a strategy most likely to work for them.

A BPI 1 to 3 might prefer repeating the name when first introduced. This also assures that you've heard it correctly. Next, use it in a sentence while you're still with the person ("Joe, I'm glad to meet you") and then again when you depart. Strive for at least three repetitions. (See **MAGIC**

OH, HOW HUMILIATING! TODAY, IN FRONT OF EVERYONE AT THE OFFICE, MY BOSS FORGOT MY NAME.

HOW DEGRADING! I FELT SO WORTHLESS, SO INSIGNIFICANT.

HEY, I UNDERSTAND. TO FORGET A NAME IS TO DENY A PERSON THEIR IDENTITY AND INTEGRITY.

GEE, I COULDN'T HAVE SAID IT BETTER. YOU'RE ALWAYS SO UNDERSTANDING, BOB.

ER, I MEAN TOM.

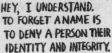

THREE MEMORY.) Another tactic is to ask for the spelling of the name of their hometown. You might also request a business card, which would bring in visual and tactile elements. When you go home or have a quiet moment, write the name on your calendar or in your address book. Adding something personal about the conversation or the person's appearance will strengthen recall even further.

BPI 5's to 9's enjoy connecting the person's name to face, body or general appearance—seeing flush-faced Jan with strawberry jam all over her face or Ray with beams of light emanating from his head; or to a funny phrase ("So long, Carp! He ho!" for Solon Carpio, engineer for Gates Rubber); or to an emotional event ("He reminds me of my first love").

To ease your concern when meeting many people, focus on a few. Then when you've heard and retained three names but forgotten one, listen for someone else in the group to repeat it. With a difficult name, ask the individual how he has told others to remember it.

> I work on many projects at one time. I forget which ones have gone out and which I'm in the middle of!

MAGIC THREE MEMORY

Canadian psychologist Donald Hebb proposes a connection between permanent and fleeting memory. In Hebb's view, short-term memory is an active or dynamic memory: Sign or sound sets off a reverberating pattern of nerve impulses in the brain. The impulses circle a closed loop of connected neurons, freezing an instant of time long enough for the brain to perceive it. But the neurons fire for only a short time, so dynamic memory will fade away unless a more permanent, structural trace is made. This structural trace, or engram, would correspond to long-term memory.

THE INDELIBLE ENGRAM

Psychologist Charles Furst compares Hebb's two processes of memory storage to the flow of water down a hill: "Dynamic traces would be like rivulets of water.... When the water stops, the pattern of rivulets disappears. But if the water runs long enough, then the rivulets cut channels and wear the pattern into the hillside, so that a permanent 'memory' of it has been formed." Short-term memories could thus be converted into long-term memories. If the nerve impulses circle their selected pathways long enough, at least three or four times with focused attention, they leave behind an indelible memory trace.[38]

Perhaps you've tried the slightly left-brain approach of noting progress on your calendar or making a flow chart report. If they haven't helped or are unappealing to you, try right-brain visualization. See the Chrysler report walking out the front doorway as you complete it. Focus on the Armour-Dial file strewn on the floor when you send the file to the bindery. If the Bureau of Standards proposal is half typed, imagine that scales (standards) are covering half of your neighbor's typewriter. By using your surroundings as reminders of these projects and their current condition, you will be less likely to forget or neglect them. This approach is a simple and dependable cure for your problem.

> Often when I get a telephone query, I'll go to the records room for the client's file and forget why I'm there. I'm annoyed with myself for this and other lapses. At times I want to bring my briefcase or calendar home but invariably forget it. And I'm always mislaying my plane tickets and the information I need for a business trip.

Try using your right and left brains with these memory problems. On your way to the file room, see the file in its drawer or stack. Once there, if you can't remember why, visualize yourself back at your desk looking at the file room scene. If all else fails, a return to your office will recapture your mission.

When you decide to bring home your calendar or briefcase, try a mediator to strengthen your recall. Throw a book in your doorway and put your jacket on top of your briefcase. Visualize the book burning your calendar and your bookcase stamping it out. As you step over the book on your way home, the image will pop out and you'll remember everything you want to take.

Use your left-brain skills to designate one specific area for plane tickets, agendas, data on your trip, etc. Reserve that drawer, desktop or shelf for those special items and always place them there. *Always* put your keys, your glasses and your bills in the same place. Then on the rare occasions when you do misplace something, that special form of cinematics, "Once More with Feeling," will help you retrace your steps and recover your lost item.

> When I complete an assignment for an outside client, I often forget to invoice them—sometimes I have ten to twelve clients not billed!

Here's another good spot for a mediator. Put a coffee cup or favorite sweater on the typewriter or calculator. Leave it there until the invoices are ready. You might also visualize a huge pink invoice rolled in the typewriter— eating it! Each time you pass by, it will call out to you: "Send me . . . send me."

> I work at Eastman Kodak Company in the office and often compile large reports. If I'm interrupted in the middle of one, I have to go back to the beginning to pick up the thread. This is frustrating and time-consuming.

Try getting a strong visual image of the last phrase (see yellow, short fellow) as you shift to your interruption. The stronger and more vivid the image, the easier it is to resume immediately—you might want to write the three last words in red to make it easier to return to your place.

If you're working with numbered items, use a phonetics cue such as "step 4—oar—a silver oar dipping into an aromatic lake of steaming, spiced tea." Hold that picture a few seconds. Now, when you return to the project, you'll see the picture and number and, perhaps, even smell the tea. This use of several senses should help you pick up right where you left off with no loss of memory.

Taking a mental picture is even faster than note-taking— and you can't always ask an interruptor to hold off during note-writing.

> I work at Gates Rubber Company and have trouble remembering numbers of any kind—telephone extensions, serial numbers, etc. When product numbers must take on a budget number, I'm really confused.

You'll need both left- and right-brain strategies here. Start with the key extensions you want to memorize and associate each to the person or department involved. Mary Hacking, new marketing assistant, on extension 9632. See her hacking and chopping the 96 down to 32. Sometimes you can be more abstract: Tony Mulkin on 3008. "Hmmm . . . he looks about 30 . . . not 08!"

If you have forty extensions to remember, set a goal of three for each day, and in a few weeks you'll have them all.

For product numbers, try to discern a pattern. Do all the belts begin with "40"? Once you distinguish such categories, you can connect the number with the class of product. The next step is to pair that product number to its corresponding budget number. Can the latter be categorized? For example, can you connect all the belts to the "40" product number to budget numbers that begin with "Z's"? If you cannot detect such a corresponding scheme, use the phonetic system to convert the numbers into words and then link them with the product. But before you take much time to devise your own plan, check with the personnel department to discover who set up the numbering system. Usually a way for correlating such numbers is already built into the system.

> My boss is a real rambler. Often, when he tells me
> to do something and goes on to many other topics,
> I forget my assignment.

When he starts winding down each time, you might review what's been said and what he expects with: "So you want me to . . ." But if time is short and a review could commence the entire conversation again, merely replay your cinematics view of the scene until you come to the beginning.

Another tactic is simply to focus on the first matter he tells you each time, then connect it to the spot where he stood, a picture on the wall or a paperweight he was handling. When he leaves, you'll have one concrete item to help you return to his beginning statement.

> I am the new district fire chief and, by the end of
> this week, I want to be able to know the addresses
> and numbers of all twenty-seven fire stations.

With the help of his wife, this very busy student devised left- and right-brain strategies while driving to and from work and memorized them all in one week. Here are some of the memory aides they created:

Station 4, 22nd and Lawrence Station 10, 32nd and Lawrence	(they paired these two by noting that 22nd was ten blocks from 32nd)
Station 8, 1616 Park Avenue	(the address has twice the station number—two times)
Station 13, 3683 South Yosemite	(they noted the ages of three males in their family, each with a three in it—one named Sam, with the nickname Yosemite Sam)
Station 14, 1436 Oneida Street Station 16, 1601 South Ogden Street	(both station numbers and street numbers have the same number of digits and both proper place names begin with O)
Station 18, 22nd and Colorado Boulevard	(they said this like a quarterback chant—18-22-hike—as they visualized the game in the middle of Colorado Boulevard)

I'm a carpenter in Aspen and often I am assigned difficult jobs—making square beams fit into a circular hole or "stretching" supports to comply with uneven walls. Recently I was given the task of fitting a three-inch circular solar valance into a forty-five-degree angled window frame. I was chosen because the client had seen other work I had done. But I can't remember just how I did the other jobs or how to start these complicated projects.

First try visualizing how you want the end product to look. Once you have a clear picture in your mind, try different approaches. Write down the steps, and if it seems that the sequence will work, use it. Otherwise, try it on a model. Here you'll be working from the right first and then the left—frame the big picture to the steps required to accomplish it.

> I must read a lot of management books for my work. After I read them, I don't remember the key points.

Try the peg or the link systems. For example, with the new book *Megatrends* there are ten key subjects. List these and then use your peg words to help you form vivid images. For example:

Pegs	Chapter
one-gun	Industrial Society to Information Society

See a gun shooting a huge manufacturing plant and all sorts of paper, books, tapes and forms exploding out of the demolished building.

two-shoe	Mass Market Technology to High Tech/High Touch

See a shoe factory producing billions of shoes—all with the same appearance. They all are running to the airline terminal, where an agent puts on a pair and smiles at you (high touch) while he punches out on the computer (high tech) where they will be shipped. Try the rest of the chapters with your own images.

GETTING PERSONAL

This chapter started with the easiest, most natural and ancient memory techniques and concluded with the newest, most complex methods. The left- and right-brain implications of each were explained. Now it's up to you to practice them. Few things are learned on the first try. Repetition is necessary, but it alone is not sufficient. You'll need your goal-oriented left brain to get you started and keep you on task, and you'll also want your right brain to help you enjoy making those fantasies and images.

Decide which methods work best for you and resolve to use them daily. Compare them to the memory goal you selected at the beginning of the chapter and ponder both for a while. Are your mnemonic methods appropriate for the level you're working on? Are you ready to raise your sights and go to a higher level? (See MEMORY GOAL SETTER; fill it out and get started.)

Purge "I forgot" and "I've got a terrible memory" from your speech. Instead, resolve to do the best you can at each opportunity and to compliment yourself for your improvements. Very soon, the rewards of a good memory will provide further reinforcement.

Scattered throughout American executive suites are men and women whose high-powered memories are held in awe by their colleagues. These executives have found a good memory to be essential to their work. To quote two:

According to *Time* magazine, Jeanne Kirkpatrick, U.S. ambassador to the United Nations, after committing to memory the names of a thirty-man committee at their first meeting, said, "I believe my memory both pleased and impressed these very influential committee members."

Steve Wickliff, chairman of Wickliff Corporation, a Midwest construction company, said, "People are flattered if you remember them . . . and clients have more confidence in you if your memory is sharp. They know you've done your homework."

No other area of mind improvement can produce the immediate and dramatic results of a better memory. Extraordinary amounts of new material come to light in each profession every year. A strategy for storing and retrieving this information is essential to your progress on the job. By adapting mnemonic systems to your needs, you can enjoy the comfort of an effective memory and make significant gains in your career.

MEMORY GOAL SETTER

At which of these memory levels mentioned earlier in this chapter are you currently operating?

___1. Subsistence (Where's my car? Where am I going?)
___2. Maintenance (What did my boss ask me to do today?)
___3. Names and faces (for the upwardly mobile)
___4. More names and faces—plus (add their vital statistics)
___5. Recalling information (grasping main ideas)
___6. Names, quotations, numbers, codes, specifications
___7. All of the above—plus (the human-relations aspects)

Which of the books mnemonic devices are you currently comfortable with?

___Patterns   ___Acrostics
___Association   ___ASOE
___Loci   ___Link
___Mediators   ___Peg
___Chunking   ___Phonetic
___Acronyms

Will you commit yourself to working toward a higher memory level? _____Which one? _____To be accomplished by what date? _____

Will you commit yourself to developing other mnemonic skills? _____Which ones? _____
By what date? _____

_____
Signature   Date

13

MANAGEMENT PROBLEMS: YOURS, MINE AND OURS

A six year-old, the youngest of three boys, said to his mother: "Mom, I wish you'd have another baby so I'd have someone to boss around!"

WHAT IS YOUR MENTAL IMAGE OF A MANAGER? MOST likely you envision a logical, articulate male sitting behind a neat mahogany desk, a left-brain person doing left-brain work. This stereotype comes to mind because traditionally management has been biased toward the left. This chapter on managing will tilt slightly to the right.

Managing is the art of effecting desired goals through planning, organizing, directing (which includes communicating), motivating and controlling. (See FIVE FUNCTIONS OF MANAGEMENT.)

Planning involves deciding what goals are sought and then specifying the steps needed to reach them. Whether

---

FIVE FUNCTIONS OF MANAGEMENT

After years of observation of the management of such diverse organizations as the Catholic Church and the military, universal management functions were defnined by Henri Fayol. He presented his view in 1900, but it was not until 1949 that his functions became part of the mainstream of American management theory. Fayol identified five functions: *planning*, *organizing*, *communicating*, *actuating* (motivating) and *controlling*. Since that time, management theorists have used different words for the functions but have agreed on the essential characteristics.

Peter Drucker, George Odiorne and hundreds of other management specialists emphasize that effective management includes these characteristics. They insist a good manager needs both logical analysis, which stresses goals and effectiveness, and sensitive, intuitive and flexible interaction with organized members.

The consensus from the voluminous material on management is that in order to manage well one must use both head and heart.[39]

---

you are opening a new sales territory or getting your favorite politican elected, these two aspects of planning are essential. Although both may appear to be dependent on rational thinking, this chapter will suggest some right-brain aids to planning.

Organizing is a process that allows the maximum utilization of such resources as people (employees, friends, customers), materials, money and time given restrictions and opportunities toward accomplishing goals. For example, raising funds for your nonprofit organization may involve efficiently organizing:

- money (augment the endowment by organizing an auction)
- time (enlist volunteer assistants to counteract tight deadlines)
- restrictions (seek approval of board of directors)

- opportunities (hold an auction at which celebrity patrons contribute)

Left dominants tend to organize by discovering the first step and proceeding sequentially. BPI 9 types, on the other hand, like to picture the final goal first and then look for ways to get there. Gifted managers integrate the two approaches.

Directing, when performed ideally, helps others clearly understand what needs to be done and how to do it. Although it is easy to see the difference between success and failure, knowing what elements contribute to these results is not so simple. However, it is apparent that good direction involves the ability to define tasks and communicate the vital steps toward their accomplishment. Successful directing also relies upon feedback. Defining tasks and methods are left-brain aspects, while communicating in a meaningful way heavily depends upon right-brain sensory talents.

Motivating requires providing incentives for others to act. Once the employee has the necessary information and tools to accomplish the task, the motivating skills of the manager set the performance in motion by instilling confidence or fear through rewards or punishment. This part of management demands a real feel for the needs and emotions of others and the ability to act and react intuitively.

EVERYONE WANTS TO MANAGE

At one time or another, almost everyone is a manager. Parents manage. So do spouses, teachers and employers. All the way up the ladder, somebody usually bosses somebody else, or at least somebody wants to boss them.

We firmly believe that everyone wants to be a good manager. We just need a fresh way of looking at the functions of management, setting goals, reducing conflict, establishing priorities, increasing productivity and coping with crisis. Becoming a good manager isn't always easy. But it can be fun.

WHOLE-BRAIN THINKING

The ability to motivate is highly dependent on the right-brain side.

Controlling consists of comparing outcomes to the original standards and objectives and taking corrective action when failures occur. This evaluation process needs the left brain's analytical, rational talents, but the right brain's hunches and flashes of insight can provide invaluable assistance.

The manager's personality and training affect the way the five functions are performed, resulting in a management style. From the many theories and criteria for determining this style, four categories seem to evolve. Following are some statements that would typically represent each style of management. As you read through them, put a check by each statement with which you agree.

_____ 1. Company loyalty and seniority are two of the most important elements to be considered in a reward system.

_____ 2. Rules are made to be followed.

_____ 3. I enjoy working hard.

_____ 4. Keeping close tabs on subordinates is a must in effective managing.

_____ 5. I like to give or get clear-cut, specific assignments.

_____ 6. I tend to be a perfectionist and am upset when things go against the plan.

_____ 7. I often criticize my own work.

_____ 8. I like formal channels, procedures, documentation and written communication.

_____ 9. I believe that fear is a strong motivator.

_____ 10. There is a right and a wrong way to do things and there is also a best way.

_____ 11. A persuasive leader is an effective leader.

_____ 12. Discussing the plans of a project is the most effective way of motivating involvement.

_____ 13. New employees should be told about company procedures, policies, goals, salary levels and career opportunities.

_____ 14. Once an employee is indoctrinated, frequent verbal checks and monthly evaluation sessions will ensure that a good job is done.

_____ 15. I like to see plans completed but am willing to renegotiate details along the way.

_____ 16. I like to delegate most of the details of a job, but I want periodic reports on their accomplishment.

_____ 17. People usually follow my directions well.

_____ 18. Most employees are conscientious if they really understand what needs to be done.

_____ 19. Compliments, recognition and good pay are the best motivators.

_____ 20. I admire original thinking if it has practical applications.

_____ 21. Jobs should be defined and then periodically redefined.

_____ 22. When work is evaluated, the object should be to discover what is successful, not who is to blame.

_____ 23. Even if all the facts point toward one decision, strong hunches against that decision should be taken seriously.

_____ 24. Group decisions are often the best because all people have something valuable to contribute.

_____ 25. It is important to me to do meaningful work as well as to make a good deal of money.

_____ 26. We are all born with the ability to solve problems and be creative.

_____ 27. Flexible work arrangements improve morale and productivity.

_____ 28. It is more important to help the new employee adapt to the relationships and the overview of the job; the details of the job will come with time.

_____ 29. Jobs can be exciting and fun.

_____ 30. Through mutual trust the needs of individuals and the demands of organizations can be integrated.

_____ 31. Work seems to flow better when each person defines his or her job in his or her unique way.

_____ 32. Staying out of the way, offering no criticism or rules will inspire employees' self-confidence and eventually motivation.

_____ 33. Hiring the best people I can find and then letting them run their own show is a successful approach.

_____ 34. The success or failure of employees' efforts is the most effective form of evaluation.

_____ 35. Loose, flexible time allows people to be free and inspires creative and innovative performance.

_____ 36. I frequently operate by the seat of my pants rather than by relying on standard operating procedures.

_____ 37. When things are going poorly, it's best to chuck it all for the day and play golf, have a drink or go to a movie.

_____ 38. When there's resistance to a project or I've had several false starts, it's best to wait until the timing is better.

_____ 39. I like to have freewheeling brainstorming sessions with my staff to form future plans.

_____ 40. Committee meetings, hierarchies and complex procedures irritate me and stifle the smooth operation of an organization.

These forty statements are grouped in tens according to the four styles of management. Sentences 1 to 10 are characteristic of analyzer-controller managers; 11 to 20 are expresser-communicators; 21 to 30 are developer-feelers; and 31 to 40 are permitter-observers.

In which group did you check the most statements? The category you chose is, of course, influenced by your brain dominance and represents both your personal approach to work and your views on how an organization best functions. (See LEADERSHIP STYLES.)

To clarify, ponder these BPI ratings of the four types,

with a recent U.S. President and a business celebrity cited in each category:

BPI 1	BPI 5		BPI 9
Analyzer-Controller	Expresser-Communicator	Developer-Feeler	Permitter-Observer
Lyndon Johnson— hard-driving, organized, articulate, rational	Ronald Reagan— outgoing, delegates, dramatic speaker, humorous	Jimmy Carter— visionary, communicates feelings, trusting, serious, sensitive	Gerald Ford— athletic, open to criticism and suggestions, casual
Henry Ford— founder of Ford Motor Company	Lee Iacocca— chairman of Chrysler Corporation	Conrad Hilton— founder of the Hilton Hotel chain	Buckminster Fuller— inventor of the geodesic dome, futurist

Analyzers function most comfortably when they can structure, schedule and control. Like a time-oriented BPI 1, they have well-defined, sequential plans and procedures for all aspects of life.

The expresser is to the left side of the BPI midpoint. This type of manager relies on some of the same management concepts as the analyzer but tends to be more expressive and concerned with two-way communication.

Developers are to the right side of the BPI. Although planning and communicating still are important to this kind of manager, they are accomplished in a less structured way, with emphasis on feelings and big-picture planning. Mentoring or coaching are favorite parts of a developer's job because he or she takes pleasure from the growth and development of others.

Finally, the typical permitter would score on the extreme right side (9) of the BPI scale, representing the type who operates on intuition and chance. This manager allows a great deal of freedom to employees and to self. Deadlines are changeable, terms negotiable. Sometimes permitters are reactive and scattered.

There are no rights or wrongs in these four management styles nor in how closely your categories correlate to your BPI. What is important is that you understand how your BPI influences the way you manage your work, others and most likely your entire life. The purpose here is not to judge or even evaluate your style but to understand the dynamics to help you solve your managerial problems.

Usually management is thought to be of interest only at the top of organizational hierarchies. However, this book takes a much broader outlook and will address management from these three perspectives: everyone is or could be a manager, problems of managers and problems with management.

LEADERSHIP STYLES

Corporate heads of personnel and management development functions have found direct correlations between leadership styles and brain preference. C. Vincent Vappi of Boston's Vappi Construction Co. states, "Autocratic, directive— Theory X-style—managers invariably have a left-brain bias." "Extreme rights practice laissez-faire or the 'country club' style of management—they tend to be 1.9's on Blake and Mouton's managerial grid," states Gordon Jones of Dow Corning Corporation.

After testing more than three hundred managers, I've discovered that the developmental, flexible and participative manager uses a whole-brain approach, shifting left and focusing on the task when needed—as when there are time pressures—and shifting right when an employee needs coaching or counseling or when engaging in a brainstorming session. No matter what his natural preference, the most effective leader is able to shift to the appropriate mode of the task at hand.

—Jacquelyn Wonder

*"Even a small operation like yours can make
effective use of our management techniques."*

EVERYONE IS OR COULD BE A MANAGER

To some degree, we are all managers of our own time,
resources, mind, actions and possessions. Of course, there
are laws, institutions, situations and individuals who mit-
igate this power to manage, but most limitations on our
abilities and accomplishments are self-imposed. If we can
understand the situation clearly and motivate ourselves to
act, we can manage our lives and jobs effectively.

Following are some of the management problems most
frequently presented in our corporate seminars and individual counseling sessions:

WHOLE-BRAIN THINKING

I am Lee, the director of training. I need guidance on how to begin planning next year's training program. My job is new—not just for me, but also for the organization. When I accepted it, I didn't expect to have to do this much advance planning, nor did I anticipate having to work with as large a committee as the VP has assigned to me. I'm very talented and have been planning and implementing programs for some time. I didn't expect to deal with so many people and so much organization. In addition, I have many other commitments in phasing out of my previous position in the company. I'm irritated, and I'm in a fog as to how to get started.

Your problem is twofold, and it is experienced in all walks of life. The first component is feeling overwhelmed, and the second is suffering anxieties about diverging from a comfortable, known role.

You sound like a dominant right threatened by what appears to be a monumental left-brain task. First, put the threat into perspective. After all, you are talented and are still highly regarded by your previous employer. An examination of your feelings of irritation and of being in a fog might provide the first step toward a solution. Perhaps your left brain is overloaded and you are trying to access the right side (à la a suspender). You may be on the verge of a big breakthrough. Frequently this state precedes a vision of a full-blown, unique solution. So relax and drift farther into that creative nexus.

Another mind mover that might help is cinematics. Review your successes on the previous job by reconstructing a particularly satisfying scene. Then visualize the new job, focusing only on its most important functions. Limit the number of people and tasks, and they will seem less threatening. Focus on the essentials.

As for your present job, this is the time to call on your left brain. When emotions start to blur your view of a problem, shifting to a left approach can release some of the tension of the situation and provide a sensible solution. So make a list of the promises you actually made when you changed positions—not what you'd like to do now, but only what you promised then. From those, extract the ones directly related to your former position. Carry out only those, then write a memo to your previous supervisor reporting the completion of those tasks and wishing your replacement the best of luck. Do not offer further assistance. You have fulfilled your obligations and have new ones to assume. Give yourself permission to enjoy your new tasks.

> I am in charge of new accounts at Osborne Advertising Agency. I need to come up with creative, inspiring and profitable programs. I have a problem completing these programs because I am afraid I will make a mess of them or that if one does get accepted there will be too much additional work for me. How can I overcome this obstacle to motivating myself?

You may be closer to the solution than you think. You've already figured out that your procrastination might have something to do with fear of failure and of the workload that might come from success.

First, answer the left brain "What if's."

"What if I make a mess of it?" "At least I produced, and with a little revision, it could be a dynamite plan." After all, the company's entire future does not rest on this one project. Management rarely assigns such vital problems to newcomers. If the task is, in fact, that important, you must be a highly talented individual to warrant such confidence.

Second, "What if the plan is accepted and it involves more time than I have?" Part of your proposal could include an escape clause that stipulates the amount of work hours required for its effective functioning. Analyze each step of the plan and note the type of assistance you will need to implement it.

WHOLE-BRAIN THINKING

Get started *now*. Just begin; the perfect moment may never come.

Self-motivation is a recurring concern for all of us. Consider applying mind movers in the following ways:

1. Bolster the left brain with reading: Read intellectually challenging books on topics you know little about (archaeology, computers, Japanese history). Biographies of great achievers will stimulate whole-brain thinking as you read about complex achievements and inspiring deeds (Eleanor Roosevelt, Booker T. Washington, Albert Einstein, Madame Curie, Benjamin Franklin).

2. Practice mind mover 2, your cinematic way of viewing the future. Picture your short- and long-term goals. See yourself accomplishing them. Commit these visions to paper and keep the list where you can see it every day. Start acting as if the goals have already been accomplished. Maintain your excitement and enthusiasm for the whole effort by reviewing your imagery occasionally, adding new details to get your vibes up.

3. Next, work at performing every concrete act possible toward achieving the desired goal. For example, if you want to attend a business seminar, even though you do not yet have your company's agreement for financing it or allowing you the time off, write for the registration details, make inquiries about the program, bone up on the topic and plan your private life as though you were going. Once the possibles are in order, you'll be surprised how easily the impossibles follow.

4. Avoid building mental obstacles. When negative thoughts occur, cancel them with positive ones. Make a habit of anticipating good results. What you deeply expect, you tend to get.

5. View impediments as challenges. Newly acquired abilities provide you with an exciting chance to overcome obstacles. Motivation often comes from the challenge of difficult circumstances. Adversity causes some men to break, others to break records.

PROBLEMS OF MANAGERS

Managers of all kinds (right- and left-brain, titled and untitled) deal regularly with problems related to the five functions of managers. (See AMERICA'S BEST-RUN COMPANIES.) The following two cases exemplify the interwining of planning, organizing, directing, motivating and controlling.

> I am a manager at Cobe Labs. We have been growing rapidly. I'm expected to do extraordinary things in my division, yet my staff and workers are simply ordinary people. How do I get ordinary people to do extraordinary things?

Perhaps these folks are not as ordinary as they seem, and perhaps the tasks are not so extraordinary. Try forming a right-brain view of your staff. Discover a little about their after-work interests and activities. You may find that the ordinary administrative secretary has a degree in writing and that your line foreman is a tournament chess player. Both these extracurricular skills could be utilized on the job. If you use an inside out to see your ordinary employees in other roles, an application to the work scene may well appear.

Another right-brain assist would be to decide what sort of climate is needed in your department to cope with the new challenges. Your company's positive growth pattern is a good aspect to dwell on when you visualize the overall picture. Now look at the details: busy employees, pleasant phone calls, the administrative secretary composing the description of your latest proposal... and the foreman designing a new, more efficient work schedule.

Then act on some of these visions. Some companies become so enamored of their managerial systems and bureaucracies that they forget how to get things done. Dynamic companies are successful because they are willing to try new things. They form task forces to act, not committees

---

WHOLE-BRAIN THINKING

to study. They have an extraordinary bias toward action.

Simplify procedures wherever possible, and be open to change. Procter & Gamble insists on one-page memos that cut paperwork and eliminate complex analyses. Memos don't get so scientific that everything must be studied. Cheap experiments are sometimes better than expensive forecasts. P&G and other successful companies use left-brain analysis, but they have the balance right. They cut loose from systems that run strictly on paperwork, and they are not worried about deviant behavior.

In view of Cobe's growth, you obviously have a desirable product and, most likely, an effective marketing program. To continue in this positive direction, remember the customer and the general public. This message needs to be communicated to all employees. You want the whole tenor of the company to be positive in dealing with the public. How the telephone operator responds to incoming calls is just as important as how the head of marketing closes the big sale. The key is that this totally positive outlook is ultimately related to individual self-image. As the manager, you can perform wonders with self-concepts by discovering employees' hidden talents and calling attention to them. You might want to exaggerate these qualities in your mind's eye so that you can use and describe them to others enthusiastically. Remember, they all know something special. Companies don't progress in a vacuum.

Share with your employees the good news about the company's growth and your desire to accomplish extraordinary things. Ask for their input, and let them share in this air of excitement.

Discovering and polishing the hidden talents of your employees not only helps your company but also makes you feel better about your management. The ideal outcome is an integration of individual and organizational needs, talents and goals.

Once you have this new view of them (and they of you) and together you've targeted the areas requiring improvement, you can wait for the ideas to grow. Soon you will be organizing their contributions and integrating them into the existing systems. Their creativity will be flowing, right along with yours.

Recently I've been made the manager of the bottling plant at Coors. I'm considering reorganizing my plant but am not sure just how to go about it. I've read about flat and tall organizational structures as well as others. I am also aware of a number of styles of management. Can you give me some pointers that could help me in reorganizing?

WHOLE-BRAIN THINKING

First, consider how well your BPI and management style relate to the flat and tall organizational structures. The flat system describes an organizational pattern in which most management functions are performed by a number of parallel divisions. It operates through managers of equal power and responsibility whose divisional activities are coordinated by one director. This system seems to suit the developer well because there is a great deal of autonomy within each division as well as emphasis on cooperation and communication.

The tall organization, on the other hand, relies on decisions starting at the top. Concrete procedures and schedules are necessary for the effective functioning of this system. If your management style is in the midrange or to the right-brain side of the BPI scale, you probably will prefer the flat organization. However, your preference is not the sole factor to be considered. The purpose of the organization also has a direct bearing on your selection.

To facilitate your choice, you should visualize your plant as it is now. Mentally go through all the steps required to make the product. Who reports to whom? Are reporting links side by side or top to bottom? Does this work well? Now try an inside out, viewing these processes as they would be performed in an opposite manner. If the current system is flat, future-view a tall one, or vice versa. You may find that the present system is fine—or eureka! The opposite approach may look great. How does the more workable plan feel to you? Comfortable? If not, what can you alter to help you be more at ease with the system?

Once you have visualized a system that seems to fit your organization's purpose and your management style, call on your left brain to extract concrete ideas. Pull out the details of your flat or your tall concept, or something in between. Look for ways to simplify and combine. As you approach your reorganization, consider how well each system will work within the structure and evaluate whether you have balanced technical and personnel efficiency.

At this point, you will most likely zigzag between scientific plotting of systems and imaginative, intuitive views of your plan.

You'll know you're finished when you have a coherent, practical plan you feel good about presenting to *your* manager.

PROBLEMS WITH MANAGERS

"Why can't a woman be more like a man?" is the plantive song of Professor Higgins in *My Fair Lady*. A similar complaint is often expressed by employees about their bosses: "Why can't he (or she) be more like me?" We tend to view our employers through our own conception of how we perform our jobs or how we feel we would perform as boss.

So assessments of managers are twofold: (1) how well the boss performs and (2) how well this performance coincides with the employee's expectations. There is a continual confrontation between boss and subordinate, parent and child, teacher and student. Mind movers can be especially helpful in remedying problems with managers.

> I am the manager's secretary and have a problem with my boss and with the new statistical typist in the office. Whenever Mr. Hill gives her work to do, she does it promptly and accurately and is all smiles when she brings the finished job to him. Often Mr. Hill gives the work to me, sometimes saying, "Get Carla on this right away." At other times, he assumes that I will automatically pass on the work. On several occasions, when I was forced to stay overtime, he remarked to me, "Why didn't you let Carla do that?" But whenever I ask Carla to do something, Carla finds an excuse to defer it. Or, if she does the work, it is sloppy and inaccurate. She invariably has a "special job" for Mr. Hill waiting in the typewriter. Often the work that I assign to Carla has priority over routine tasks

that Mr. Hill had given Carla to do at her leisure. But Carla is insistent about completing Mr. Hill's work first, putting aside with a smug smile the rush jobs I give her. When I discussed this situation with Mr. Hill, he was surprised. He said, "I've always found Carla willing and efficient on any work she's done for me." What do I say or do now?

To help clarify the situation, you might start by getting the three of you together to verify duties, reporting lines and expectations. It appears that all three of you have different images of Carla's job, your job and Mr. Hill's job.

Using your right brain, imagine Carla and Mr. Hill working. What were they doing? How were they doing it? What did they look like? As you visualize each job, draw it on a piece of paper or a blackboard and put two or three adjectives by it. For example:

Carla's job as Carla sees it:

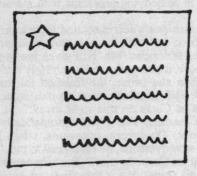

Clear
Big-Important

Carla's job as Mr. Hill sees it:

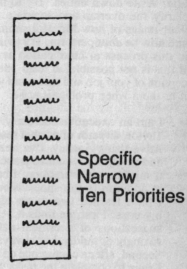

**Specific
Narrow
Ten Priorities**

Carla's job as you see it:

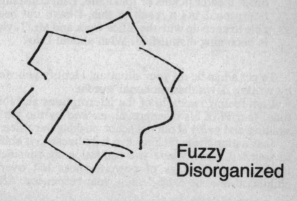

**Fuzzy
Disorganized**

Now with your left brain, review each person's job description. Write down duties. Try to fill in unclear areas. Also clarify the overlap and separate. Be sure to synchronize your image of how Mr. Hill *should* perform as a manager and how he *does* perform. Try to involve Mr. Hill and Carla in this process of clarification at any step along the way. If this is not possible, at least you will have a clearer perception of your job and theirs and you will be able to express it to them when problems arise.

> I am an executive secretary working for Richard Taylor, director of market research at the Osborne Advertising Agency. I've been here three months and would like to make a success of this job, as it is my first big promotion. I have other work to do in addition to the supervision of two secretaries. I have learned two things about Richard Taylor, my boss. First, he finds it very difficult to accept suggestions of a critical nature, reacting either strongly or mildly, but always reacting negatively. Second, after a conference on the day's work, when I start to complete the tasks we have agreed upon, Mr. Taylor interrupts me with a stream of personal requests. Whether it is to get coffee for his guests, order theater tickets or find a file, I am constantly interrupted. As a result of this, I have not been able to keep up with the office work and Mr. Taylor is becoming dissatisfied. What should I do?

To get a handle on your situation, identify your feelings by writing down the emotional words:

I am feeling *resentful* of the interruptions and this attitude, *fearful* of his disapproval, *excited* by the job's possibilities and *guilty* about not accomplishing the office work.

Just listing these feelings can help because it shifts you to your left brain, where you can rationally consider their implications. Feelings of powerlessness left over from childhood may be exaggerating your responses. After all,

DAMN IT! JUST GIVE IT TO ME STRAIGHT— WHAT DID JENKINS SAY ABOUT ME?

Since criticism seems to trigger Mr. Taylor's right brain, it will be useful to get him to move to the left also. Write out the goals you believe need to be met in the next month, listing a time schedule and priorities. Make a copy for each of you and set up an appointment to go over these with him. At this meeting, clarify what is really important. You may find that some of his interruptions are vital to his being able to operate smoothly. At this point you can explain what happens physiologically when you are interrupted and must switch jobs. (See REFOCUS.) Be clear about the time it takes to concentrate fully again. Offering him facts about what happens and how you feel will be less aggravating than direct criticism.

Richard Taylor does not have unlimited power over you, and he has a vested interest in improving the situation also.

You two may agree on a signal (red file placed on the desk) when you are deep in a project as an impersonal reminder not to interrupt unless it is truly urgent.

Now that you have helped Mr. Taylor understand the emotional and pragmatic effects of his behavior with this whole-brain approach, perhaps you can direct him to the long-range matter that affects the situation: your career and how it ties in with his.

He may end up being your mentor if the process can be comfortable and helpful in fulfilling his own goals. As you grow, he grows.

REFOCUS

Extensive research has been done by the U.S. government's Office of Personnel Management and the National Institute of Health on the time required to refocus after an interruption. Researchers found that it took from five to twenty minutes for a person to reach a level of concentration where outside distractions and events were not noticed. After the interruption of a phone call, a question, a request, etc., it again took an additional five to twenty minutes. Right dominants being extremely sensitive to the world around them took longer to refocus than left dominants.[42]

Although there are many more management problems that could be addressed in this chapter, these touch most of the areas that typically arise in the workday. You can use these mind movers as guides to solving your own managerial problems, be they personal or professional. Once you have tried the techniques suggested here, experiment with others. Adapt and innovate. Have faith in your own abilities. After all, you have managed for many years. You have the power within to manage yourself, a job and others wisely and effectively.

14

STRESS AND YOUR WORKWORLD

Stress is the body's nonspecific response to any demand placed on it, whether pleasant or unpleasant.

—Hans Selye

Behold the turtle. He makes progress only when he sticks his neck out.

—James Bryant Conant

SITTING IN A DENTIST'S CHAIR IS STRESSFUL, BUT SO is exchanging a passionate kiss with a lover. During the latter, your pulse races, your breathing quickens, your heart rate soars. Who would forgo such a pleasant pastime simply because of the stress provoked?

Indeed, there are several kinds of stress: pleasant and unpleasant, helpful and damaging, productive and wasteful. Every time you eat, your body undergoes mild stress. Every time you drive on a new road or meet a stranger, you undergo minor to severe stress (depending upon how you handle the situation). In fact, stress is essential to achieving healthy adulthood; it helps you learn and grow.

The aim in this chapter is not to tell you how to avoid stress (that would be impossible), but to help you find the draining stress in your work and life and then minimize it. Then you can use stress rather than be a victim of it.

Generally, stress, an engineering term, is the result of putting an object under pressure. For instance, a steel beam can handle only a certain amount of weight or stress. Similarly, when you are in a new situation, you can handle only a limited degree of mental pressure. Moreover, the same amount of stress can provide a challenge or titillating excitement to one person, but an overwhelming burden to another. In any case, how you cope with stress determines, to a great extent, how effectively you can handle your work.

HYPER HORSES AND TURTLE LOVES

Are you the racehorse type, happy only with a vigorous, fast-paced life-style? Do you feel comfortable in an atmosphere in which phones are ringing, people are coming and going, and you are in a position of importance? Or are you a turtle, who requires a generally tranquil environment? Lying on a beach day after day would be a fate worse than death to a racehorse, yet to a turtle, it would be the ultimate pleasure.

Understanding your style is the first step toward using stress positively. There is no clear correlation between your BPI and your work-style preference because persons at all points on the scale react to stress in individual ways. A better way to determine your stress-style is to note carefully the times when you feel comfortable and peaceful and when you don't. In addition, the cases described in the second half of this chapter will describe stress with which you might identify.

There is a direct relationship between negative stress and the imbalances that exist in your job. You can make concrete, constructive alterations in your work that will

© 1982 United Features Syndicate, Inc.

remove most of these. Or, if you have the authority, you can restructure the activities of others in your workplace to produce a well-balanced, productive unit.

Before you can implement either of these solutions, however, you must review that much-reviled and much-revised job description. What tasks do you perform each day, week and year on the job? On the following pages you will find two lists that describe many kinds of work. Underline those activities that describe any part of the work you do.

As you completed this exercise, both sides of your brain probably were examining its implications. You've got it! List 1 lists left-brain chores; list 2, right-brain ones.

The functions listed in list 1 are best performed by the left brain and primarily by left-dominant persons. They include quantifying, qualifying and activating.

The activities in list 2 are more typical of sensory, spatial, intuitive tasks performed by the right brain and epitomized in the behavior of the right-dominant type.

WHOLE-BRAIN THINKING

List 3 includes tasks that must utilize both sides of the brain. Take, for instance, forecasting and designing. You can possess the intuition of a great psychic, but without the ability to analyze situations and statistics, you will fail to put your extra information to practical use.

With regard to selling and meditating: You can be articulate and literate but never be able to persuade another to your way of thinking if you have no feel for attitudes and needs.

With regard to teaching and researching: You can commit librariesful of books to memory but have no understanding without hands-on experience and emotional interaction.

LIST 1

accounting
administering
advocating
allocating
analyzing
appraising
assessing
assigning
bookkeeping
budgeting
buying
calculating
clarifying
classifying
collecting money
comparing
compiling
computing
contracting
controlling
copying
critiquing
debating
deciding
defining
detailing
detecting

directing
discussing
dissecting
editing
enforcing
evaluating
examining
expediting
explaining
expressing
filing
graphing
guiding
identifying
implementing
initiating
judging
leading
lecturing
managing
memorizing
modifying
motivating
ordering
organizing
persevering
planning

policymaking
preaching
prioritizing
purchasing
reading
reasoning
recommending
reconciling accounts
recording
recruiting
reducing
reporting
reproducing
reviewing
scheduling
screening
self-motivating
speaking
summarizing
supervising
systematizing
tabulating
talking
updating
validating

LIST 2

adapting
addressing
assembling
assisting
building
caring
catering
climbing
composing
counseling
counting
creating
dancing
decorating
delivering
demonstrating
discovering
drafting
drawing
enlisting

exercising
farming
feeding
fixing
gathering
humoring
innovating
installing
manipulating
mapping
negotiating
nurturing
observing
operating
painting
performing
preparing
processing
proposing
reacting

reflecting
relating
repairing
restoring
scanning
servicing
shaping
simplifying
singing
staging
styling
supporting
surveying
symbolizing
tending
translating
troubleshooting
typing
visualizing
wishing

LIST 3

acting
advertising
anticipating
arranging
balancing
bargaining
canvassing
changing
collaborating
conducting
consulting
contributing
cooking
cooperating
coordinating
curing
delegating
designing
developing
diagnosing

driving
educating
encouraging
experimenting
facilitating
finding
forecasting
fundraising
hearing
helping
hosting
influencing
inspiring
interpreting
inventing
joking
learning
listening
lobbying
mediating

perceiving
persuading
programming
promoting
proofreading
proposing
public speaking
publishing
remembering
researching
risking
selling
stimulating
studying
teaching
thinking
training
traveling
troubleshooting
writing

WHOLE-BRAIN THINKING

The next exercise is designed to help you acquire a graphic view of your job's characteristics.

In the following chart, put in the appropriate slots the words you've underlined; put those from list 2 on the right, from list 1 on the left and from list 3 in the middle.

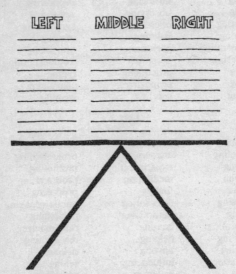

To determine the left- or right- brain character of the various jobs in your workworld, list the duties of each, with left-brain types on the left, and right on the right:

LEFT   MIDDLE   RIGHT

If one side far exceeds the other, then there is a clear indication that the job is out of balance. The balance must come either from after-hours activities or by changing the job itself.

How's your work balance? Does your workload look ready to tip one way or the other? If so, go back to the lists and see which tasks you could add or eliminate to help rectify imbalances; then write these in. (For examples of imbalanced jobs, see BALANCING JOBS.)

Go through your list again, visualizing your work, your workplace, your routine as it occurs daily, weekly, monthly, seasonally. Visualize your co-workers performing their tasks. Is there a chore you could do for them that would bring more balance to your job? To theirs? Are there things they could do for you that would eliminate some of the imbalance of your job? That would stabilize their jobs?

Add balancing tasks, wherever possible, to the underweighted side until your assignments come into equilibrium.

A PERFECT MATCH

A dominant left working a career weighted to the left might seem to have a fortuitous combination of talents and job requirements. The same assumption might be made for a dominant right in a job with a tilt to the right. However, "doing what comes naturally" for a long time can lead to negative stress just as surely as a mismatch can. The tedium of repetition and lack of challenge can lead to boredom and burnout, as can too many demands and too much adjusting. The exception is the highly lateralized person who thrives on total involvement in a task. But for most of us, change keeps the process of renewal going and prevents stagnation. Making compensations and pushing a little beyond your comfort level, in most cases, keeps you vital. (See AMOEBAS.)

As you restructure your job, your fellow workers will be affected. If it is possible to balance each job within the system, the whole organization will operate more efficiently and creatively.

BALANCING JOBS
ACCOUNTANT

Left	Right
1. computing	1. devising new tactics for collections
2. organizing	
3. monthly, daily tasks	2. settling disputes between bookkeeper and stenographer
4. balance sheets	
5. tax planning	
6. sales analysis	
7. P&L statements	

COACH

Left	Right
1. evaluating strengths	1. developing personal relationships
2. compiling statistics	2. encouraging teamwork
3. planning strategies	3. motivating self-improvement
4. reviewing plays	
5. analyzing films	
6. writing to schools	
7. disciplining	

ARTIST

Left	Right
1. learning lines	1. visualizing and *being* one's own art
2. being on time	
3. getting contracts	2. connecting with people
	3. creating aura
	4. synchronizing verbal and nonverbal messages
	5. displaying uniqueness and independence
	6. flamboyant image
	7. disregarding time and money
	8. displaying emotions and senses

AMOEBAS

Stewart Emery describes two tanks of amoebas in a California research center. In one tank, the temperature, humidity, level of water and other conditions are constantly adjusted to provide the environment most conducive for proliferation of the amoeba. In another tank, these organisms are alternately subjected to extremes in heat and cold, fluid level, protein, etc.

To the researchers' amazement, the amoebas in the tank meant to induce rapid growth died faster than those subjected to extremes.

Emery theorizes that having things too perfect, too set, too *comfortable* actually causes us to decay and die, while being forced to adapt promotes growth.[43]

If you are the boss and can implement broad changes, then all jobs can be balanced, to the improved health and performance of all concerned. But if you are a cog in the machine or work in a rigid organization where new approaches are discouraged, you might need to use a less visible means of bringing balance to your work. Leave the job description as it is but find balancing ways to perform it.

Through cinematics, see yourself performing your tasks as you do them now. Then replay the film and watch for opportunities to alter it. You might try reversing everything with an inside out.

If you're accustomed to doing accounts receivable on Monday mornings and stewing all weekend about the prospect, shift the task to Friday afternoon. There are fewer interruptions then because some people have gone for the weekend. Plan to do the chore in a different part of the office, perhaps one with a view. Bring yourself a flower in a bud vase, pack a snack to reward yourself midway and play relaxing background music. Take your shoes off, loosen your belt and plunge. Schedule a few mini mind-vacations and other stress reducers. (See ON-THE-JOB STRESS REDUCERS.)

ON-THE-JOB STRESS REDUCERS

1. *Time-out-for eyes*. Turn your face to the wall or look out the window (whatever is less conspicuous). Close your eyes and roll your eyeballs upward. Take two deep breaths.
2. *Mini push-ups*. Put your arms at your side, hands pointed forward. Now bend your hands backward as far as possible and hold them rigid. Count to twenty (if you have time) and release. Put your hands in your lap for a few seconds and enjoy the feeling of release.
3. *Roll-arounds*. Roll your head in a circle several times and then reverse direction. Repeat for as long as you can comfortably, each time rolling more slowly and fully.
4. *Lean-tos*. Lean from side to side in your chair until your hands are touching the floor with each lean. If observed, you can always pretend you're picking something off the floor.
5. *A mini mind-vacation*. Close your eyes and visualize yourself in your favorite place—the mountains, bed, etc. Stay there until your body feels it's there too. If you have cold hands or feet, visualize yourself in a warm, friendly place and warm those extremities.
6. *Standing room only*. If you must stand for extended periods, shift from foot to foot, exaggerating the movements by bending your knees and ankles.

If you have a job with little structure, build in systematic components or perform it in a left-brain way. Many sales representatives working from their home find their freedom difficult to deal with. They have no office to report to, no hours to keep, no limits to lunch hours and, as a result, they often have no sales or income. The successful ones learn early that they must schedule, commit and report. They keep regular office hours, whether at home or on the road. They maintain records of all client calls and have a highly structured schedule of appointments and chores to accomplish each week. They set aside regular times to review accounts, learn new products and explore new prospects. Although selling itself requires left-brain verbal skills and right-brain intuition, the freedom of being your own boss requires left-brain discipline and structure.

ACCENTUATE THE OPPOSITE

If your job is totally one-sided and is impossible to restructure, you might bring variety to your life in another way. Choose evening and weekend activities that are in the opposite sphere. If you're an accountant, do something physical or artistic. If you're a highway construction worker, go to the theater or library. This doesn't mean that you must give up your favorite recreation—just be sure to add new and contrasting activities.

So far you've learned about broad changes that can balance your job, your workworld and your private life to correct unhealthy stress and strain. Although some people love everything left (organized and scheduled) or right (spontaneous and open-ended), the long-term effects of such one-sidedness is still negative. The left-brain perfectionist will lead a limited social life, and the right-brain slob will sink into a morass of self-gratification. In the following cases, you will learn about actual problems and their brain-balancing solutions.

> I've recently been made managing partner of a large national organization and am simply overloaded with work. I perform all the managing functions, have retained old accounts and get the usual personnel problems. I'd like to have someone else do part of my old work, but my subordinates seem to lack the experience and overall knowledge that these clients require. Also, my position enables me to get results faster. I'd like my office to serve as a model for others. I want to take care of existing clients, add new ones and run the office in a modern, humanistic way. Instead, I'm feeling stressed, burdened and panicky.

Well, you said it: You are experiencing stress, and it's from overload that occurs when stimulation or demand exceeds the capacity to process or comply with it.

There are four major contributors to overload: time pressure, excessive responsibility, lack of support and unrealistically high expectations. Any one or a combination can result in stress.

Time-pressure stress often stems from working against deadlines and can be alleviated through the left-brain skill of effective time management. This helps you set priorities and schedule tasks into the most efficient order possible.

Cramming too much into a short amount of time also leads to overload. When you schedule appointments back to back, there's no time for error or complications. Since you want to do everything, you set up unrealistic goals. Pad your schedule with extra time to cope with complications—and to catch your breath. Allow for driving time, exercise time and thinking time.

Excessive responsibility causes overload: serving on too many boards, taking on too many clients, accepting too many obligations.

One solution is to learn how to say "no." Assertiveness pays off when you start feeling better physically and emotionally. It also frees you to do a better job with the responsibilities you do accept.

The second solution is to delegate work. Someone not so burdened might do it better. Allowing a subordinate to develop skills saves you energy and helps that person grow.

A third solution for excessive responsibility is to break down an overwhelmingly long and complex project into small, feasible parts. Then treat each part as a separate task with its own deadline. Concluding more projects faster gives you energy. Be sure to note each finished task and reward yourself.

Lack of support from subordinates or superiors is a source of stress. Have you ever felt you're the only one who cares if a project is completed on time? If all efforts fail to achieve support, change your attitude to reduce this kind of stress.

Ask cold, hard left-brain questions: "Can my single energies complete the project?" "Do I care enough about the project to expend that much energy?" Your answer to both might be "no" more often than you would imagine.

Unrealistically high expectations lead you to set unobtainable goals and result in stress. Allow yourself to make mistakes. They are part of life. Once you accept that neither you nor your organization is infallible, the major cause for stress with disappear.

Although there is nothing wrong with striving for excellence, perfectionism has an extremely high price tag: ulcers, depression and a sterile existence. (If you are a perfectionist, you probably already know it, but to check out the more virulent strains, see WHAT'S YOUR PQ?) Then commit yourself to trying some of these strategies:

1. Visualize several successful persons. Did they get there without ever making mistakes? Did they ever fail? Of course.
2. Another technique is thought-stopping. Simply shout the word "Stop!" as soon as you are aware that anxiety and perfectionism are creeping in. Then try switching abruptly to a cinematics to imagine a relaxing scene.
3. Try to surround yourself with nonperfectionists so that you won't constantly have to compare yourself to those other overachievers.
4. Employ your left brain to make a list of the costs and benefits of each of your goals. You may find it's not cost-effective to be perfect in everything.
5. Closely evaluate the goals you set for yourself to be sure they are reasonable.
6. Don't base your self-esteem solely on your work. Although it is desirable to have pride in your work, too much ego investment causes hostility toward yourself and others, and eventually this results in stress.
7. Consider your expendability. What would happen if you took another job, retired or even died! Use a hearing 2 to talk with yourself, and listen to your answers.

WHAT'S YOUR PQ?*

1. Are you ashamed or reluctant to talk to others about mistakes you've made?
2. Does losing a game, any kind of game, make you angry? With the winner? With yourself?
3. Do you discount the validity of criticism others give to you?
4. Do you feel helpless when you don't accomplish all you have set out to do in a day?
5. Do you believe others will think less of you if you pronounce a word wrong or spill a drink on yourself, on the floor or on someone else?
6. Do you do crossword puzzles with a pen?
7. Does making an error saying something stupid keep you awake all night?
8. Do you jog or play tennis or backgammon for reasons other than personal enjoyment?
9. Are you always trying to win, always trying to beat someone even if it is only yourself?
10. Is the thought of being average frightening to you?

You know you're a perfectionist if you answer yes to more than three of these questions.

*perfectionist quotient

Perfectionists often try to be all things to all people. Of course you can sign letters, talk on the telephone and give instructions all at once, but the stress is tremendous. Often too, this overload causes confusion and leads to mistakes.

Luckily you are in a position to balance your job and thereby reduce stress for all your employees. This will ease the way to the high standards you have set for yourself and your office, and it will relieve the sense of burden and panic.

I feel more and more isolated in my new job as a research analyst. Though I am vitally interested in

my work, my interaction with others is minimal.
I spend most of my time in a library or research
office and end up feeling irritable and snappish.

You seem to be suffering from deprivational stress—an
internal bodily reaction to understimulation. Some American
soldiers imprisoned during the Korean War used complex
mental imagery to lessen the stress of solitary
confinement. You can use cinematics for the same purpose,
but obviously your options are much greater than theirs.
Start by balancing that left-brain job with some right-brain
elements: Make luncheon appointments several times a
week. Call someone each day about your project. Join a
professional group so you have some human connections
related to your work. Use mini mind-vacations and other
stress reducers to relieve the stress that is subtly growing
while you're at work.

Then, in your private life, talk to your spouse or best
friend about your job so that another personal element
carries over into your isolated, sterile workplace.

Finally, make certain you have after-work activities with
a variety of people.

A note of caution: The stress suffered as a result of
understimulation is as exhausting as that caused by over-
stimulation. You feel just as nerve-wracked and have the
same urge to get away from it all. But a traditional vacation
is often of no help. Doing nothing is a *real* stress if you're
a racehorse type and is disappointing if you're a victim of
boredom. So make sure you understand your feelings and
needs before you make elaborate compensations for stress.

I am a sales manager with a huge territory. I make
two or three calls each day and meet with clients
of all kinds. Some are slow, deliberate and in no
hurry, while others are very task-oriented and hard-
driving. Some want to linger over lunch, but others
won't even take a coffee break. I am constantly
driving to their offices or seeing them in new set-

tings and find myself worn out by the interaction, which I always thought would be stimulating. What's going on?

Stress results from increased demands for adaptation that accompany any change or novelty, and it seems that you are making too many adjustments daily. But some strategies can help:

1. Maintain as many of the same clients and as much of the same routine as possible. Establish a route and schedule so that each day won't seem so much like breaking new ground. Keep notes on your meetings and clients, which you can review before the next visit. Try to adjust to them via the right brain instead of feeling you have to meet an intellectual challenge every minute.

2. Decide when your energy is at its highest. Are you a morning or an afternoon person? Do your diet or sleeping habits affect your energy level? Schedule your meetings for the best times for you and leave the less demanding part of your work (perhaps making reports) for your low-energy times. (See BRAIN CYCLES.) Sit in your car for a few minutes before each appointment and relax. Suspend that left and move right to see yourself adapting easily and enjoying the variety of your work. It's especially important for you to have a suspender that works, but does not require physical energy. Driving when you're revved up leads to recklessness and impatience.

3. Establish at least one day a week as your mental health day. Reserve it for true rest and relaxation. Participate in your favorite and most restful activity, whether it's golfing, reading, riding or just loafing. Don't depend on a yearly traditional vacation. Build in short getaways to diminish the stress and replenish your energies.

4. Get the big picture of the way you live your life. Do you change jobs or raise the ante on your job just as you are about to conquer it? Simply for excitement, highly motivated individuals who enjoy challenges often

BRAIN CYCLES

The brain operates in ninety-minute cycles, alternating between performing verbal and spatial processes (left- and right-hemisphere tasks) more efficiently.

Similar cyclical shifts between hemispheres is evident during sleep. Dreaming occurs during REM (rapid eye movement) cycles approximately every ninety minutes throughout the night.

Daydreams and other wakeful flights of fancy also manifest in ninety-minute cycles.[44]

move from jobs they do very well to areas where they lack expertise. They are stress freaks who are hooked on the rush of adrenaline that comes from pursuing a goal that's out of reach.

5. Laugh a little. Don't take yourself, your job, your clients or life so seriously. The world won't come to an end if you're five minutes late for an appointment or if you trip over the rug at your sales presentation. Laughter will lower tension for you and your client and will establish a valuable rapport that can't be achieved as well or as easily in any other way.

Look at your life and your goal-setting style. Be sure that you aren't putting stress on yourself. Are you a perfectionist? Then do everything you can to structure your job so it will call for less moment-by-moment adaptation. Finally, develop some great escapes from stress on the job through suspenders, and get away from the job through real recreation.

Four years ago I joined a large organization with an attractive reputation for low employee turnover, excellent benefits, a fatherly concern for employees and a prestigious postion in the community. Now I am disillusioned and depressed by the company's rigid, bureaucratic ways. There is no flexibility, no altered working hours and no comp time. Procedures are cumbersome—everything must be in triplicate! Advancement is tied to a strict schedule with no allowances for exceptional work. I'm fed up and I don't know what to do next.

Large organizations are almost inherently bureaucratic and maddening. Most of your frustration stems from feeling that you are at the mercy of inflexible corporate policies. You might consider moving to another job where you would have more freedom. If you choose to stay for personal or financial reasons, keep in mind that you have *chosen* to stay, so you *are* exercising your own judgment and freedom.

Then decide to change your attitude toward the company. Write down all the advantages the company offers: security, benefits and prestige. Next, write down all the disadvantages. No doubt structure will be at the top of your list.

Now focus on the flip side of those disadvantages. Have you considered that the predictability of structure allows you to put more energy into creative activities? The comfort of a secure, low-demand job may permit time and energy to write poetry, join a performing-arts group, become a marathon runner or build an addition to your home.

Balancing a job with outside activities isn't your only option. You can use innovative techniques on the job—just recognize that implementing them will take longer in your rigid organization. When you do achieve a work goal, reward yourself: Tell family, friends and your supervisor, report it to the company newspaper or do your favorite thing. The first two might not appeal to you because of modesty, but often good work will go unnoticed without a little nudge. You can be subtle about tooting your own horn with your boss by writing a report with outcomes and statistics to point out your achievement.

Your most important need is to recognize that you *are* directing your own life. So set your course and those structural walls will come tumbling down.

I moved from New York recently to a very enviable position in Colorado. (The whole thing is too good to be true!) But now I am constantly torn between the job and the attractive outside activities I've found here. I feel I should do some reports and other work after hours and on weekends, but there's always the pull of the mountains or the bicycle trails. The more I vacillate, the more drained I feel.

Vacillating between options can be exhausting. Use a hearing 2 to find out the pros and cons of working on your own time. Listen to those voices within to find out:

Is it really necessary to work overtime? Is that "should" coming from the boss—or from you? If it's self-imposed, are you compensating because you don't feel you're doing a good job?

Visualize the pros and cons on a scale like this one:

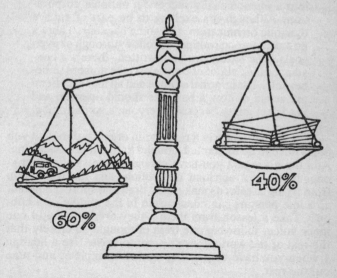

If it's 60 percent for mountains and 40 percent for reports, then go to the mountains that weekend. Go through the weighing each time to make sure you are deciding each case separately. If it's fifty-fifty, then toss a coin for your decision.

There's another possibility: You might still be experiencing the stress of success! Your promotion and move should make you the envy of all those you left behind. Right? Wrong. There's always some guilt and self-doubt involved when things go very well. Besides, the demands of a major move can be debilitating.

Your feelings can be attributed to the stress of ambivalence and adaptation with a little guilt thrown in. So stop agonizing; decide each weekend priority separately, and remember that you deserve your success.

I work for a spice and herb company that started as a cottage industry in the 1960s and has grown into a phenomenally successful national corporation. Although it's exciting to be part of such a dynamic organization, I'm going bananas. There's no structure, no routine, no follow-through or even goals. The letters are handwritten, there's a constant milling about of people and the noise is unbelievable. The informal attitude and all the rest offend my sense of how a business should operate, and yet I feel guilty because everyone's so darn nice.

You are definitely in a right-brain organization, and you don't have to be too far left-brained to find it disconcerting. Add the noise and you have enough to stress almost anyone. Noise is a constant distraction, and the frustration from trying to refocus makes you tired and short-tempered.

Some persons can concentrate in the middle of a hubbub. Take a lesson from them—they are listening to one inner voice, following one train of thought so closely that the rest of the world doesn't seem to exist. Use a hearing 1 when you have demanding work to complete, and tune out the rest.

Your boss might be receptive to goal-setting if you propose some right-brain methods. Suggest a visualizing session in which groups of your fellow employees try to envision where they would like the company to be in one year and in five years.

To provide certainty, organize and structure your own job and ways of performing it. Perhaps some kindred souls will follow suit.

Finally, take a step back from your company and get the whole picture. Perhaps you will find some pattern in the seeming chaos. Reflect on the company's success and the reasons for it. Can you see the overall pattern as a playground or swimming pool teeming with energy and goodwill? There are rules and regulations in those settings too, but they are not as obvious as the structure of a typical business. Remember, there is no one best way to run an organization, and your company has found a path to success. So relax, get rid of preconceived notions and you'll soon find yourself a comfortable member of the zoo.

A HAPPY ENDING

This chapter ends without examples to illustrate the beneficial effects of stress (eustress). It is obvious why: No one complains about good news, and our examples represent problem situations. Productive stress is the tension that builds as you look forward to an awards luncheon honoring you; your alive feeling when you're totally involved in a work project; the thrill of making a super presentation at the annual meeting. Your heart beats extra fast and you perspire madly. These are all signs of stress, but they have a happy outcome. The contrast is well described by Tom Ditmer, a trader for the Chicago Mercantile Exchange: "It's on the slow days that I feel down. When I'm really busy, it's exciting. I remember every trade—it's buy, sell. I get in a rhythm and feel more and more competent. At the end of the day, I feel exhilarated and refreshed."

Such eustress situations are duplicated when you are dancing, playing games, jogging and doing aerobic exercises. The stimulation increases bloodstream levels of endorphins, substances that have an opiatelike quality. Your way to a natural high!

Diet and medication also affect your stress levels, but the most important element in keeping it at manageable, healthful levels is your attitude. As society becomes more and more complex, it is natural to feel less in control of one's life—and the feeling of powerlessness is the greatest stressor of all. But realizing that you are able to control even the slightest actions and reactions of your body can help firm your determination to direct your life. Resolve to balance your workworld as well as possible, and then develop strategies for using stress rather than allowing it to use you.

From the split-brain point of view, much of your stress arises from an imbalance between the right- and left-brain aspects of your particular job, within your work setting or between your job and private life. How far can you balance your job or corporate culture may be limited, but you have many options in balancing your own life. The next and final chapter refocuses on helping you chart your future course in a changing world.

15

THE BOTTOM LINE: YOU, YOUR BRAIN AND YOUR FUTURE IN A CHANGING WORLD

To be is to do.
—Immanuel Kant

To do is to be.
—Sigmund Freud

Dooby, dooby, do.
—Frank Sinatra

FUTURISTS JOHN NAISBITT, ALVIN TOFFLER AND MARilyn Ferguson have identified our present state as one of transition from an industrial society to an information-dependent culture in which most jobs and energies are spent producing, disseminating and retrieving data. Today's environment requires vastly different skills than the ones developed in our training—even for the youngest among us.

Therefore, it behooves us all to look at our present skills to determine if they match the career needs of the times. Are you continuing to count on work abilities that will soon be as obsolete as the dinosaur? Will you do something to improve your chance of success and happiness in this emerging information society?

You may plead that it is impossible to form individual plans based on your personal perceptions. You may claim there is no big picture to perceive, no nugget of self-realization to discover.

A right-brain perspective can produce a surprisingly clear vision that is not readily apparent to the naked eye. Once you can see the patterns, you can direct your efforts most advantageously.

John Naisbitt in *Megatrends* bases his patterns on events described in local newspapers. Daniel Yankelovich in *The New Rules* predicts largely from the study of public opinion gleaned from polls and mass media. Naisbitt describes his method of detecting trends as simply a matter of noticing which new topics were replacing old ones. He and his cohorts collected and analyzed data, then discovered the overall pattern of changes, and presto! A trend was detected.

This whole-brain approach to divining history as it occurs can be a helpful strategy for plotting your future. Take what you know about your workworld, your city, state and country, project it onto a cinematic screen and forecast your

AVAILABLE JOBS

UNEMPLOYED WORKERS

own life-trends as they fit into your milieu. Then be ready to adapt to your scenario.

You need not be mired in the past or in the present. You don't have to be consistent. When a newspaper reporter pointed out to John F. Kennedy an inconsistency between his current stand on an issue and the opinion he had expressed a year earlier, JFK blandly replied, "I changed my mind."

To have JFK's flexibility is not easy for most of us. It derives from many experiences and the comfort of high self-esteem; it enabled him to adapt to change, an essential talent in a world so rife with it.

How can you be more flexible than you are? By perceiving the overall direction of your life in comparison with the trends going on about you and making specific adjustments to them.

Which areas of your life you want to alter may depend upon your stage or station of life. If you are a young married man who has been working in a right-brained job since school and are about to become a father, you may suddenly feel impatient with your work. You might want something more structured and financially rewarding; you will certainly need more money and security in your life. Your first steps toward a new left-brain career might be more schooling, associating with professionals in the field or merely reading about it. Focus on the left-brain aspects of your job. Volunteer to organize the billing procedure, be the spokesperson for your department or gather data on the new word processor.

A middle-aged woman who's reentering the business world after twenty years as a homemaker experiences the same sort of shift left. From attending the parallel crisis of homemaking, she moves to a much more focused way of thinking. Although she will still need her intuition, she will have to work within facts, figures and business structure.

On the other hand, the late-middle-aged male may be ready for a shift right. If his career has been successful and satisfying, he may feel entitled to reward himself with travel, recreation, art or learning for pure pleasure. Another man, who is not yet set financially, may still have less-expensive but far-ranging adventures.

There are many variations of these life passages, but all demonstrate the tendency to move back and forth between hemispheric dominance to maintain equilibrium. The times are replete with examples of famous persons who have experienced similar brain-balancing stages. Sandra Day O'Connor moved from immersion in the right-brain activities of her youth to Stanford University Law School and later to the left-brain rigors of the U.S. Supreme Court.

Dianne von Furstenberg wedded her sense of drama and design to a left-brain flair for finance and became head of her own successful clothing design company.

President Ronald Reagan's effective communications style can be attributed to his balanced method; each speech includes concrete examples of facts and figures; warm human-interest stories; and visuals to demonstrate plans and problems.

John De Lorean, the automobile maker, exemplifies the dangers of shifting to one extreme and staying there. His early successes were, no doubt, due to his flamboyant, innovative abilities; but as he became less and less restrained by left-brain strictures, he lost touch with the realities of the business world.

Besides the left/right brain model, there is another brain model that suggests how the human brain adapts to changing demands. It is the triune brain theory, proposed by Dr. Paul MacLean, chief of the Laboratory of Brain Evolution and Behavior of the National Institute of Mental Health. According to Dr. MacLean, the human brain has three layers, which developed over the long history of man's evolution. Each represents a different type of mentality and is geared to the needs that prevailed during its growth.

The oldest and most primitive, called the reptilian brain, is located in the very core of the human brain. It is the site of our impulsive reflexes that respond to danger. It is the part of you that makes self- and species-survival decisions. The primal mind guides your mating, nesting and socializing behaviors. It is more than instinctual, but not much more.

As creatures evolved from reptiles to mammals, the limbic system was added to the human brain, Dr. MacLean theorizes. This midlayer added such abilities as memory of personal identity, enabling mothers to recognize the care for their newborn. The survival benefits of this feature are self-evident. Learning and communication at an emotional level became possible, and the taste and smell senses developed more fully. This layer added the ability to care about and for others of the same species. The negative side effect of this refinement was the introduction of a weakness in the survival game that pure reptiles surely exploited; giving one's life to save an offspring could imperil the species and, therefore, MacLean says, the third layer of the brain developed to compensate. Enter: the new mammalian or neocortex.

This outer stratum has two specialized hemispheres, the intellectual left and the emotional right, which combine to produce complex, sophisticated thinking. The new layer is capable of balancing practical skills with altruistic urges. The push and pull of survival necessitated the brain's progress from the reptilian to the limbic brain and from the limbic to the neocortex. A similar dynamic goes on between the two hemispheres, resulting in even higher levels of abilities, including foresight.

Several recent California studies show that individuals who score highest on predicting future events had "balanced brains"—that is, were adept in both hemispheres and used them in combination. Says one researcher, David Loye: "Current failures of economic forecasting by economists, a predominantly left-brained specialty, indicate the need for forecasting methods that employ more balanced brain usage."[45]

At times, adapting to an ever more complex society seems an unbearable burden, but in reality it is the constantly adapting to change that keeps us vital and growing. Jerre Levy, a leading brain researcher at the University of Chicago, believes that the human brain thrives on challenge. She says: "Normal brains are built to be challenged. They operate at optimal levels only when cognitive processing requirements are of sufficient complexity to activate *both* sides of the brain."[46]

The heartening suggestion of all the theorizing and research is that the human brain has been adapting to the needs of its environment throughout the ages and that you and your particular brain are the outcome of this long-range improvement. Also, you, in your time and life, are capable of making your life better by stimulating brain growth and vigor. It truly is a do-it-yourself project.

Never before has it been more important for individuals to keep their thinking flexible, their brains vital. Just making the weekly and monthly changes contemporary humans do would have staggered the abilities and imagination of a Socrates or a George Washington.

You ignore these demands at your peril. You will miss the excitement and pleasure of broadening your interests and discovering more facets of your abilities.

The split-brain theory is an easily understood model that can help you extend and improve your mental capabilities and enjoyment of life. It can serve you well in coping with burgeoning information as the necessities of the times require. It offers a road map or software for bettering your life now and in the future. So step back, get the big picture and fit yourself into it. Make your mind do push-ups each day and you will be like a Pablo Picasso, who worked with pleasure and ability till four hours before his death at the age of ninety-one. By using his whole brain through his whole life, he died a beloved, fulfilled man who left an artistic legacy of a right and left brain in harmonious accord—a life's work well done.

> The human mind, once stretched to a new idea, never goes back to its original dimensions.
> —Oliver Wendell Holmes

NOTES

1. R. W. Sperry, "Lateral Specialization in the Surgically Separated Hemispheres," *The Neurosciences Third Study Program*, eds. F. O. Schmitt and R. G. Worden (Cambridge, Mass.: MIT Press, 1974), pp. 5–19.

2. M. C. Wittrock et al., *The Human Brain* (Englewood Cliffs, N.J.: Prentice-Hall, 1977).

3. Beryl Lieff Benderly, "The Multilingual Mind," *Psychology Today* (Mar. 1981); Sally Merrill, "The Japanese Brain," *Science Digest* (Nov. 1981).

4. Elliott D. Ross and Marek-Marsel Mesulam, "Dominant Language Function of the Right Hemisphere? Prosody and Emotional Gesturing," *Archives of Neurology* 36, pp. 144–48.

5. Staff, "Just How the Sexes Differ," *Newsweek* (May 18, 1981); Jo Durden-Smith, "Male and Female—Why?," *Quest/80* (Oct. 1980).

6. Jack Fincher, *The Sinister People: The Looking-Glass World of the Left-Hander* (New York: G. P. Putnam's Sons, 1977).

7. Thomas R. Blakeslee, *The Right Brain* (Garden City, N.Y.: Anchor Press, 1980).

8. B. Shapin and L. Coly, eds., *Brain/Mind and Parapsychology* (New York: Parapsychology Foundation, 1979).

9. "Neat/Sloppy Linked to Left, Right Brain," *Brain/Mind Bulletin* (July 13, 1981), p. 1.

10. Jerre Levy, "The Mammalian Brain and the Adaptive Advantage of Cerebral Asymmetry," *Annals New York Academy of Science* 299 (1977), pp. 264–72.

11. Richard J. Davidson and Nathan A. Fox, "Asymmetrical Brain Activity Discriminates Between Positive and Negative Affective Stimuli in Human Infants," *Science* 218, pp. 1235–37; Marcel Kinsbourne, "The Brain/Sad Hemisphere, Happy Hemisphere," *Psychology Today* (May 1981), p. 92.

12. "Breathing Cycle Linked to Hemispheric Dominance," *Brain/Mind Bulletin* (Jan. 3, 1983), p. 1.

13. Dina Ingber, "Brain Breathing," *Science Digest* (June 1981), p. 74.

14. Eric Peper and Elizabeth Williams, *From the Inside Out: A Self-teaching and Laboratory Manual* (New York: Plenum, 1981).

15. Carl Sagan, *Dragons of Eden* (New York: Random House, 1977).

16. Winn Wenger, *How to Increase Your Intelligence* (New York: Dell, 1975).

17. "Brain Size in Species Linked to Adaptation," *Brain/Mind Bulletin* (January 4, 1982), p. 2.

18. Edward de Bono, *Lateral Thinking for Management*, American Management Association, New York, 1971.

19. Alex Osborn, *Applied Imagination* (New York: Charles Scribner's Sons, 1963).

20. Jerome Singer, *The Inner World of Daydreaming* (New York: Harper & Row, 1975).

21. Betty Edwards, *Drawing on the Right Side of the Brain* (Los Angeles: J. P. Tarcher, 1979).

22. Virginia Adams, "Mommy and I Are One," *Psychology Today* (May 1982).

23. Thomas R. Blakeslee, *The Right Brain* (Garden City, N.Y.: Doubleday, 1980).

24. Paul Bakan, "The Right Brain Is the Dreamer," *Psychology Today* (Nov. 1976).

25. Thomas H. Budzynski, "Tuning in on the Twilight Zone," *Psychology Today* (Aug. 1977).

26. Frank Putnam, a study of EEG's of multiple personalities, National Institute of Mental Health, 9000 Rockville Pike, Bethesda, MD., 20205.

27. Elizabeth F. Loftus, *Eyewitness Testimony* (Cambridge, Mass.: Harvard University Press, 1979).

28. Beryl Lieff Benderly, "The Multilingual Mind," *Psychology Today* (Mar. 1981), p. 10.

29. Jack Fincher, *The Brain* (Washington, D.C.: U.S. News Books, 1982).

30. Francis Robinson, *Effective Study*, 4th ed. (New York: Harper & Row, 1970).

31. Douglas Dean et al., *Executive ESP* (Englewood Cliffs, N.J.: Prentice-Hall, 1974).

32. Dr. Seuss, *On, Beyond Zebra* (New York: Random House, 1955).

33. Richard Bandler and John Grinder, *Frogs into Princes: Neurolinguistic Programming* (Real People Press, 1979).

34. M. C. Wittrock et al., *The Human Brain* (Englewood Cliffs, N.J.: Prentice-Hall, 1977).

35. Julian Jaynes, *The Origin of Consciousness in the Breakdown of the Bicameral Mind* (Boston: Houghton-Mifflin, 1977).

36. Beryl Lieff Benderly, "Flashbulb Memory," *Psychology Today* (June 1981), p. 71.

37. Seymour Kety, "Adrenaline: A Secret Agent in Memory," *Psychology Today* (Dec. 1980), p. 132.

38. Jack Fincher, *The Brain* (Washington, D.C.: U.S. News Books, 1982).

39. Peter Drucker, *The Corporate Society* (New York: Warner Books, 1976); Muriel James, *The O.K. Boss* (Reading, Mass.: Addison-Wesley, 1975).

40. Thomas J. Peters and Robert T. Waterman, Jr., *In Search of Excellence: Lessons from America's Best Run Companies* (New York: Harper & Row, 1982).

41. Terrence E. Deal and Allan A. Kennedy, *Corporate Cultures. The Rites and Rituals of Corporate Life* (Reading, Mass.: Addison-Wesley, 1982).

42. "Brainstorms," *Forbes*, June 6, 1983.

43. Stewart Emery, *Actualizations* (Garden City, N.Y.: Doubleday, 1978).

44. "Rhythm Found for Cognitive Style," *Brain/Mind Bulletin* (July 16, 1979), p. 3; Jack Fincher, *The Human Brain: Mystery of Matter and Mind* (Washington, D.C.: U.S. News Books, 1981).

45. David Loye, Institute for Futures Forecasting, Carmel, California, tested management students at the Naval Postgraduate School in Monterey, California, and undergraduates at the University of California at Berkeley and the University of California at Los Angeles.

46. "Jerre Levy: Human Brain Built to Be Challenged," *Brain/Mind Bulletin* (May 9, 1983).

INDEX

About the Authors

JACQUELYN WONDER is a management consultant who conducts seminars on whole-brain thinking for major corporations across the country.

PRISCILLA DONOVAN is a program director in the Continuing Education Division at the University of Colorado at Denver. She has also conducted brain lateralization research at the Biofeedback Institute of Denver.